To dear Ashton
with admiration
and great affection
Brooke

June 1980

FOOTPRINTS

By the same author

FOOTPRINTS
A PATCHWORK CHILDHOOD
THE BLUEBIRD IS AT HOME

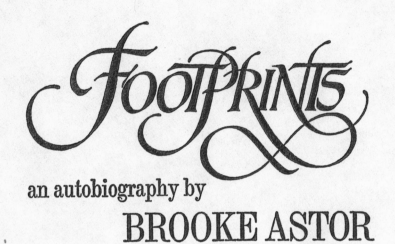

FOOTPRINTS

an autobiography by

BROOKE ASTOR

Doubleday & Company, Inc.   Garden City, New York
1980

Library of Congress Catalog Card Number 78-20053
ISBN 0-385-14377-X

Copyright © 1980 by Brooke Astor

In Memory of Anne
and
For her children,
Mary Armour, Fergus, Brooke

That exquisite poise of character which we call serenity is the last lesson of culture—it is the flowering of life—the fruitage of the soul.

anon.

FOOTPRINTS

PROLOGUE

June 1st—Peking 1979

This visit to China has been one of the great experiences of my life. To begin with, so many people urged me not to go. It was also said that most people who visited the country were unaccustomed to the climate and food and got sick. Well, I thought to myself, so what? What have I to lose at my stage in life—one is not immortal and if I live a little bit longer by never leaving the beaten track, and losing all sense of adventure—then life will close in on me and I will become an introspective old bore.

One of the reasons the visit has been so magical has been that constant sense of déjà vu. From that first morning in Peking when I walked by myself in the fresh soft air of the early morning and found Old Legation Street and the American Legation gate and looked up at the windows of Mother's room—it made everything come alive for me. I was not a stranger here. I was moving back through the long years and felt the freshness of my childhood. It filled me with happiness because I felt so close to the two people who made me what I am, and I thought of them as young and gay and vital and full of life—and passing it on to me. What a gift they gave me.

Standing at the gate, I saw myself astride my donkey, jogging along the path through the cornfields of the Western Hills, riding to a picnic at the Eunuch's Temple. So much has happened to that child since. So much she never could have imagined in her wildest dreams. And she was a dreamer.

In a way that dreary-looking Marine barracks house, now abandoned, with a coal heap in front of it, is the only concrete thing that remains of my childhood. Here is the only solid evidence that a family called Russell really existed. But, of course, no one knows that but me.

PART I _____

Dryden

1

My father was a Marine officer, and one of his questions about a man in the service was, "How did he react under fire?" It is a simple question, but a penetrating one. Anyone who leads any sort of an active life with a certain amount of power to make decisions is always "under fire." This fire can come from the outside: from competitors, from the jealousy and envy of those less successful (or less lucky). It can also come from the inside: The fire of one's emotional conflicts can be devastating. One must learn to "face fire" with courage and not to become hard or cynical. Life is a lonely game to be played out alone. No one can help us make inner decisions. A game without rules is no game at all, only chaos. In thinking over my own life, I realize that I am one of the lucky ones. I was taught that life can be a good game if played well and with certain rules. My mother used to say that I was like a bird, and that I would never lose my balance. Of course, it hasn't always been true: But if it has been true at all, it is because, by what they said and what they did, my parents provided me with a survival kit. If I land on my feet like a bird with a strong sense of equilibrium, it is because I was taught to fly long before I left the nest.

My family strengthened my wings in preparation for storms ahead, although they probably expected me to have a very tranquil and uneventful life. If they expected me to be a quiet, easygoing person, they did not take their own natures into account. Mother was mercurial, fascinating, and intellectual. Father was steadfast, stern, and endlessly compassionate and loving. With these two totally dissimilar characters, how could life be simple for me?

I had the priceless advantage of being an only child. All the love that I might have had to share with rival siblings was mine alone. The nest was mine, so that the affection and interest of these intelligent but totally dissimilar people was concentrated on me. "I never wanted another child," said Mother, "I stopped at perfection" (not a bad thing to have said about one). For sixteen glorious years I was totally secure. Love was everywhere, and I knew that I was the living link between Father and Mother. Sixteen years of that kind of security helps one withstand almost any blow that life can deal. One is firmly rooted like the bamboo, one bends, but does not break. Although as a child I often thought that my parents were too strict, and did not understand me, I knew in my heart their love was deep and unflinching, though certainly not blind, because there were rules that I had to adhere to. I was made to realize when I was very young that life is a two-way street and that no one has it all to himself. To receive, one must give. I was never allowed to sulk, to be impudent, or to be rude. Good manners come from a good heart, I was told. Remember to be kind and pleasant. If people are rude to you, pay no attention, they simply don't know any better. Good manners are in fact a protection. Why argue with rude and aggressive people? It simply weakens and eats away at the spirit.

Mother used to say that good manners and good humor made for a good marriage. In my middle life I was to find this to be true. Another axiom was that even if you know that you are right it is sometimes better to give in than to be stubborn. To preserve peace in a relationship is often more important than winning a point. This last advice served me very well in my contact with my first in-laws.

As a child, I was made to feel that I should create an

atmosphere of goodwill around me. It is certainly a much pleasanter way to live than to have a chip on one's shoulder or be continually looking for flaws in someone else's character. It is also, in a strange way, a defense. It is like a moat of still but deep water, that keeps one in tranquil isolation without appearing to. It is hard to fight with a person who puts up with rudeness and is not offended. Never to sulk and never to be rude, which was difficult to achieve as a child, has become a part of me: not second nature, but nature itself. The French say, "To know all is to forgive all." Well, one can never know all, and one cannot in one's heart forgive everything; but one can appear to do so, and then eventually one forgets.

Next to being an only child the greatest gift my parents passed on to me was marvelous health. They were two of the most vital, healthy people I have ever known. To be fit to them was an absolute "must." "When you feel lazy and tired," said Father, "that is just the time you ought to go out and play tennis, or take a brisk walk, or a canter on your pony, anything to blow the cobwebs away. Don't mope around the house." "Keep a bowl of apples always near you," said Mother, "and eat one instead of candy." "Don't be a stick-in-the-mud, for goodness sake *do* something."

To be on the go from morning to night was their code. These admonitions had their effect, and unconsciously I learned the value of disciplining my body. That has been a great asset to me. If you feel well, you are certainly better equipped to deal with problems; and my "rude health" has made me quick to recover from despondency and despair.

This wonderful health led to mental activity. Mother read the Goncourts, Walter Pater, Walt Whitman, and Henry James—while Father stuck to higher mathematics and books such as Mahan's *The Influence of Sea Power*

upon History and Spengler's *Decline of the West.* Mother
read Walter Scott to me, and Dickens and Thackeray,
while Father insisted on Dana's *Two Years Before the Mast*
and *Tom Brown's School Days.* I became an omnivorous
reader and have remained so. I also became a very fast
reader, adept at skimming through a book in no time at all.
This became a bad habit of mine as I often only remember
little bits and pieces to be stored away, quite out of con-
text.

It was because of this slapdash way of reading that at
the age of fifteen I rather fancied myself as a scholar, and
wanted to learn Greek. This idea terrified my mother, my
grandmother, and my aunts. What if I turned out to be a
bluestocking—a wretched woman who ran about in a
baggy tweed skirt and tennis shoes and bored civilized
people (men) to death with arguments and facts? In my
mother's eyes a woman should know only what made her
attractive to an intelligent man, and even then she considered that a woman should hide how much she really knew.
"Men don't like women who know more than they do."
Mother said that but she did not entirely believe this herself,
since she and my aunts all felt that they were far better in-
formed than their husbands. Mother, true to her credo,
promptly took me out of Miss Madeira's in Washington,
D.C., and sent me to a school more interested in French
and drawing than in Greek and Latin. I did not like the
new school and dawdled the time away.

After giving me love and health, my parents instilled in
me a deep respect for the truth. "I will never punish you if
you tell me the truth," said Mother, and Father (who
never punished me at all) took it as a matter of course that
even a child could understand that truth and honor went
hand in hand. Two instances of what truth can mean stand
out in my memory. The first occurred when I was seven
years old in Peking. It was my parents' wedding anniver-

sary and we were having lunch together. Mother, who had been in particularly high spirits for a week or so, became rather intense during lunch, and asked Father if he really loved her. "Of course I love you," said Father quietly, "more than ever." "More than ever?" "More than ever," repeated Father, smiling. "Have you ever been irritated with me?" Mother asked. Father did not answer. Mother's eyes began to flash. "Answer me, John," she said. "Have you ever been irritated with me?" Still Father did not answer. "Then you don't love me," cried Mother throwing down her napkin and bursting into tears. "Here I am in China with you, thousands of miles away from my family. I have given up my life to you, and you don't love me." Father started to speak, but she jumped up from the table and running upstairs to her bedroom slammed the door violently. "Oh, Father," I cried. "What are we going to do?" Father looked white and shaken. "Don't worry, Little Woman"—his nickname for me. "It will be all right," he said, and he left for his office.

But it wasn't all right. When he came home that evening, Mother was still locked in her room and refused to answer when he tapped on the door. He took refuge in the study, where he sat in the darkness gloomily smoking his cigar. My whole world seemed to be falling apart, and I could bear it no longer. I dashed up to my mother's room and knocked loudly on the door. "Oh, Mother, dearest Mother, please come out," I pleaded. "Father is all by himself and is like a snail without a shell." These words seemed to have an effect on Mother. She opened the door a crack. "Wait," I said, "don't close the door, I'll go and get Father." Father must have been very near because he appeared almost at once and threw his arms around Mother. I felt like the Good Fairy and was overjoyed that my world had been saved. Even then, in the midst of my happiness, I realized that Mother did not repeat the question she had asked Father, and that he did not volunteer to answer it. She knew, and I must have sensed it, that even at the risk of breaking his heart, he could not tell an untruth. Mother's flirtations and flightiness must have driven him mad at times. But he preferred silence to admitting it, or denying it. Mother, with all her charm and vivacity, knew her limitations. "Do as I say, not as I do," she used to say to me. And so I did, as long as I lived at home.

The other incident occurred after we had returned from China and were living in Washington. We lived in a funny old-fashioned house which had belonged to my Grandfather Russell. It stood on the corner of the street and had a little iron railing around it and a garden gate that clicked loudly. Next to it was a small brownstone house that was a place of mystery. The shades were always half drawn, and two elderly ladies and a very old gentleman came out of it occasionally to take a drive in a hired car. They wore out-of-date clothes and in winter the ladies wore aging fur capes garlanded with masses of small fur tails. I noticed that my very outgoing family never spoke to these people and always managed to avert their heads when passing the house. It was only when I was about fourteen and one of the ladies died that I learned the reason for this unusual behavior. It seems that they were an English family and that one of them had been mixed up in a great scandal to do with cheating at cards during the reign of Edward VII. "To cheat is as bad as stealing," said Father. "It is taking something which is not yours." "No matter where one's sympathy might lie it is not permissible to accept a cheat as a friend." "One of the most important things in life is to have the respect of the people who know you. Everyone may not like you, but you should conduct yourself in such a way that all will respect you." These words meant little to me as a child, but when I grew up I realized that not to be respected is to forfeit something of primordial importance.

One of the advantages of being an only child is that one becomes—without knowing it—the repository of grown-ups' aspirations, hopes, fears, and joys. An only child learns early on in life that nothing and no one can be taken for granted and that one has to work constantly to keep a relationship going. One of the ways I was taught this was by conversation. Not just talking, but *conversation*, by which was meant talk that had real meaning and flavor and would bind people together, that would help them exchange ideas, facts, viewpoints, problems and laughter. And where better than at the family dinner table? "Having a meal together is like going to a market place," said Mother. "Each one of us should bring something to it." There were only three of us, but we did a lot of talking. Like all families, we had our problems. We had very little money, but as a child I was never conscious of it. It was never mentioned that so-and-so was rich or that so-and-so was poor. My parents considered that bad form. That was fortunate for me, because my grandmother, in her old-fashioned Southern way, cared very much about material things, as did my mother's oldest sister. A "good marriage" to them was a rich one.

To return to the dinner table: My mother was really an extraordinarily attractive woman. She was so full of health, intelligence, and fun that she transformed the atmosphere the moment she entered a room. Looking back, and being now a veteran of many family meals, I marvel at her generosity and kindness in using those fascinating assets on just Father and me. Of course, I realize now that there must have been a strong physical bond between them. No matter what flirtations she indulged in on the side, she did not want to lose Father. As for me, I was an

adoring sponge, sopping it all up and longing to be like
her. She was a marvelous raconteur and a wicked mimic
and I used to beg her to repeat some of my favorite stories
over and over. She never told them in exactly the same
way, so I hung on every word as I waited for the dénoue-
ment. She talked so much about what she saw, read, and
heard, that to this day I do not know if *I* saw Nijinsky
dance in the *Spectre de la Rose,* if it was *I* who watched
breathlessly as he made his great leap, or if it was Mother.
Did *I* meet Maurice Rostand? Had *I* known Saint-
Gaudens, and did I have tea with Edith Wharton? I think
not. But thanks to Mother, I *did* lunch with Henry Adams
at his house on Lafayette Square in Washington. I was
only twelve, and I was terrified at being the only child
there, but Mother had told me so much about him that although I was totally tongue-tied I drank in every detail. I
still boast about having been there, and I remember his
small study, looking out on the square. Two of the walls
were covered with William Blake drawings, and Mr.
Adams, a tiny man with a well-kept goatee, sat on a red
leather sofa, while a relation of his, Miss Aileen Tone,
played tinkling French bergerettes on the clavichord. "Mr.
Adams has written so much about education," said
Mother, "that perhaps you can learn something from
him." I did learn that truly great people are always kind.
Mr. Adams must have given up his after-lunch nap in
order to be nice to a shy child.

My parents' emphasis on talk forced me to think, to
look about me, to find new interests, and to become interested in other people's ideas. "If you are not interested in
what is going on, there is nothing to talk about." It is not
easy for a grown-up to make a child participate in a
different world, but Mother made it seem easy. I was like
Alice in Wonderland; and even if things were "curiouser
and curiouser" and I did not really understand them, they

aroused my interest and stimulated me. It was a wonderful gift that Mother gave me, because I now find it impossible to be bored. Mother made a story out of everything. She never saw anything as drab or dull; she turned it into something to feel sorry about or to laugh at. She may have shown off a bit for us, but she aroused in me an interest in people which I have never lost. Because I was brought up to express myself, I feel that, given the chance, I can talk to, and get on with, almost anyone.

Sometimes I feel that children today are shut off from the mainstream of their parents' lives. They hardly speak, or are spoken to, at the table, and the moment that the meal is over they are expected to go as far away as possible to a place where they can immediately turn on the TV or a rock music cassette. "Aren't children awful these days?" moan the parents. "We can't do a thing with them." I ask myself if those parents have tried. Have they ever thought how very important every adult word and action is to a child? Have they ever tried to relate to their children and stimulate them?

I cannot help but think how lucky I was. It seems to me that the mind must have muscle, like the other parts of the body; if it is not used, it grows flabby. No one would ever dream of keeping a perfectly healthy child in bed day after day; we know that lack of exercise would atrophy its legs. How frightful then to create a mind that only receives and can never give out, or initiate anything on its own, but functions as a useless and dull instrument inside one's head!

My mother was an omnivorous reader, and one of her pleasures was to read aloud to me the books she had enjoyed. I loved to be in bed with a mild sore throat, a cashmere shawl over my shoulders, while Mother read to me. "Shall I stop?" she would ask hopefully after a couple of hours. "No, no, please, Mother, go on," I would croak,

and on she would go. Miss Betsey Trotwood and the donkeys, the fascinating Steerforth, Dotheboys Hall, poor little Paul Dombey, the wicked Becky Sharp, the Elephant
Child by the Great Grey-Green Greasy Limpopo River,
the industrious and knowledgeable Swiss Family Robinson,
Pendennis, Dr. Proudie, Heathcliff, Rebecca and Rowena
in Ivanhoe—on and on. My whole world was filled with
them, and Mother and I would argue about Micawber and
Mrs. Grundy and Mr. Rochester as if they were real people—so they became a part of my own life. I sensed that
when I was grown-up I would find the world an exciting
and challenging place, full of Pendennises, Micawbers and
Heathcliffs (especially Heathcliff, that wild and untamed
spirit). I was thus prepared for the even more exotic types
whom I was to meet later on, and who proved the axiom
that "life is stranger than fiction."

Learning life through great books has its advantages.
The first advantage is obviously an appreciation of the
beauty and power of the written word. English is one of
the most varied and subtle of all tongues; in England it is
written and spoken as it should be, with all its nuances and
savor. Here in America I feel that we now have only a
much diminished notion of it. And even those who should
teach English have but little command of its potential. I
know that my own vocabulary was more varied and my
writing better phrased at twenty than it is today. I am myself a victim of televisionese. Reading good books has the
advantage that even if one's own life is limited one still
learns a great deal about human nature. My mother would
never let me read the comics, or any form of what she
called "trash." "It is such a waste of time," she said. "Let
people who have no intellectual curiosity read what they
like, but I want you to stretch your mind." She was right.
Intellectual curiosity is one of the greatest gifts my mother
gave me. Even now, in the autumn of my life, I find new

interests and new challenges almost every day. My education is still not complete, and I hope it never will be. It
seems strange to me, in view of what one sees and hears today, that I was so totally innocent about sex. I used to read
about love, and I would hear Mother and her friends saying, "He is madly in love with her," or, "It is disgusting, he
has left his wife and gone to the South of France with
another woman." Father and Mother always had separate
rooms because he was a dreadful snorer, but when I sometimes saw them sitting up in bed together, I thought nothing of it. It was like me with a sore throat and Mother
reading to me. Children are learning sex in school today,
complete with diagrams, from the age of six. At that age I
was making clothes for tiny fairies and hiding them in
match boxes in the trees or sitting under a rose bush talking
to a bee.

Little boys, however, did start kissing me when I was
about six, and I was constantly interested in them from
then on. They were mysterious and different and I wanted
them to like me. But I was not experimental until I reached
the age of sixteen. I sometimes think that this long childhood was a benefit. I grew up slowly and my sex urge took
the form of writing plays and poems and stories. I was
constantly scribbling. I organized little literary clubs
among my best friends at school and published a magazine.
I was like a plant growing steadily and strongly, fed by
my parents' interest and not forced to bloom. "Boys don't
really like girls like *that*," said Mother about girls who
wore lipstick and sat in the back of cars at parties. I almost
believed her—but not completely. Why were those girls so
popular, and why was I so often stuck with a boring boy?
Fortunately, it did not make that much difference to me. I
knew when the time came someone who was really interesting would come into my life. Someone with Father's
character and Mother's wit. But I thought of a person, not

of sex. It all seems totally absurd and very old-fashioned, but I feel sorry for the young girls of today who must have a "steady" boyfriend (dreary phrase) from the age of twelve on. It makes them into old people before their time and turns off the creative urge.

My parents liked nature for the obvious reasons. They liked good weather because of exercise. "Red sky at night," said Father, "sailors delight. Red sky in the morning, sailors take warning." Having graduated from Annapolis and gone to sea after graduation he knew the heavens intimately. He tried to teach me the map of the night skies and the names of the clouds that we saw in the daytime. I could never learn them. Mother loved flowers, and we always had flowers in the house, but she was not interested in how they grew. It was not until their old age, when they were living in California, that either of my parents really took an interest in gardening: then it became a passion for them both. They created a charming little garden and it brought them great pleasure.

With me it has been different. I feel an affinity with every natural thing—the sky, the sunsets, the moonrise, the flight of birds, the moving branches of a tree, the rain beating against the window, the quiet fall of a snowflake. I feel a part of them all.

I attribute this to the four years we lived in Peking—beginning when I was seven. As children do, I picked up the language very quickly and in no time at all I spoke Chinese fluently. This opened a whole new world to me. They say that a Westerner cannot live in China and not be changed by it. What then could it do to a responsive, only child, during the most impressionable years of her life? I feel that it really changed me, and, in doing that, changed my life.

Strangely enough, the two important values that my parents neglected to instill in me were the love of nature and the comfort of religion. But I should not have been aroused by either if it had not been for my mother's insistence on intellectual curiosity. I learned to "stretch my mind" as she told me to and, in doing so, found interests that were not theirs.

To them nature was to be enjoyed because it was healthy to be out of doors. One took it for granted. It was nice to feel the sun on one's body, to walk in the rain and snow, to exercise in all weather; but to sit and contemplate the landscape and to day-dream, to feel a mystical bond with nature, was not something that they wanted or needed.

As for religion, Mother grew up in a household that was deeply divided in religious conflict. My maternal grandfather was English. He came to Baltimore with his mother and brother soon after he had graduated from Cambridge. His mother was a Miss Hornby, a Protestant, his father, a Howard. They came to Baltimore with letters of introduction to the "best society," and the two brothers started a law firm. My grandmother's name was McGill, and her mother was descended from the Protestant side of the Carroll family. My great-grandmother was born a Spence, and was a cousin of James Russell Lowell. Granny, who was a beauty and "the belle of her year," fell madly in love with Grandfather. She was intrigued by his English accent, the way he dressed (impeccably cut suits, huge gold watch chain hung with fobs, an immaculately tended beard, and beautifully manicured hands). He waltzed and played the piano and sang. These were not very sound reasons for marriage, and so it turned out.

Nevertheless, they were married in St. Thomas' Church, the Episcopal Church of Garrison Forest (just outside Baltimore), and moved to a house on G Street in Washington, which my great-grandfather gave them as a wedding present. There they proceeded to have three chil-

dren in rapid succession. Then Grandfather—either because of the boredom of domestic life, or because of
business—took a trip by himself to England. He returned
with a chest of silver for the table and three family portraits. But to my grandmother's fury and horror, he also
returned a Catholic—"a papist." "All English Howards are
Catholics," he said. This was an abomination to her, a
staunch Episcopalian, and from then on Sunday was a day
of dissension and vilification. Grandfather went off to St.
Matthew's, Grandmother to St. John's. He lingered at the
Metropolitan Club on Sunday and came home just in time
for the two o'clock mammoth Sunday dinner. Grandfather
had his way in that all five children (they had two more
after Grandfather's visit to England) went to Catholic
schools, but the children all very much disliked going to
church. My mother never went to church except when I
was confirmed and married, and for Father's funeral and
the funeral of two of my three husbands. She did, however, provide me with a very conscientious and upright
godmother, Miss Elsa Bancroft Bliss (a descendant of the
famous historian George Bancroft, who wrote a ten-
volume *History of the United States*, was Secretary of the
Navy under President Polk, and established the U. S.
Naval Academy at Annapolis), who saw to it that I was
instructed, and later confirmed, by Bishop Harding. My
father came from a long line of Protestants. His father,
who was a rear admiral, had been a vestryman at St. John's
Church in Washington and had married the daughter of a
minister. But although Father was the most upright, honest, and kind man I have ever known in my long life, he
was not a churchgoer. His life was an example of what the
impact of a totally honest and decent character can make
on those around him. He was, as Mother said, a merry
saint. However, Mother's influence was stronger in his life
than his desire to go to church. So if it had not been for

my godmother I would never have known the beauty of the King James Version of the Bible, nor the consolation of ritual, nor the mysticism of communion. My spinster godmother saw to it that I read my Bible and my prayer book. Her religion was pragmatic and unequivocal. It was fortunate for me in many ways, because without her unwavering and loyal faith in the Episcopal Church I would have had no firm foundation on which to build my love of God. For by the time I came under Aunt Elsa's guidance, I already had, at the age of twelve, my own brand of Christianity.

At the age of seven I went to Peking. We lived in that beautiful city in the winter, but in the summer we had several courtyards in a Buddhist temple in the Western Hills, just outside of Peking. The temple was called The Temple of a Hundred Courtyards and except for the courtyards rented to us it was an active center for Buddhist priests. As an only child who had no one to play with and was full of curiosity, I got to know all the priests very well. They were gentle, kindly people and their days were divided between prayer and work. The older ones held classes of instruction and spent hours before Buddha asking for guidance. The younger ones went to classes, worked in the gardens and fields, and prepared the meals. It was, in effect, a monastery. I would often sit in a corner of an incense-filled room listening to their chants before Buddha on his altar. As I breathed in the incense, I was possessed by the feeling that behind Buddha there must be another presence. It seemed to me a symbol of something very mysterious, but very real. These gentle priests also pointed out to me the beauty and excitement of nature. To watch a pomegranate ripen through the summer, to see a flower grow, to listen to the singing wind and the rippling of a stream—these were to them an important part of their lives. Everything had a life of its own, they told me, every plant and tree, and it should be loved and cared for, as one would care for a person.

When we came home to Washington and my religious education was put into Aunt Elsa's hands, I was still young enough to find Buddhism and Christianity compatible. The love of one's fellow man was a cardinal point in both religions. And as God created the universe, why should one not revere all his creations? I do not pretend to be a philosopher or an intellectual, but to find God in nature has been very helpful to me. How can I ever be lonely when the cloud that passes overhead, or the pigeon on my window sill is as one with me?

I sincerely believe that to have no faith is to be unhappy. I feel that adversity and tragedy are sent to test one's faith and courage. I do not believe in besieging God with prayers for oneself—we should never beg, but we should instead be thankful for our blessings. We should be an example to those around us in our good humor, goodwill, courage, understanding, kindness, and self-discipline. Self-pity is the most ignoble of emotions.

It took me a long time to live up to this philosophy. I knew what was right, but as a young girl and a young woman, I was often overeager and impulsive. My present happiness surprises me because I realize now that with such parents I really should have been a wiser person from the beginning.

2

There is a legend in my family that an ancestor of ours, while fighting in the wars in Tripoli, became so impatient to get into action that when the cannon he was firing did not go off the moment he set the fuse, he jumped astride it, pulled out the cannonball with his bare hands, and hurled it at the enemy.

I feel that my entrance into adult life was rather like that. I was dragged from the warmth and security of a happy and protected childhood into a world that was, if not hostile, at least totally foreign.

It all happened in a most conventional way. One of my best friends, Janet Harlan, had been asked to go to the Princeton Commencement Prom by her older brother, John Marshall Harlan (who later became an associate justice of the U. S. Supreme Court). Janet and I had discussed this great event and were wildly excited that she, at sixteen, was considered sophisticated enough to be invited to such a glamorous occasion. But, alas, Janet's luck did not hold out. She got the mumps just a few days before going to Princeton. So Mrs. Harlan called Mother to ask if I could fill her place. Mother was all against it because I was only fifteen, had never worn a real evening dress, and still had my hair in a braid down my back. But my aunts (one in Washington, one in Baltimore) were in favor, and Mrs. Harlan was insistent because she was desperate. At that late hour John could not possibly get a re-

ally attractive girl of the right age—so they said—so why
not ask his little sister's friend? The telephone was kept
very busy while I sat by not knowing whether to be
pleased or terrified. "She has nothing to wear," Mother
said, speaking to my youngest aunt on the telephone. "I
have a white and silver chiffon dress that has shrunk in
cleaning," replied my youngest aunt, "Tantee." "We can
get the dressmaker to fill in the decolleté with tulle and
shorten it. Do let her go, Mabel, it will be fun for her."
"She can wear my red mohair cape to the dance," Granny
said, who always thought Mother was too strict with me.
"Do please say yes," begged Mrs. Harlan. "John has to
know at once so that he can fill in his dance card." I
was never asked what I felt about the matter or consulted. I
was still a child and supposedly incapable of making
decisions. Father was in South America, Grandfather
stood aloof from the argument. So in the end the women
of the family (who had all the power anyway) decided that
it was right and proper to let me go. Mrs. Harlan was a
tower of propriety, and would watch me like a hawk.
John, a very good-looking young man, was extremely
serious and conventional, so there seemed no possibility
that I would "get into mischief."

In those days a prom was taken very seriously, and invitations to the various clubs at Princeton were sought
after months in advance. John seemed to have everything
perfectly arranged, and all Mrs. Harlan and I had to do
was to take the train to Princeton Junction. After twenty-
four hours of mad preparation with the whole house in an
uproar and Stella, the dressmaker, ensconced in the sewing
room, I was considered properly equipped for the Princeton visit. My equipment included Tantee's white chiffon
and silver evening dress, Granny's cape, two cotton dresses
miraculously whipped up by Stella, a pair of silver high-
heeled slippers, and, most exciting of all, my long hair

rolled into a bun at the nape of my neck. To have my hair "up" made me feel that I had attained a new status. However, I had no makeup, no perfume, nothing but my own dumpy little self and a tremendous desire to please even though I was surging with a mixture of fear and a sense of adventure and anticipation. I still felt a bit like a bathtub toy that is thrown out to make an Atlantic crossing. So off I went into the unknown with Mrs. Harlan, who seemed pleased with my demure outfit.

Princeton was at its very best—all the beautiful trees in full leaf on the campus and along the streets, Lake Carnegie sparkling in the sunshine, but above all, the laughter and the gaiety of young voices. The windows of the dormitories were flung open and young people were hanging out of them, waving to their friends below and sometimes singing along with the Victrola. Only a few years before Scott Fitzgerald had been there, and the campus seemed to retain the aura of his personality. People were cramming themselves nine in a car—"cut-outs" off and tops down. There was movement everywhere and a sense of joy in being young and irresponsible and protected. At the Ivy Club the very cream of Princeton was gathered. We lunched there where they all talked and laughed and sang and some wandered away in twos. Instead of any flirtatious goings-on, John, Mrs. Harlan, and I visited Nassau Hall, had tea with some old friends of Mrs. Harlan's, and dined that night at Mrs. Moses Taylor Pyne's lovely old house "Drumthwacket." After that came the highlight— the prom itself, held in the gymnasium, with Meyer Davis leading a full orchestra. I hardly knew what I was doing; and when I went to the dressing room to leave Granny's cape, my heart sank as I saw the chic sophisticated girls around me. Girls who had already "come out" who wore backless, beaded dresses and carried ostrich feather fans. I could talk precociously to Mother's friends and giggle with my girl friends, but I had no "line," no shield of protection between me and this intense competition. Fortunately, in those ancient days, there was the "dance card," and as John was extremely popular I had every dance taken with a suitable partner. We danced cheek to cheek to tunes that still jingle in my head although I can no longer remember them by name. What I do remember was that I suddenly had as a partner a young man who could not dance at all. He held me at arm's length as we shuffled about the floor, and he paid no attention to the rhythm of the music. I should have been warned by this. He lacked rhythm—a very important lack.

He did, however, do something none of the others had done. He looked into my eyes, and I looked into his. He had the bluest eyes I had ever seen, and they were alight with an interest in *me*. The others had all said, "This music is great, isn't it?" How do you like Princeton?" "Where do you come from?" "What school do you go to?" and oh, horrors, "How old are you?" Of course, I lied about the last. "Seventeen," I said glibly, "almost eighteen." When he—his name was Dryden Kuser—asked me that question I answered him in the same way, "Almost eighteen," which started our relationship all wrong and was exactly what my parents had told me not to do. If I had told him my real age he probably would have lost interest in me as being far too young for any Princeton senior and I would have been saved many heartaches. As it was, he proceeded to talk to me as someone on his own level. He talked about himself, asking my opinion as he talked. He told me that he was managing editor of the *Daily Princetonian*, a member of one of the two Debating Societies, president of the New Jersey Audubon Society and the author of a book, *The Birds of the Somerset Hills*, which was illustrated by Louis Agassiz Fuertes. He was, in addition, one of the seven neorealists who were studying under Professor Spaulding. This was heady conversation. I had only a foggy idea of who Audubon was and had never heard of neorealism; but I smiled and hung on every word he said with occasional interjections of, "How fascinating." "How marvelous." "Do tell me more." "It must be wonderful to do all that." And soon we were not dancing at all but just rocking on the floor, and he was telling me that I was "awfully pretty" and that he "certainly wanted to see more of me." The music stopped, John came up to introduce me to my next partner, and then they were playing "Good Night, Ladies" for the third time and the prom was over. As we were leaving, Dryden rushed up to me, card and pen in hand, and asked for my address. I wrote it out for him while John looked on rather impatiently. (Dryden was the only man on my card who was not Ivy Club!)

When I got back to Washington my family wanted to know all about Princeton and the prom. What were the names of the boys I had met, did people like my dress, did I remember to always be near Mrs. Harlan and John, did anyone say I looked pretty, was Princeton an attractive place—this from Mother, who thought that Harvard was the only really intellectual college. I answered as best I could, saying I had met one particularly attractive and intelligent man called Dryden Kuser. Mother laughed uproariously at my use of the word "man" instead of "boy" and Granny said, "Kuser—what a funny name. Where on earth does he come from, who *is* he?" I could not answer these questions, and the subject was dropped. They were pleased I had enjoyed myself. Now that it was over I would probably never go to a Princeton prom again or hear from anyone called Kuser.

I had already been taken out of the senior class at Madeira without graduating because Mother thought it too pedantic. I had even left the more easygoing school, and it had been decided that the best thing for me to do was to

settle down to my studies at home. I could then perfect
my French, learn more American history, and try to play
the piano. These tasks, with golf and a few tennis lessons,
would keep me well occupied. But that return to childhood was not to be. Within a few days I was being bom-
barded with letters. First came a copy of the *Oxford Book
of English Verse*, beautifully bound in blue leather, tooled
in gold and inscribed to "Miss Brooke Russell from Dryden Kuser." A very nice, correct gift according to
Mother, but those letters went on coming every day. Of
course, I answered them (my first reply began with "My
very dear Mr. Kuser"), and soon I received a bunch of vi-
olets with a rose in the center. Mother did not know that
in the language of the day this meant "I love you." Oh,
heavens, what a thrill that was, and how I boasted to my
friends of my mysterious Princeton beau! They, poor
girls, only knew wretched boys who went to the Cathedral School and had to take a bus to school instead of riding around in a Stutz Bearcat as Dryden told me he did.

After a firm entente had been established, telephone
calls started, and I was whispering and laughing on the telephone for an hour at a time. Then I would call Janet or
Evie Wadsworth or Nancy Hoyt, and relay a highly
colored version of these exhilarating conversations. They
were all "livid" with envy, but fascinated that I had
achieved this sensational triumph, and they hung on my
words. Not so Mother. She became irritated that none of
her friends could ever reach her on the telephone as it was
always busy. "You are getting beyond yourself, Brooke,"
she said. "You are becoming a silly little bore, this boy has
gone to your head. Tell him that he is only to call once
every other week, and then only over weekends. Your
tutors say that your marks are all going down—and quite
apart from all this we have never heard of the Kusers and

have never seen this boy. He can't be very well brought up, calling the house all the time." Mother's word was law to me and I relayed her message to Dryden.

The one adult who took me seriously was my grandmother. Sitting in front of the coal fire in the "Green Room" of my grandparents house on N Street, I told and re-told the story of my Princeton visit to her, embellishing it more each time for Granny's interest and delight. Granny had been my confidante ever since we had returned from Peking, and about once a month Mother let me spend a night there. My grandparents' house was a five-story brownstone with a large bay window on the drawing room and main bedroom floors. That house was full of mystery and dreams to me, although it was slightly gloomy and not really attractive by today's standards. The front room on the ground floor, which was separated from the hall by double velvet portières, was called the Green Room because the portières and sofas were green and the Axminster carpet was green, with red roses all over it. There was a large mantelpiece with a coal grate, and on each side of the mantel, mahogany bookcases with glass doors which were always kept locked by my grandfather. There was a large stair hall with a fireplace, and at the back was the dining room. The pantry had a dumbwaiter, and we communicated with the kitchen and the servants by a speaking tube built in the wall which wailed eerily when used. The stair walls were covered with rubbings from famous medieval English tombs, while the second-floor hall was hung with steel engravings of scenes from Shakespeare's plays and a mammoth painting of "The Return of the Prodigal Son." The drawing room in front was done in faded blue velvet, with gray damask curtains, and was crowded with Dresden china figurines and a tray and tea set of Dresden china. All the china was a present from Granny's sister who had married a man who for a long

time was U. S. Consul in Dresden. There were a pair of vit-
rine tables filled with curios—mostly presents sent by rela-
tives who had visited the far corners of the world. These
curios were fascinating to me—a tiny silver slipper, some
netsuke, a little porcelain egg with an infinitesimal chicken
at its center. No one went into the drawing room, except
on rare occasions when Granny had an "At Home"; but I
sat there sometimes and tried to imagine how it had looked
when Father and Mother were married in that very room:
Mother all in white satin and Father in his full-dress blues
and his sword buckled at his side. How romantic it must
have been! The back room on that floor, called the morning room, was my favorite. It had fat upholstered armchairs, Grandfather's upright piano with its swinging brass
candlesticks, and again two large bookcases which, unlike
the ones downstairs, were kept unlocked. Here I found
Sherlock Holmes, Edgar Allen Poe, Wilkie Collins and
Histories of Famous Crimes. All his life Grandfather was
engaged in writing a history of crime. His many other activities included a workshop on the fourth floor where he
worked on clocks and made over old furniture he had
bought at junk shops. He also tried to make things of his
own, such as a little chair for me, which stood close to the
fireplace in the Green Room. This house had a great impact on me, because it was so unlike our own house. It was
always quiet, and one could hear the many clocks ticking
the time away. I felt as though I was in a cocoon, caught
up in a bygone era. Looking back I suppose my grandfather was a bit of an eccentric. He considered that Washington in the summer was a tropical city and dressed ac-
cordingly. He wore a white pith helmet lined in green,
called a topee (made popular by English colonials in tropical climates, as a protection against the heat). He also
carried a pongee parasol lined in green and wore pongee
suits and white shoes. As I have said, he had a passion for

clocks and there must have been at least five in every room
—all running, and striking the hours. It was total pandemonium at midday and midnight. He didn't neglect his two
pocket watches, either, but kept them hanging on a little
stand when not in use; he claimed to lay a watch flat was
bad for it. He was a great clubman, one of the earliest
members of the Chevy Chase Club and a staunch member
of the Metropolitan Club where he went every Sunday
after church. He was a lawyer by profession and was fond
of arguing and probing into why such and such a thing
was possible or impossible. He was full of curiosity about
people and life, and was a marvelous storyteller. All of this
bored my grandmother. She only cared for a few friends
to gossip with and never read anything except what was
then called a "light novel." I loved her dearly because she
doted on me, and we wove dreams together. One saying of
Grandfather's made a great impression on me, and I have
often quoted it to myself. It was on a Sunday when Grandfather was quite late for lunch and Granny was furious.
"The roast will be ruined," she said. "Whatever kept
you?" "I was talking to so-and-so," replied Grandfather,
naming a certain man, "and I forgot the time." "Law, Mr.
Howard," said Granny, "why bother talking to that
bore?" "Now, now, Bertie," Grandfather responded, "I
know that he is a vain man, a limited man, a damn fool,
but I like him." What more can one say about a friend?

Meanwhile Dryden responded to Mother's boycott by
coming down to Washington, meeting Mother, and taking
us out to lunch. Mother thought him a delightful young
man. He had set out to charm her, and he succeeded. Having accomplished this, he proceeded to sweep me along on
the wave of an emotion I had never experienced before.
When we were alone in the drawing room of our house,
just before he was leaving to go back to New York, he
kissed me. He kissed me not once but many, many times,

making my head reel, and only stopping when we heard
Mother coming down the stairs. After he had gone I
remained in a dreamy haze, looking at myself in the mirror
to see if I had changed. Was I really pretty, was I really attractive, could such a person love me? Love to me was
Shakespeare's sonnets, Swinburne, moonlight, starlight,
soft music, and someone telling me over and over again
how lovely I was. It was not a very good background for
marriage, but marriage never entered my head. Marriage
was something that older people liked and had something
to do with having children—all of *that* had nothing to do
with *me*. I, Brooke, was embarking on a romantic career
and learning how to flirt as I had seen Mother do. I
remained in this delicious state for a couple of months, and
only really woke up after my visit to the Kusers in Bernardsville, New Jersey.

The Kusers would not be easy for me to cope with
even today, after a long lifetime of coping. On that first
visit I was incapable of judging them. They lived in a huge
Italianate house in Bernardsville, New Jersey. The floors
were marble and the double staircase had a red carpet with
a white linen runner held down on each step by a shining
brass rod. The decor of the house was frightful, what
Mother called Early Pullman. Stiff brocade armchairs with
fringes around the bottom were scattered through the main
rooms at such a distance that it was almost impossible for
conversation. The bedrooms were all "suites"—in other
words, identically matched wood furniture with Tiffany
glass lamps by the bedside. Even I, young as I was, thought
it very odd. I was accustomed to shabby, pretty furniture,
lots of books and sofa cushions, and good reading lights.
In any event, I survived that first weekend, dazzled by the
hideous grandeur—the butler and three footmen in the
dining room, the personal maid, the four chauffeurs. It
was quite awe-inspiring to me.

I was equally overcome by the attention the Kusers showered on me. No grown-up had ever taken me seriously before. Mrs. Kuser admired my simple dresses, my lack of makeup, the curtsey that I still made when introduced. She compared me favorably to Dryden's friends who she thought were not the right sort for him. These girls were a far more sophisticated group than I had ever known. They were "chic" New York girls, quite different from the Washington girls, whose social life in those days was controlled by the old-world Diplomatic Corps and the arrogant but dowdy Washington families who were known as "Cave Dwellers." "Party calls" were paid the Sunday after a party. There still were "At Home" days and when a diplomat was leaving Washington he usually made a round of "Pour prendre congé calls"—the corner of the card turned down in order to show he had called "in person." In New York things were still a bit formal, but the young had far more freedom. In Bernardsville the girls all had their own cars. They smoked and drank occasionally and played highly competitive sports. To be young and rich in those days was to live a perpetual holiday. No one worked until they had finished college, so all the holidays were spent at home or at resorts, and all the summers were given up to sports and parties.

My life had been so much simpler. We never left Washington for more than a month in the summer, and we never thought of going away in the winter. I had spent more time with older people (longing to be like them) than I had with people my own age. In spite of my father urging me on to play tennis and golf (he was a first-class tennis player) I never really was much of an athlete. And so I was completely out of my depth in this new world of New Jersey, which seemed to be so preoccupied with indoor and outdoor games. But Dryden's attentions and the Kusers' flattery quite turned my head. I felt that I was really a grown-up person, and rather an extraordinary one at that! Things went on faster and faster, as in *Alice in Wonderland*, until by the end of the summer they culminated in Dryden's asking me to marry him. I could not even say yes or no—as I had never thought of such a thing—so, after I returned home, he wrote Mother, saying not only that he loved me and wanted to marry me but that his father and mother totally approved of me.

Mother was aghast. "What is all this talk about marrying?" she said to me. "This whole thing is absolutely crazy. Don't they know that you are just sixteen?" I had to admit then that I had lied about my age. I cried on Mother's shoulder because I was frightened. It was the only time in my life that I was glad that Father was not there. "There is only one thing to do," Mother said, giving me a kiss. "Don't cry, Brooke dear, write Dryden and Mrs. Kuser, tell them that you are *just* sixteen and that you told a fib (it was dear of her not to call it a lie) about your age. The whole thing is a comedy of errors, there is nothing to cry about, so be a good girl and write the letters, but let me see them before you post them." Ignominiously I had to write the two dreary letters, and when Mother sealed and stamped them, I felt that I had reached the end of a saga. I was rather relieved in a way, as I knew in my heart that the situation was more than I was capable of handling. The Kusers, however, were not to be held off. Colonel—complimentary title given for favors done for the Governor of New Jersey—and Mrs. Kuser came down to Washington in their private railway car and had a long talk with Mother and Grandfather and Granny. I was the perfect girl for Dryden, they said. They loved my "girlish simplicity," my "good manners," and my "sweetness." In addition, they found me very mature for my age (which I certainly was not), and they said that I could easily have been eighteen. They mentioned money quite often.

Mother said in later years that they were *nouveau riche* and vulgar, but at the time she must have been dazzled by the sums they mentioned. I would have material security for life, and I am sure that she, never having really had it, felt that this was a great thing. I was making a "good marriage"—especially as my future in-laws seemed to be as much in love with me as Dryden.

Although my parents were not rich, we had lived out of America so much that we had always benefited by a good dollar exchange, and had lived in a way which we could not have possibly afforded at home. We had spent a year divided between Panama and Hawaii, then we had returned to the U.S.A. for two years in Newport, where Father was teaching at the Naval War College. There we had a tiny little house on Bellevue Avenue sandwiched in between "The Reading Room" and the Park—and I went to school for the first time. My father had a small income beside his pay, and in those days Mother was young and not really extravagant. It was only when we went to Peking that we lived in a way that accustomed Mother to a more luxurious mode of life. She reveled in the Peking life, but I, being a child, simply took it for granted. We had a large household ruled by the "Number One," or what one would call the maître d'hôtel, or steward. He engaged the numerous servants and was only rivaled by "cook," who presided over a horde of underlings in the kitchen. To complete the summit trio, there was Amah, Mother's personal maid, who kept an eye on me, too. Father had polo ponies, Mother had a horse, and I a little Mongolian pony, on whose back I rode to school with the "mafoo," or groom, running by my side.

Mother was able to send to Paris for clothes and had them copied by the tailor who lived in our house. He was also kept busy making dresses for the numerous fancy dress parties that were given at the various legations. I went to children's parties dressed as a rose, or a Quaker girl, or as a forget-me-not (which costume I wore to dance around a Maypole). We lived on a lavish scale, not only physically but mentally. I say this because in Peking the Legation Society was quite fascinating. In the French Legation there were the de Margeries (Madame de Margerie was the sister of Edmond Rostand, the poet, and author of *Chantecler*), and there were also the Picots, well-known for a famous treaty. Max Müller, Patrick Ramsay, and Sir John and Lady Jordan were at the British Legation, while at the Belgian Legation there was a Lambert, and at the Italian, Brambilla. At the Banque de Chine was Maurice Cazenave, and there was also Willard Straight, who married Dorothy Whitney and came out to Peking on his honeymoon. There were Russians and Danes and Poles—all of them sending around a "chit book" every day which carried invitations to the never ending rounds of parties. The "chit book" was very helpful, because one could see who else was invited and then decide whether one really wanted to go or not.

Mother was then in her very early thirties, and she absorbed all this glittering world of Continental and British sophistication with a hearty American appetite. The totally different outlook which had made Grandfather so attractive to Granny was even stronger in Mother because she was Grandfather's daughter. She had been brought up on Dickens and Thackeray, and Gilbert and Sullivan, but now she became at home with Proust and Baudelaire, Richard Strauss and Poulenc, Pierre Louÿs and Bertrand Russell. Instead of the waltz, she danced the tango in a dress slit to the knee, and an aigrette in her hair. While all this was going on, Father hobnobbed with his brother officers and some Chinese mandarins. He took a Chinese lesson every day and learned both to speak it and write it. The Chinese city with its color and movement was even more fascinating. As Lin Yutang, the historian and writer, once said to me, "When you lived in Peking, Peking was twenty-five years behind the rest of China, and China was twenty-five years behind the Western world." Writing of Peking as I do now, it is as though I were writing of a city of a hundred years ago. I remember the fairs at the Temple of Agriculture, so full of varied and intriguing booths, with foods steaming away in braziers, candied red apples strung on poles, little crickets in bamboo cages, marvelous dolls and colored stilts and traveling players, and magicians strolling through the crowd. I spoke Chinese fluently; and I chattered away with everyone, and found the Chinese so kind and patient with me, and so full of humor.

There was the Temple of Heaven where we used to ride—so incredibly beautiful that I can shut my eyes and still see its lapis lazuli tiled roof, its marvelous white marble steps, and its huge open marble altar said to be the center of the earth. Then the noise and color in the streets, the mingling of carriages, Peking carts, rickshaws, vendors, ordinary pedestrians walking their birds in cages, camels, mules, and donkeys, all combined to make any stage production pale beside it. Not the least colorful were the nine ranks of mandarins who were distinguished by the color of the stone they wore on the top of their hat, and the liveries of the outriders who accompanied their carriages as they dashed through the narrow lanes.

When this mosaic of splendor (and squalor, too) was combined with the elegant and sometimes reckless gaiety of the Legation quarter, it could not fail to affect an impressionable and vital woman of thirty; and as it changed my mother, so it filtered down through her to me. She wished to bring me up like a *jeune fille* of the nineteenth century. I was always to make a curtsey when meeting an older person. I was never to speak unless spoken to. I was to wear high laced boots to keep my ankles slim. I had to walk with a board strapped to my shoulders and a book on my head to improve my posture. This I refused to do when I was about thirteen, as my bosom had begun to sprout, to my great embarrassment, and I preferred to slouch to hide this dreadful disfigurement.

When we returned to Washington our "life style" had to change. We no longer had the huge entourage—there was no maître d'hôtel or head chef, or live-in tailor—instead, we had a housemaid, a cook, and, for Mother and me, that great extravagance, a French maid (provided by Granny). Mother insisted that the French maid had to walk with me to and from school. I absolutely detested this supervision. By the time I was in my teens, most of the other girls would stop off at a drugstore and even dare to linger to have an ice-cream soda in order to take a look at the boys who in their turn were engaged in looking at *them*. Mother brought with her from Peking some very strong ideas of what she wanted to do, and Granny agreed with her. So, thanks to a little pinching on Mother's part, and to financial help from Grandfather and Granny, I was sent to the best schools, went to the best dancing class, and always had the sort of dresses Mother liked.

These are all superficial things, I know; however, I still consider them as nice fringe benefits. There was very little talk of what I would do when my education was finished. Certainly the good school was important, not only for the education it gave me, but for the friends I made. I loved school, and I never guessed that it might be hard for Mother to make ends meet. She was so gay, and she enjoyed life so much. There was nothing of the martyr in her, and I took it for granted that I should be dressed well, and that I could always bring friends back to the house from school for a potluck meal or some hot chocolate.

The maid was really what I hated most, and I made her life as difficult as possible, sometimes running full tilt, dragging my feet at other times. But she, Catherine by name, was absolutely conscientious and took me straight home down tree-shaded Connecticut Avenue, past the British Embassy on N Street to our own little tree-lined street. We lived on De Sales Street, and where the Mayflower Hotel now stands was a convent with a huge walled garden. There were horse chestnut trees on both sides of the street, and the convent garden was full of lilac bushes, snowball trees, and syringa. From our upstairs sitting room, and from my bedroom on the third floor, we could look down and see the nuns walking in pairs through the garden paths. I often thought I would like to be a nun and live in a lovely garden. I would tend the flowers as the priests did in the temple, and as Mother was fond of saying to her friends, "I could invite my soul." But these thoughts were rather fleeting, and I took to writing poetry à la Swinburne instead. This, then, was the silly young miss who was considered to be ripe for matrimony.

All in all the idea of my marriage seemed an extraordinary piece of good fortune, and Mother convinced herself that it was the best thing for me. She told the Kusers that if I really wanted to marry Dryden she would give her consent and she wrote to Father, who was in South America, telling him the marvelous news.

I, too, became intoxicated with the idea of marriage. Dryden promised me my own house, and all the dogs I wanted, and a car of my own as soon as I was old enough to get a license. I began to think that I would want a pale lavender bedroom with a huge four-poster bed like Granny's and a grand piano in the drawing room. Of course I said "Yes" and Dryden kissed me a lot and wanted to make love, but I held him off—not being at all sure what he was really talking about! His suggestions seemed very weird to me! The wedding date was decided and Father arrived home a few days before and seemed to-

tally bewildered by all the confusion in the house. Grandfather gave me Meyer Davis and his orchestra to play at
the wedding reception at Rauscher's. The family pooled
their money and gave me a complete set of table silver in a
mahogany chest from Tiffany. Mother had a marvelous
time choosing clothes for me, including the wedding dress
and the bridesmaids' dresses. My wedding dress, as I
remember it, was a plain white satin with long sleeves and
a square neck. The bridesmaids' costumes were prettier—
pale green chiffon with large leghorn hats trimmed with
apple blossoms. We had wedding pictures taken which I
tore up after our divorce. I enjoyed showing off my huge
sapphire ring to my friends, and with it the sapphire and
diamond necklace which was the Kusers' wedding present.
It was not the value, but the fairy-tale glitter that attracted
me. I was really a princess.

On a sunny April afternoon, flanked by a wedding
party of eighteen, I walked up the aisle of St. John's Episcopal Church on Lafayette Square in Washington on my
dear father's arm. With the aid of Bishop Harding, the
Bishop of Washington, and the Reverend Roland Cotton
Smith, rector of St. John's, I became, in half an hour, Mrs.
Dryden Kuser, which was to be my name for ten years.

3

Nothing in my previous life had prepared me for the combination of circumstances with which I had to deal as a
young married woman—or more exactly, as a married ex-
schoolgirl.

The wedding trip to White Sulphur Springs was a disaster. It began with a frightful night-train trip down. The roadbed seemed unable to hold the train, which lurched from side to side with all its couplings clanging. The situation in our drawing room was somewhat comparable when in my white nightgown with blue ribbons on my shoulders and a blue satin sash around my waist I tried to avoid Dryden's grasp. It was a losing battle; and at six in the morning when we got off at White Sulphur junction, I was feeling very sorry for myself indeed. Was this what happened to everybody? Was *that* what grown-up ladies did behind closed doors? How could they come out smiling, or flirt, or be gay when they knew what a dreadful ending was in store? To face the facts fairly, we were a totally miscast pair. Dryden was oversexed and completely inexperienced, and I was hopelessly ignorant and unprepared in any way for this great adventure.

To make matters worse, Dryden's father's valet had forgotten to pack a dinner jacket for him. In those far-off days a man was not allowed in the dining room of a good hotel unless he wore a dinner jacket. So every night we had to dine in our suite. I dragged my feet slowly as I went up the stairs listening to the music and the sounds of laughter as people gathered in groups for cocktails and Dryden stayed behind for a drink or two in the bar. I was not allowed in the bar, because of my age, and I did not drink anyway until I was over twenty-four. So, forlornly, I went up to the suite, where my brand new evening dresses were hanging unused in the closet.

Although I was totally ignorant of sex, I knew what love was, and I quite certainly knew that there was more to a relationship between a man and a woman than just sex. How could Father and Mother be so happy if it was such a violent act? I was no longer ignorant but I was still innocent. I was greatly relieved when at last the wretched ten

days were over, and we were back in Washington for an
overnight visit to my family. When I saw the dear little
drawing room, with its toile de jouy curtains, and all the
pretty familiar things, and Father and Mother standing in
front of the fireplace, I rushed to Father, and throwing my
arms around his neck, burst into tears.

"There, there, Little Woman," he said, patting my
back. "I've missed you terribly," I sobbed. Father gave me
a hug, and then, turning me over to Mother, shook hands
heartily with Dryden. When Mother and I were alone
before dinner, she asked me if I was all right, and I said,
"Yes, but I'm homesick." "So was I when your father and I
were first married," said Mother. "But I got over it. Besides,
you can always come to us for a visit." But that was not
to be; within a month Father was ordered to Haiti, where
he and Mother stayed for ten years. The first two years
he was in command of the Marines, and for the next eight
he was High Commissioner with the rank of Ambassador.
I was left to make out as best I could.

Dryden and I spent our first summer living with the
Kusers. We had a huge sitting room and a bedroom. The
bedroom was all freshly done up for us in gray-blue velvet. There were twin walnut beds with velvet backs, and
spreads. Velvet curtains, two velvet armchairs, a walnut
dressing table and bureau and a lamp on the bedside table,
between the beds, which was a cluster of opalescent glass
calla lilies, a tiny bulb in each lily, and a dozen or so weird
leaves springing from a gold stem. I remember every detail
of that room to this very day. The sitting room, which had
been Dryden's before our marriage, was oval, and had
huge repoussé red velvet sofas and green, yellow, and red
Tiffany lamps with bead fringes. There was nothing anywhere that was even faintly reminiscent of what I thought
of as home. I was not even allowed to keep my Pekingese,

Lulu, as Mrs. Kuser thought it was not properly house trained.

That first summer I did not know really where I was, or what I was. I was still only a young girl making my curtsey to older ladies, jumping up when any older person came into the room. I had been brought up to respect my elders and I had no idea of asserting myself. Dryden had a sister, fourteen years younger than he was, who was the apple of the Kusers' eye. One night a week, when the governess went off, it was called "treat night" because Mrs. Kuser had six o'clock supper with the little girl and spent the night in the nursery. It was on those evenings that I began to learn something about the Kusers. When Colonel Kuser was alone with Dryden and me he talked and talked. I grew very fond of him. Although he was hard and tough he had the most brilliant blue three-cornered eyes—sailor's eyes, although he never sailed—and a nice smile. I had never met a self-made tycoon before and I found him fascinating.

First of all, I learned from him that the very rich think that they are never wrong. The arrogance of big money is one of the most unappealing of characteristics, and it goes very deep. Most very rich people think of themselves as simple and undemanding. I was astonished, too, that Colonel Kuser, who had started from nothing, had no use for anyone who had not succeeded in life. This included his group of male secretaries (they did not have women secretaries in those days). The way he barked out orders to his secretaries used to upset me. "Never be rude to someone in your employ who cannot fight back," my family had told me; but here I saw it before me every day. It did not make me wish to do the same: On the contrary, I used to try to smile and pretend that I had not heard his rudeness. Colonel Kuser's attitude was as effective in its way as my family's admonitions. It made me want to be polite and kind—

to put myself in the other person's shoes. To see a grown man groveling in order to keep his job is a horrible sight.

On the other hand, for the first time I began to learn about free enterprise and how it works. My family on both sides had been, for generations, professional men—lawyers, soldiers, plantation owners or members of the foreign service. None of them had ever made much money, although Charles Carroll, barrister, had not done badly financially, nor had the Spences. Nevertheless, they were certainly neither among the robber barons nor among the big spenders. So for the first time I was talking to a man whose family had come to this country penniless from Austria in 1848 and who had climbed the financial ladder from poverty to opulence in one generation. Colonel Kuser and his twin brother John became the two wealthiest members of the large Kuser family; and of the two, Colonel Anthony R. Kuser was the richer. As youths they had lived in Trenton, New Jersey, where Colonel Kuser had started his career as a "pants presser," and then as a streetcar conductor and I can't remember what else, until suddenly (as he told it) he became involved in New Jersey Light and Traction, which eventually became Public Service of N.J., was the largest stockholder in Fox Films and married Miss Susan Dryden, the daughter of Senator John F. Dryden, the founder of the Prudential Insurance Company. She lived in a huge private house on Broad Street, Newark, had had several "seasons" in Washington when her father was Senator (which meant that during those winters she had mingled with what was then Washington's most exclusive society) and would have nothing to do with any member of Colonel Kuser's family, including his twin brother. "A farm" outside Trenton was several "classes" below the stately home on Broad Street and the title "Senator" many cuts above Colonel Kuser's mother—Mrs. Rosalia Kuser, affectionately called "Gross-

mutter," who ran the farm. I only visited her on her farm
once and was called down by Mrs. Kuser, who would not
speak to me for over a week.

Colonel Kuser had one hobby that was surprising. He
was intensely interested in ornithology. Because of this interest, Dryden was taken on early morning bird walks
with a trained ornithologist from the time that he was old
enough to carry binoculars. This started Dryden on his career as an ornithologist. Unfortunately, he lost interest in
birds while at Princeton, but in our early married days he
could still, while lying in bed on a spring morning,
write down the calls of seventy-eight birds, either resident
in New Jersey or migrant. I think that one of Colonel
Kuser's first disappointments in Dryden was that Dryden
did not continue and become a dedicated ornithologist.
Just a few years before Dryden and I were married, Colonel Kuser attempted to nurture that hope by buying a
12,000-acre estate called "High Point." It was a beautiful
untouched bit of land, and it was crowned by a rambling
house which rode the crest of a rocky crag overlooking
three states—New Jersey, New York, and Pennsylvania.
Soon after we were married we were sent up there to look
it over. It was quite the bleakest place I had ever seen, and
seemed a million miles from anywhere. Only an ideally
suited couple with six perfect self-sufficient children could
have ever survived there. We were certainly far from that,
and the sight of a poised rattlesnake arising from his sleep
near a rock did not add to the charm. Dryden and I were
totally united in agreeing that this was not the place for us.
Colonel Kuser was quite distressed, but eventually he gave
it to the state as a park, and Dryden at the end of his life
returned there to marry the widow of the resident care-
taker. How lucky we are not to know the future!

Colonel Kuser was upset by Dryden's lack of enthusiasm, but he never lost his own. He had found William

Beebe at the New York Zoological Society in the Bronx
and had persuaded him to take time off from being the Curator of Birds to go out to India to study the pheasant.
The result was the definitive four-volume monograph on
pheasants, illustrated with beautiful colored plates which
took Beebe eleven years to complete. It is a prized item
among collectors today and is a monument to both Beebe
and Colonel Kuser.

The great social event of the Kusers' life was to go to
the Zoo Members Garden Party in June and to talk to
Will Beebe and Dr. Hornaday, the director, and Frederick Edwin Church, the artist, and Madison Grant, the
anthropologist, Dr. Ditmars, the herpetologist, and other
colleagues. For these annual occasions a large striped tent
was erected just at the top of the steps outside the Administration Building, and ices and soft drinks were served.
Colonel Kuser was really in his element. I tagged along,
never dreaming that one day the Zoo would become an
important part of my life.

At home in Bernardsville, at "Faircourt" there was
a huge eliptical room called the pheasant room. The ceiling
was made up of polychrome squares with a different spe-
cies of pheasant in each square; and along the entire length
of one side of the room was a glass case filled with stuffed
pheasants. These birds were assembled as though in their
natural habitat, grazing and nesting among the snows and
crags of Mount Kanchenjunga.

At Faircourt I found it rather dreary to sit drinking
Darjeeling tea and peptonized milk, facing a display of
birds who never moved in a room where the sun never
penetrated. I often felt like one of those birds, behind
glass, in a never changing landscape.

Dryden and I played golf and tennis and drove madly
over the winding roads. We saw other young people but
we always had to be home for meals, and we had to be on

time. If we were not, Colonel Kuser had his watch on the
table and $100 was taken off our allowance for every min-
ute that we were late. My original charm for the Kusers
began to wear off. Dryden was drinking on the sly, not
getting drunk but being a bit loud and talking back to his
parents. This was not at all what they had bargained for. I
was supposed to have changed his habits, and by my
maidenly behavior to have transformed the wayward son
into a model of filial piety and devotion. On the contrary,
I am afraid, the very qualities they liked in me were
Dryden's undoing. I literally drove him to drink, and his
parents into retiring to their upstairs sitting room and lock-
ing the door behind them.

As autumn drew near Colonel Kuser arranged that
Dryden be made a vice-president of the Lenox China Co.,
which Colonel Kuser controlled. He and Mrs. Kuser
thought that it would be a good idea if we rented a house
in Princeton in order to be near the factory, which was in
Trenton. This arrangement was more than agreeable to us
all. Dryden and I found a house in Princeton, and a
French couple to run it, and with a huge newly acquired
Airedale called Sandy McTavish we moved in during the
month of September.

What a joy it was to have a house of our own! It was
an old person's house, furnished with mahogany rocking
chairs and stiff Victorian sofas. But that really did not
matter much to me when my friends began streaming up
from Washington to go to the football games and the Tri-
angle Club shows. As a married woman, I was the perfect
chaperone. Dryden's friends, an older and racier group,
poured down from New York and up from Philadelphia. I
forgot my parents' admonitions, and every day I ordered
all the things I had been forbidden to eat at home—
creamed sweetbreads, hot chocolate with whipped cream
(Lenox China made special chocolate cups), and ice cream

with chocolate sauce. While Dryden drank, I ate and ate, and at the end of the winter I weighed ten pounds more than Dryden.

It was quite a winter. Dryden went off to the factory, and I sat in on some classes and walked Sandy McTavish around Lake Carnegie. I really cannot remember it all now, in fact I think that having all that extra weight put me into a sort of hibernation. The French have a saying "*Reculez pour mieux sauter* [Withdraw to advance further]." I suppose that was what I was doing without knowing it. I hid behind my fat, and in doing so, continued in the role of a little girl. It was a form of refusing to admit that I was grown-up and should take on responsibilities.

We left that house on one early summer day. The blinds drawn down neatly in every room, as though there had been a death in the house. We certainly had no regrets on leaving. Dryden was no happier than I was. So ended the first year of my marriage. I never asked myself if this was all there was to life. It was certainly not the way my parents behaved together, but then *everything* was so different—my surroundings, the new people, being a married woman and a chaperone. I was neither unhappy nor happy. I was in limbo.

4

That second summer we Kusers set forth on a visit to Europe. We crossed on the *Olympic* and the jolly little group consisted of Colonel and Mrs. Kuser, Dryden,

Cynthia, and me. To support us we had a trained nurse, a
governess, a valet, and a personal maid. On arriving in
France we were met by a Swiss courier called Fazenac
who was probably one of the greatest rascals ever to conduct rich and helpless Americans around Europe.
Strangely enough, Colonel Kuser, so tough and so sure of
himself at home, was meek as Moses with Fazenac. Instead
of going either to the Ritz or the Meurice or the Crillon,
we went directly to the Grand Hôtel du Louvre, a totally
commercial hotel. But Colonel Kuser thought it must be
the best because it was three times the price of the Plaza at
home. Fazenac could pull the wool right over his eyes,
since none of us ever saw a bill or handled any cash.
Fazenac moved like a prince, paid for everything, and
every day or so had to guide Colonel Kuser to the bank in
order that he could draw on his letter of credit.

After four days in Paris, the Kusers were to go off
with Fazenac to Carlsbad and Marienbad (cure and after-
cure) and be gone three weeks. It had been arranged that
we were to stay on at the Grand Hôtel du Louvre, but I
had other plans. Mother had not talked to me about the
Goncourts and Stendhal and the pleasures of the Left
Bank for nothing—I wanted to go where I could drench
myself in the atmosphere of these famous people. I wanted
to tread the streets they had trod, to sit at the cafés they
had frequented, and to stroll along the Seine.

When we had been in Paris six years before on our
way home from China and stayed at a tiny hotel behind
the Place Vendôme, Mother had said at that time that the
best restaurant in Paris was Foyot, across from the Palais
du Sénat at 33 rue de Tournon. She had been there several
times, but I, of course, being only eleven was left at the
hotel with a properly accredited maid, found by mother's
friend, Lady ffrench (who had also chosen the properly
priced and rather inconvenient hotel). Now, however, as a

married woman of over a year's standing, *I* wanted to go
to Foyot. Dryden and I had sneaked away and dined there
one night when the Kusers were still in Paris. The shabby
red velvet banquettes and the dark wood paneling were
quite unlike the dining room of the Grand Hôtel du
Louvre. Dryden and I feasted on the specialities and then
went up to see the few rooms above the restaurant that
constituted the hotel part of the establishment. I was
thrilled when, looking out of the window of our future
bedroom, I saw the Théâtre de l'Odéon and the Café Voltaire. The café was supposedly frequented by Voltaire
and, of course, by the theatrical people connected with the
Théâtre de l'Odéon. Dryden was not overcome as I was
by the drama of being in this literary atmosphere, but he
liked the idea of our doing something on our own, and so
we booked the room for a ten days' stay. When we got
back to the Grand Hôtel du Louvre and told the Kusers of
our plans, Colonel Kuser immediately said that as we had
chosen to give up the accommodations made for us by
Fazenac in the finest hotel in Paris, and preferred to stay in
some disgusting second-class filthy place, he would not
pay for it and we were to be entirely on our own until we
joined him in Switzerland. He and Mrs. Kuser both felt
that we would contract some vile disease, and they were
appalled by our ingratitude. We felt rather insecure as we
had no letter of credit; but Fazenac, though looking extremely sour, took Dryden to the bank, where Dryden
was able to cash a fairly large check. The Kusers left in a
huff, but we were elated. Looking back, I realize that we
did the craziest things and that the Kusers were quite right
to have been perturbed. We picked up people at the Place
du Tertre at the top of Montmartre. We went to a costume ball at the Opéra, all alone, met an expatriate American couple there, and became so attached to them that we
rented a car and took them with us on a motor trip to visit

the châteaux of the Loire. The car was a little bright yellow open Citröen, and I sat in the back seat, carrying a parasol. The couple, as it turned out, were not happy, and Dryden had the first of his many love affairs with the wife. She dressed in a mannish way with a man's hat pulled down over one side of her face, and smoked constantly, holding the cigarette in long nicotine-stained fingers until the ash dropped off. At first I had thought her fun, but when she started flirting with Dryden and they took turns driving, laughing uproariously in the front seat as the tires screeched around the curves, I no longer liked her, or enjoyed the trip. I was hurt, upset and furious. The husband had said that he was a writer, but early on I realized that his books would never be written. He talked as though he were going to be a second Proust, but his powers of observation would not have been up to one of the novels in the Rover Boys series.

At Langeais Dryden and I had a dreadful fight—again, the first of many—and I cried and said that I wanted to go home, and that I would never be happy again. Fate was with me. Dryden got tight after the row, insulted the husband and we awoke the next morning to find that the couple had left at dawn leaving us to pay the bill.

We were lucky to have gotten off so easily. We had never seen these people before the Opéra Ball, and had not the faintest idea who they were or where they came from. Once alone, Dryden and I were happier than we had ever been. Thinking back to Granny and Mother and Father, I remembered Granny's words, "Who were they?" Who were they indeed? I thought perhaps these new friends had been sent to teach me a lesson. Hadn't I been brought up never to talk to strangers? I clung to Dryden and forgave him. Unconsciously I felt that his parents had not taught him what mine had, and that I should have known better. In this mellow and hangdog mood, we rejoined the

Kusers in Basle. Eventually, after going over the St. Bernard Pass in cars so large they had to go forward and then back up in order to go forward again to get around a curve, with Dryden and me sitting on the "jump seats," we ended up in Venice. There we spent a ghastly few days with all of us wearing surgical masks made by the trained nurse, as the Kusers were fearful of infections arising from the polluted waters of the canals. We must have been a strange and eerie sight as our gondolier lazily propelled us around the canals and lagoons. Colonel and Mrs. Kuser, Cynthia, Dryden and I, the governess and nurse lay back in our gondolas, our faces swathed in white gauze. We had our own gondolas and our own gondoliers in smart white costumes topped by straw hats garlanded with long red ribbons. Their songs and other songs floated across the waters to us, all so full of amorous invitation; but all that melted like ice in the sun, when Colonel Kuser said, "These Italians are damn fools. Let's get out of here."

What they must have thought of us was another matter. I only knew that the sound of ribald laughter mingled with the impassioned sounds of "*Sole mio*" and "*Parla mi d'amore, Mariu*" as we glided by. They laughed at us while we remained in masquerade to them. We were in costume out of season. We cut our visit short; and as soon as tickets could be procured, on we went to the Savoy Hotel in London. Fazenac only functioned on the Continent, so once rid of him we fared better, but only in one way. The hotel was better but the service was frightful. Colonel Kuser did not deign to learn another currency beside the dollar and usually tipped tuppence or a halfpenny. Finally I made Dryden get some money so that we could surreptitiously leave it on the dining room table as we lingered behind his parents. My family having very little money put no value on it. They were always generous tippers, and it depressed me to be surrounded by scowls,

and to be seated each meal at a less and less desirable table.
The London visit over, we piled once more into the
Olympic and returned to Bernardsville. "Never again,"
said Colonel Kuser as he sipped his peptonized milk in the
pheasant room. "There's nothing over there that you can't
get better here. This is God's country." "It was a tiring
trip," added Mrs. Kuser. "Cynthia needs to stay home to
get the roses back in her cheeks."

Dryden and I were glad to get back too. Even though
we were still living with the Kusers at Faircourt, we could
always go down to the Somerset Hills Club for golf or
tennis, and see some people our own age. I began to feel a
little more at home, even though it was difficult to have
much contact with other people when the Kusers were so
strict about meal times. Dryden had been able to live a sort
of life of his own before he was married; but now that he
had acquired a wife, life was supposed to be different. I
was supposed to fill his life completely. I knew that they
expected something I did not know how to give. I was not
a staid married woman. In fact I did not feel married at all.
I was homesick and lonely. There was no one I could talk
to or get guidance from. I had friends, but I was a new
friend to them and was too shy to take them into my
confidence. I wondered how it would all end, and if this
dilemma ever could be solved. It was solved for me in a
mysterious way. I found that I was pregnant; and this time
I sought advice from some girls in Bernardsville who were
near my age, and went on my own into New York to a
doctor recommended by several of them. I wanted to get a
good doctor and not one of the fussy old men that the
Kusers imported from Newark. I had a question to ask and
I wanted the right answer. Having not participated very
willingly in this future event, I was perturbed. "Is it possible," I asked in a quavering voice, "to have only *half* a
baby?" I remember Dr. Ward roaring with laughter, and

giving me a big hug. "Don't worry," he said, "a fine healthy girl like you will have a splendid bouncing baby."

I was much relieved, as in my abysmal ignorance, I felt that I had failed the Kusers in the worst possible way. However, at the end of nine months, and although I am not a very big person, I produced as Dr. Ward predicted a, ten-pound bouncing boy! But before that happy moment a lot happened. In the first place, when we broke the news to the Kusers they were all smiles, but when they heard that I had seen a New York doctor and not their favorite from Newark, and that I actually intended to have the baby in a hospital, they were horrified and reacted in the familiar way. "If you refuse to have the best doctors in the country, and insist on going to a hospital instead of having the baby in your own home, we don't want to hear any more about it." And that was that—I was terribly upset, and so was Dryden. "It is our baby," he said, "and you must do what you want. I don't care what the family says." He was very sweet to me and I was proud and happy.

The Kusers did have some good news for us. A house on the corner of their thousand-acre estate had become conveniently vacant. Colonel Kuser had bought it to round out his property, and Mr. Kramer (Colonel Kuser's executive secretary) had gone to a sale in Newark and been instructed to buy the entire contents of a Broad Street town house, lace curtains and all, to furnish it. It had been rented to an old lady, but now it was free, and they were going to give it to us. It was quite monstrously furnished as Newark was not famous for taste, but it had a large, square welcoming hall and lots of windows through which the sun poured. A Colonial porte-cochère rising up to the second floor gave it a grandiose appearance which soon fell apart, as the wings on each side were done in a haphazard way with windows placed without design. It

consisted of three stories—eight master bedrooms on the
second floor, four on the third, and twelve servants' rooms
in a wing complete with laundry and servants' sitting and
dining rooms. It seemed absolutely huge to me. I wandered
through it with Dryden, trying to imagine what I could do
to it, and whether I could be happy there on a rainy day.
In the end, we decided that with a little painting, and some
chintz and no lace curtains it would be habitable. Anyway,
it would be our own.

The Kusers were quite willing to make improvements
to brighten up the house for us (anything to get rid of us,
I would imagine); and in the meantime they suggested that
we go to Florida at their expense to find a winter home for
them to buy. Kramer had arranged the trip, starting at St.
Augustine and going straight on down to Palm Beach. As
this was our first trip on our own since our marriage, Mrs.
Kuser said that I must wear a money belt, and from a
Tiffany box she took out a strange contraption—a sort of
sporran-like pouch of gray chamois, strung on a gray silk
belt. She fastened this around my pregnant waist, leaving
the pouch to hang down between my legs under my petti-
coat. It was frightfully uncomfortable and made me wad-
dle like a duck to avoid its swing. However, being still
much in awe of the Kusers (secretly, I thought they might
use witchcraft on me), I wore it during the entire Florida
trip, thereby incurring a vicious attack of prickly heat. In
the wretched pouch were only one or two little trinkets,
such as a holly pin with two rubies that Granny had given
me, a small necklace of turquoise beads bought in China,
an add-a-pearl necklace and some ten-dollar gold pieces.
All my newly acquired jewelry was left in the safe-deposit
vault in Newark. I also had some travelers checks. Dryden
was similarly equipped but his belt went around his waist
under his shirt, and so was not the nuisance that mine was.
I often wonder why they sent us off to find a house. It

must have been sheer desperation, but the strangest part
was that when we *did* find a house they rented it sight unseen, and bought it that very first season.

I really loved that trip—in spite of the money belt—it
was fun being greeted by eager real estate people in every
place, who whizzed us around, not only to the houses but
to all the sights, and wined and dined us into the bargain.
In St. Augustine we stayed at the Ponce de Leon Hotel,
where the Kusers had spent their honeymoon, a rambling
bougainvillea-covered place, very attractive in its way. I
have never been to St. Augustine since, but then it struck
me as being a delightful town, with the romantic advantage of having the oldest house on this continent—at least
that's what we were told. We moved from there to Day-
tona, then Ormond Beach, and across Florida to St. Peters-
burg and finally to Palm Beach. In Palm Beach I found
a house—houses bored Dryden, but I have always been
keenly interested—and this house had such a marvelous
situation. It was called "Los Incas" and stood on the North
County Road between the Howard Phipps and the Edward Stotesbury estates, and the property went from the
ocean to the lake, with a magnificent avenue of royal palms
in the lakeside gardens. We called the Kusers and told
them that our quest was ended. We were told to come
home and by the time we were back at Faircourt, action
had already been taken to rent the house for the following
winter with the option to buy. The Kusers then departed
for Aiken, South Carolina, to spend their last winter in
their house there, which they had already sold to the
Fermata School. Dryden and I rented a house on East
Ninety-fourth Street and Mother came up from Haiti to
be with me. I had a wonderful time with her, going to
concerts, visiting museums, having her friends to lunch
and sometimes dinner. The winter passed. On my birthday in March Dr. Ward called on me and I wrote in my

diary how kind it was of him to come to see me and bring me a bunch of daffodils (particularly as Mother had gone to Washington and I was feeling lonely). I grew fatter and fatter and began to jump off the kitchen table and down every step of the stairs in the hope that the baby would arrive. He was very late in appearing. Father came up but could only stay two weeks, so had to return to Haiti. Mother came back from Washington the first week in May although there was no sign of a swift arrival. On the night of May 29 I was at the theater with Mother, Dryden, and the trained nurse, Miss Billington, when I suddenly felt a strange new pain. "Miss Billington," I whispered, "something is happening." She asked me to describe it, then said that we had to leave at once. We climbed over a row of people, and I must have looked quite a sight, as I was in a bright red dress and weighed fifty pounds over my normal weight. At last we arrived at Miss Lippincott's Hospital on the seventh floor of the building (still standing) on the corner of Madison Avenue and Sixty-first Street. I was rushed into a little delivery room and then after holding the hands of Miss Billington and Dr. Ward, and responding valiantly to the command "push" for six hours, I produced Tony. Half an hour after his birth, and just as the sun rose on May 30, I was back in the large corner room that had been engaged for me, laughing with Mother and Dryden and looking with wonder at the baby. He was certainly not half a baby. He was perfect! And what was more, I would never be alone again. We were two. No witchcraft could touch me now. I had to become the Defender, and to begin to know my own worth; if I were to be responsible for another life I had to become someone myself. I had to be like my parents. I returned to Bernardsville quite a different young person from what I was when I left; without really knowing it at the time, I had taken a giant step forward in my life.

5

As I have said, all my life I have loved houses. When I was young I had a recurring dream of houses, houses with secret rooms and many corridors. Sometimes I have thought of my life as a house—the foundation was what I inherited, the roof was the faith that sheltered me, and the rooms of the house were the different phases of my life. Leaving the door open in some rooms, closing the door on others. Even now, to put myself to sleep, I often redecorate a house I have seen or design an entirely new one. I remember all the houses I have ever lived in, how the furniture was placed and what I saw from the windows. I am a nest-builder. Whether my taste is good or bad, I must make the nest my own. This I inherited from my mother. She could take a banal government house like our house in Peking, all green plush and fake mahogany, and with the aid of slip-covers of coolie cloth and a few ornaments and flowers transform it into an attractive and welcoming setting. I believe that if you like where you live you will be an adjusted person, better able to face the more difficult passages in life. In my later life I have felt this to be especially true of government-subsidized housing. The total lack of planning for the fundamental human needs and the grimness of the architecture can only lead to discontent and unrest. The graffiti on the walls are a subconscious sign of contempt for the kind of pseudo-involvement that finds expression in the second-rate and the shabby.

Civic thoughts were far from my mind in those distant days. I was the average young person, interested above all in myself, and now I had a house all my own.

In the last month that we had lived with the Kusers we had been chloroformed and robbed while we were asleep in our beds. Even my engagement ring had been taken off my finger, and my sapphire necklace and bracelet and several pins were all stolen. There was a night watchman in the house, supposedly making his rounds, and our rooms were all closed from the inside by "gem" bolts. There were also heavy screens in the windows. How the thieves got in (leaving one brown leaf on our bedroom floor—it was November) was a mystery that was never solved; and for a year or two every time someone gave me a strange look on the streets of New York I wondered if it was he who had lifted my inanimate hand and taken the sapphire off my finger. There was, however, a silver lining in this catastrophe. Although the jewels were not fully insured, I did get some money by way of compensation, and I put it into an account in the Hanover Bank. It was mine. The first money I had ever had that I could do as I wished with, and to me at that moment the most important thing was to make my home attractive. We had ten in staff in the house —two chauffeurs and three gardeners outside—and yet we were short of cash. The Kusers wished us to live as well as all the other young people in Bernardsville and were very generous, particularly as we seemed to be settling down. Dryden had also inherited quite a large trust fund from his grandfather. We were really very rich, but, somehow, there was a hole in our pockets. Not only was Dryden a heavy drinker, but he was an inveterate gambler—and, alas, a constant loser. He did play superb golf, as he had spent all his winters before going to Princeton in Aiken, South Carolina. There he had a golf lesson every day with the professional, who at that time was considered one of the

top men in the golfing world. I can see Dryden now, his
swing beautifully co-ordinated as he sent the ball straight
down the fairway of the verdant golf course of the Somerset Hills Club. I used to follow him around when he
played in a match and was proud of him, but it soon became a torment. He would get up from a lunch where he
drank one martini after another and go on to bet a couple
of thousand dollars on every hole. Often he would end up
by paying $36,000 for an afternoon on the golf course. It
was agony to watch him, and I wonder now if it was quite
fair on the part of his fellow members to take his reckless
bets. We also played bridge at ten cents a point. I have a
natural card sense and Dryden was a good player; but I
remember that once when I became rattled I trumped
Dryden's ace. He threw the pack of cards, and the rest of
his drink, in my face. We also played a game called red
dog, which made it even easier to lose. You can see from
this brief explanation that we were often short on cash and
that the insurance money seemed heaven-sent.

I made quick use of it. I tore down the porch which
made the west room and drawing room so dark, and with
the friendly help of an excellent architect, Musgrave
Hyde, we (or rather he) made an inviting terrace looking
onto the garden and two french windows in my bedroom
opening onto a balcony. There were too many ugly features in the house itself for us ever to overcome them
without spending a great deal of money; but as the climbing roses grew over the low wall of the terrace and the
flower beds blossomed, the terrace became more and more
a part of my life. I sat there constantly and rejoiced. It was
a marvelous investment, far better than sapphires!

We called the house by the very corny and inappropriate name of "Denbrooke," but I suppose that that was
what it really was, because it was from this den that I set
forth in search of friends.

I made this move for the first time in my life since I had left school, and I found truly wonderful friends, what my mother called "friends of the heart," without whom I might have been totally submerged. Because of these people who gave me their affection and understanding, I became in the end almost indifferent to Dryden's drinking, to his affairs and to his continual attempts to humiliate me. I cannot pretend to have been a model character. In fact I was really a hopeless wife for Dryden. I lost my temper with him and fought back. But I hid my ill temper and disillusion from the world as best I could, wiping the tears of rage away with a cold washcloth and going downstairs with a smiling face. I had friends among the young marrieds, all a few years older than I was, and I made friends with, and became quite a protégée of, the older ladies. In those days the older people really controlled the community, partly through the purse strings, but mostly through family feeling.

Although Bernardsville was a hunting and shooting community, it was also a churchgoing community. The older people went to church every Sunday and noticed with a sharp eye if the young marrieds did not go, too. The Kusers were not church-goers. In fact they were so entirely self-sufficient that they needed no outside interests. Colonel Kuser could have been more gregarious, I think, but Mrs. Kuser was one of those intensely jealous women who considered any outside interest of her husband's as a threat to her security. She was, I think, a little like Queen Victoria and was as wrapped up in her Anthony as the queen had been wrapped up in her Albert. In fact, Mrs. Kuser with her pompadour, her pigeon breast, and pouting sensual lips was a true Victorian woman.

I started going to church in Bernardsville on my own, right after Tony was born, and only sickness ever made me miss a Sunday. I began to draw great comfort from the

church and from the kindness of the older people to me. I
also began to take part in the activities of the community
and found them very comforting. It was just what I
needed at that point in my life. There is a great deal to be
said for a community. It creates strong ties, and acts as a
protection. The young married people looked up to their
parents, and the grandchildren, at that time, were being
brought up in the same way. It was as though a group of
nonwarring tribes were all gathered together in a securely
walled city. It may have made for a certain irre-
sponsibility, a certain taking for granted of the material
comforts of life, but on the other hand it gave security
when one needs it most, and that is when one is young, inexperienced, and bringing up a family. It is so difficult for
young families today who live far from their parents, and
often in a totally alien setting, to be able to cope with the
continual problems that a young family faces. However,
even in this utopia, there was some rebellion—young
mothers resented interference from their own parents or
in-laws regarding the upbringing of children; and some
sons refused to go to their father's alma mater or enter the
family firm, thereby forfeiting "fringe benefits" from the
family.

Of course, there were flirtations. We could not have
had so many parties, including dances on moonlit nights,
without a little extracurricular dalliance. We were always
ready for a "good time." I remember once George Post
giving a dinner dance that was such a success that he kept
the band over and gave exactly the same party the following night. As time went on there were divorces. Underneath all this lavish life style of the late twenties and early
thirties people were much the same as the present-day
commuter. Being driven to the eight-fifteen in the morning
in a chauffeured car did not change entirely the emotions

and motivations of the young man sitting in the back seat with his straw hat jauntily on one side of his head.

I loved this new life, and as I say, particularly the older people. They replaced Father and Mother, and it was one of my mother's guidelines that gave me the entrée to this formal society—the system of good manners that she had insisted on. What the Kusers had liked in me at the beginning was also what won me the affection of the older people. I became in fact something of a "pet"; and as Dryden grew more and more difficult, *they* liked me more and more. With this sound backing I was able to endure the fact that he either did not appear at dinner, or would have to leave hurriedly. He did, however, do one thing that was way ahead of his time. He went into politics and became assemblyman for Somerset County. The people of our age thought it was a joke, but Dryden persevered and eventually became a state senator. We campaigned together, and in the beginning I was very active and enjoyed it enormously. I loved meeting the undertakers, the farmers, the bootleggers who lived up in the hills, and all the other assorted types. It was only later on, when Dryden seemed to have guaranteed every bad loan in the county that I became skeptical.

I began to reach out on my own. I was on the Board of the Virginia Day Nursery and the Maternity Center Association by the time I was twenty. By working for the Maternity Center and going the rounds in New York with a trained nurse, I learned what it is like for a family of six to live in a "railroad flat" with one toilet down the hall. I also went to the first government housing at 125th Street and the East River Drive. Whenever I pass that low-rise housing, I think how much more intelligently planned it was than the huge impersonal buildings one sees today. The President of the Maternity Center Association was Mrs. John Sloane (incidentally, the mother of Mrs. Cyrus

Vance). She and the Director, Miss Hazel Corbin, were more far-sighted and imaginative than I realized at the time, even though I was sensitive enough to appreciate their quality. They brought Dr. Dick Read, the author of *Childbirth without Fear*, from England to introduce natural childbirth and the M. C. Clinic is still extremely active in that domain.

We had spent a winter with the Kusers in Palm Beach the year after Tony was born; and there, for the first time, the Kusers let us off the leash. The Edward Stotesburys, who lived next door, were inveterate entertainers and Dryden and I got on their list. The Kusers never wished to go anywhere, but they really seemed pleased that we were invited to the Stotesburys and so we were there a great deal. Mrs. Stotesbury was what the French call *Une belle femme*, tall and stately with her hair piled on top of her head and a "dog collar" of seed pearls with diamond slides around her neck. Mr. and Mrs. Stotesbury stood on a Persian rug beneath the palm trees and received their guests. She was truly an extraordinary hostess. With sixty or eighty people at a sit-down lunch or dinner, she remembered exactly where each guest was seated and would say, "Brooke, you are sitting between Addison Mizner (who created Palm Beach with his Spanish architecture) and Paris Singer—or on one glorious day next to Joseph Hergesheimer. Joseph Hergesheimer was a very well-known novelist at that time—particularly for *The Three Black Pennys* and *Java Head*—and I was overcome at sitting next to a real live best seller. He took a great fancy to me and wrote me from Havana that whereas at fifty he thought that he had built a stockade around his emotions, all that had changed when he met me. He felt alive again—at least, so he said. I hung on his every word. At nineteen, fifty seemed very old to me, and he was not very handsome—in fact, quite the reverse. He looked a bit like a walrus with large yellow teeth emerging from each side of his mouth. But I was captivated by his way with words, his beautiful voice and the fact that he considered me worthy of such fascinating remarks as "women should have charm, men should have courage." All this exhilarated me beyond words. He would also ask me, "Who would you like to know?" as though the whole world was his to command for my pleasure.

I met many interesting people through Hergesheimer. Dryden and I went down to stay with him and his wife Dorothy at their house "The Dower House" in West Chester, Pennsylvania. We went to a band concert that Stokowski used to conduct once a year and had supper afterward with Stokowski, H. L. Mencken, Alfred Knopf, and George Jean Nathan. Unfortunately, I cannot remember a word they said. All I remember is the blue of Mencken's eyes, and how they sparkled with wit and malice, and Knopf's saturnine looks and Stokowski's ebullience. I wrote it all down in my diary, but my second husband asked me to destroy the diaries I kept from sixteen to twenty-three, and we burned them together. I have never kept a real diary since. Each year of my life I seem to have less time to myself.

At the Stotesburys I also met Oswald and Rhoda Birley. Oswald was a well-known English portrait painter, later to be knighted, and she was one of the most beautiful and exotic-looking women I have ever met. We went on picnics on the Loxahatchee River with them and fed the manatees lobster mayonnaise. Zuloaga, the Spanish painter, was a friend of the Birleys, and our picnics were great fun as they all had so much to say about the world of the Arts. Oswald had a marvelous sense of humor, and his stories of life as a student in Paris were like something out of

Maupassant. I remember writing in my diary, "At last, I am really living."

I drank it all in. I was fascinated by Mrs. Stotesbury's dinners, and by her dress books which her maid brought to her every morning so that she could choose her costume of the day. She showed me these books, which contained sketches of her dresses in color with all the proper accessories on each page. Mrs. Stotesbury would leaf through the book and then tell her head maid, "I will wear costumes 170, 162 and 82 today." All would be laid out in her dressing room. She had only to choose the right jewelry. Her underclothes were kept in drawers which slid out easily, and each nightgown or chemise was covered with a thin satin cover filled with sachet. I reveled in all this, just as I reveled in the solid gold dressing table set, encrusted with a sapphire monogram, which a maharajah had given to Rhoda Birley when Oswald had painted him in India. I was sorry that the maharajah had never seen Rhoda brushing her shining black hair back from her lovely face, laughing as she did so. What joy it would have given him! But it could have given him no more than it did to Oswald, who watched her every movement with the eye of a man, and an artist.

Encouraged by these fascinating·people, I was quickly out of my depth. I pretended to be very musical, and I must have picked up some sort of musical patter from someone, because Addison Mizner invited me to a series of afternoon recitals by a string quartet at his apartment on Worth Avenue. I went there with the arrogance of youth to find that only six people were invited, and that we were all given scores to follow. When mine was handed to me, I hardly knew what to do. I had only got as far as playing MacDowell's "To a Wild Rose" on the piano. However, as they say now, I toughed it out, and sat with a rapt expression on my face while glancing slyly now and then to see if anyone had turned a page. It was a dreadful ordeal, but I think that Addison Mizner must have caught on. After two sessions he very nicely said that he thought that a young person like myself should really be outside on a fine day, instead of cooped up indoors. He knew how much I loved music, but even so, he thought I should take advantage of the Palm Beach climate. It was a good solution, and we remained friends. Unfortunately, I did not profit by this lesson, and it was not until later that I saw the wisdom of the Chinese saying "A man of two thousand characters can never fool a man of ten thousand characters."

6

When we returned to Bernardsville in the spring, the impact of the exciting winter lingered on. I was eager to keep open the doors to a new outlook upon life. There was in Bernardsville an especially interesting and attractive older lady who was also one of my champions—Mrs. Larocque. She was the sister of Alice Duer Miller, the poet, whose *White Cliffs of Dover* was so popular during World War II. Another sister was Miss Caroline Duer, an editor of *Vogue*. I had met Miss Duer quite often when she had been staying with her sister for the weekend. She was a small birdlike person with sparkling eyes and a vivacious manner who usually came accompanied by either Condé Nast, the publisher, or Francis Crowninshield, the editor of *Vanity Fair*.

I was very pleased to be asked by Mrs. Larocque to lunch with her and Miss Duer that spring. I was determined to ask Miss Duer for a job. Since the age of seven I had either been writing or reading and I felt that I could combine the two. At seven I started a diary—and from then on I wrote plays in verse, sonnets and short stories. Everything was grist to my mill, and at Miss Madeira's School I started a monthly magazine called *Facio*. I approached Miss Duer and in her particularly endearing and attractive way she said that she was delighted to hear that I would like to join Condé Nast and that she had just the job for me. I could review books.

It was a marvelous opportunity and I felt that I was starting a career. *Vogue* had no book reviewer up to that time. I could do the reviews any way I liked. I chose to do them in the form of letters to a friend whom I called "Anne." I received about sixty books a month and picked out the ones I liked best. I also tried to give the reader a choice: a book of philosophy—a book of poetry—a memoir —a novel. A sort of literary smorgasbord. Anne was supposed to be living somewhere out in the sticks, and had an unsatisfied craving for culture. Of course I shudder to think back on those reviews. They were so girlish and unprofessional. However, those were still the days of innocence for *Vogue*. Boutet de Monvel and Erté and Pierre Brissaud did delightful sketches of clothes, and there were photographs of what a woman with taste would want to wear.

The association with *Vogue* brought me in contact with a different world. I met a couple who lived at the Chelsea Hotel on West Twenty-third Street. He was French and a poet. She was American and a painter. It was a *ménage à trois*. A very masculine lady lived with them and seemed to dabble in both poetry and painting. I met them at a cocktail party at Condé Nast's and was very much impressed by their talk of Gertrude Stein and Ronald Firbank and Rosamond Lehmann.

I went to the Chelsea several times. It was a funny old-fashioned place even then, and it delighted me. I went up as far as the lift would go, dashed up a precipitous staircase which led to the roof, and found their penthouse studio. The wife did a watercolor sketch of me, saying as she did so that I looked like an "opalescent kitten." The husband read French poetry aloud to us as the sketch was being done, and the friend smoked long cigars and never spoke at all. It was such a different life from the one I normally led that I was mesmerized. After the last sitting, when I was about to take the sketch home, they asked me to let my hair down; and when all three of them started to comb it while calling me their "dear kitten" I decided it was time to go and fled with the sketch under my arm.

With Hergesheimer it was different. He asked me to lunch with him in New York. He was so well known he said, that we would be besieged by autograph hunters if we lunched in a restaurant. He told me his friend Mischa Elman, the violinist, who was out of town, had kindly lent him his apartment. I went there undaunted (this was no Chelsea), trusting to the attraction of my intellect and a little light persiflage. We were served by a Chinese butler, and Joseph was a model of propriety. Kissing my hand on my arrival, he told me all through lunch that I had inspired the creative instinct in him and that he intended to dedicate his next book, *Tampico*, to me. I thought how satisfying it was to have inspired such a man, and felt well on the way to establishing a literary salon. I would be a combination of Julie de Lespinasse and Mrs. Thrale. As I left to go to a Maternity Center meeting, he told me that I had the prettiest knees in New York. A very delicious compliment —particularly as it was the era when the dresses were just above the knees, and the waist usually a huge sash, just a couple of inches higher.

Shortly after this he invited us to come down to spend the weekend with him at a cottage he had rented in Cape May. "I will be charming to Kuser," he said, "and I think that you will enjoy yourself."

I do not need a diary in order to remember that weekend. It was a nightmare. We arrived quite late on Saturday, intending to stay until Monday. The cottage was one of a long row, all identical and quite hideous. But that did not matter, for Joseph was sitting on the porch smoking a cigar, and immediately welcomed us with great courtesy. He and Dryden knew each other, but they had very little in common. Nevertheless, he was extremely cordial to Dryden, and immediately asked him to come down and help him mix the drinks as soon as we had unpacked. "I have given you a room to yourself, down the hall from Kuser," he whispered to me, and I thought how dear and sensitive of him. Dryden snored dreadfully and I had told him that. I unpacked slowly, looking from time to time at the sun setting over the sea. How glorious to smell the sea air, and to sleep with the sound of the ocean filling the silence! What a peaceful, happy night I would have!

The first shock was when I came downstairs and found Dryden and Joseph busily stirring something in stone pitchers. "What are you making?" I asked. "Martinis," answered Joseph. "This gin eats right through the metal mixers." With this explanation, they both set to work with renewed vigor, sampling their concoction from time to time to see how it tasted—it was still Prohibition, and drinking was quite hazardous. There was a table with a white tablecloth on it in the dining room. On it were a few dishes of greasy-looking peanuts, a large bucket of ice, and some glasses. There was no sign of food, or of anyone preparing it. This was quite different from The Dower

House, where Joseph lived with Dorothy, and where all was order and serenity. I did not know what to do, so I went upstairs and changed my dress.

When I came down again quite a few people had arrived, and they were standing around with drinks in their hands and talking loudly. Dryden had already found a girl and was going out on the front porch with her. Joseph came to me and started introducing me around, but these were not the intelligentsia that I had associated Joseph with—these resort people, chattering ceaselessly about nothing and going nowhere. I, who had come to sit at the feet of an idol, felt very out of place. It was all local talk—who had done what last night, who got drunk, who made a pass at whom, and which couples fought the most. As I knew none of these people, I couldn't enter into the talk at all and felt totally left out. Also, I began to get hungry—seven o'clock came, eight o'clock, nine o'clock, no sign of food. I wandered out to the pantry and found some Uneeda Biscuits, and with these in hand went back to the party.

There was no sign of Dryden anywhere. Joseph was wedged on a sofa between two giggling women. No one had even noticed my absence. I felt very depressed and let down, and so decided to go to bed. Up in my room I cried. I was dreadfully disappointed and humiliated. Joseph didn't even seem to know that I was there, and nothing had been said by anyone that I could write in my diary. I knelt on the floor by the window and looked out at the sea. A freighter went slowly by on its way south. Perhaps it was going to Haiti, where my parents were. How I wished I were on it! What a mess my life was! Mother had often spoken of a "divine discontent," but my discontent was anything but divine. At last I cried myself out in a dreadful state of self-pity, and as I was young and healthy I fell asleep. I awoke suddenly with a sensation that someone was in the room. I listened, and sure enough I heard the padding of bare feet.

Thinking it was Dryden I reached over and turned on the light. It was not Dryden, but Joseph—Joseph arrayed in crumpled black silk pajamas with a red monogram on the pocket. "Joseph!" I exclaimed, reaching for my bed jacket. "What's happened—what do you want?" "You," he answered, trying to put a large hairy leg into the bed. I gave him a terrific push which knocked him sideways to the floor. He was very fat and not very agile. "Go away," I said. "You are crazy." "It's you who are crazy," he retorted angrily. "You little fool, you certainly couldn't have thought that it was your mind that interested me. You are an absolute little bore." I jumped over and across him onto the other twin bed and walked to the closet. "I am leaving," I said. "You are a hateful, hideous old man, and I am going to get Dryden and leave." "You can't get Dryden," he said as he rose unsteadily to his feet. "He passed out long ago. It would be like trying to wake the dead." By this time I was behind the closet door. "Go away!" I repeated. "You are perfectly horrid." Go he did, slamming the door behind him.

I packed as fast as I could, and when I shut my suitcase and opened the door of the room I could hear Dryden snoring down the hall. I went downstairs and out to where the car was parked beside the garage. Dryden fortunately had left the keys in it and so I got in and drove off. I had had my license for two years, thank heaven. I had qualms about leaving Dryden as I drove through the dawn; but I need not have, as he stayed until Monday morning and brought back the girl he had met at Joseph's to spend a night at our house in Bernardsville. Needless to say, *Tampico* was not dedicated to me, and I never saw Joseph again.

That episode ended my search for unusual characters—

I think that I had reached out to try and show Dryden that I could have friends all of my own away from Bernardsville. He was constantly telling me that people in Bernardsville only liked me because they were old friends of his whom he had grown up with. "You never would have known any of them if it weren't for me," he would say. "Every single person you know you have met through me." That was true, of course, because I had never lived in New York or Bernardsville. But to have it rammed down my throat while at the same time he often had to be carried upstairs drunk before a dinner party and was forever having a "love affair" with one of a very odd assortment of characters was certainly not something to build up my ego. I knew that I was making friends—particularly among the older people—but only the toughest person could have withstood such a daily onslaught without having misgivings about herself. Perhaps no one really did like me? They say that all nice people have an inferiority complex. Well, after four years of marriage, I must have been very nice indeed.

I did have my book reviews, and two other young women and I read Greek plays together once a week. I was also an enthusiastic beagler—meeting with Mr. George Post's pack, and eventually became a "whipper-in," which meant that I had to keep a sharp eye on the beagles and not let them stray off the scent. We met every Sunday in the autumn at different houses and were told exactly what our course was to be. I loved it. The beagles "gave tongue" and wagged their tails, and seemed to have such a good time, and fortunately it was not often that we "found" a rabbit. I didn't like that part. It was more fun for the rabbit not to be "found." I was a whipper-in for several years, and wore khaki gaiters, a bramble-proof khaki shirt, a green jacket with brass buttons, and a jockey cap. I have always been a tremendous walker, but when beagling I had to run, and run I did, through glades and streams, plowed fields and briar patches, all over the hills around Bernardsville. Even if the beagles did not "find," the beaglers did. As dusk fell, we reassembled where we had started from and went into the house of the host of the afternoon for a gourmand's tea of buttered scones and crumpets, small sausages, cinnamon toast and heavenly cakes. Our hosts vied with one another in providing these teas, and we were well rewarded for our efforts. Eventually, I resigned as a whipper-in and began to free-lance in beagling. Sometimes I joined Dickie Gambrill's beagles in Peapack. At other times I stayed with Mr. Post. This free-lancing turned out to be a very good move, as the countryside was different, and I met more people.

The greatest thing in my life was my Tony. He was an adorable little boy, round and rosy, and he had what his Scottish nanny called "grand legs for kilts." I think that to have a child when you are very young is a good thing. Tony and I played together and I loved inventing games. It also gave me a chance to do amusing things. When Tony could hardly walk he had a little pony and sat in a small basket chair on top of the pony while I led him around. Then he and I graduated to a wicker governess cart, which I used to drive through the Kuser estate and across the road to their pheasant and deer park. Once we were chased by two angry stags during the rutting season and just made it through the gates in time. The pony and I were terrified, but Tony loved it. "Do it again, Mummy," he cried in delight.

The other day for no reason at all I began to sing "Rock-a-bye, Baby" while I was pulling some snow and ice off some overladen pine branches in the woods in Westchester. A wave of nostalgia came over me as I remembered Tony sitting high on my knees while I was in bed; and when I sang "Down comes the cradle, Baby and all," I would let my knees fall and Tony would shout with laughter. I can never recapture those joyous moments. I felt suddenly very old, and went back into the house for a cup of tea.

The Kusers were never really interested in Tony. "He seems to be improving," said Colonel Kuser when I would bring him up there, all dressed up in his white linen shorts and ruffled blouse and red shoes. This phrase infuriated me, and he repeated it each time he saw us. As for Dryden, he was not interested in Tony at all. He was far too busy with his politics, his girl friends, and his golf. So I profited by their indifference and had Tony to myself. Only when my father and mother came to visit could I really show Tony off. They adored him, and later in life he was able to return their love in the most touching and heart-warming way. So, with Tony, and with friends who I began to feel were, in spite of Dryden's words, really *my* friends, I began to settle down. I wrote not only for *Vogue*, but for a magazine that no longer exists called *Pictorial Review*, whose editor was Percy Waxman. I remember the first article I wrote was called "Do Women Dress for Men or Women?" I got six hundred dollars for it. (If you want to know the answer, I said that women dressed to make other women envious.) I bought a little Chippendale table with the money, and I have it to this day. It is part of my lares and penates that I have dragged around with me through my life.

I sometimes feel that like Marley's ghost in *A Christmas Carol* I am shackled to my belongings. A great many of them are absolute junk, but they have been with me through good times and bad. I feel that I cannot desert them. They are my friends and I cannot throw them out just because they have become outdated and shabby. Perhaps it is the years in China that make me feel this way. I feel that even inanimate objects have a life, and that I must be good to them because they trust me. Whenever I take a trip I always bring something home to show that although I was away I was thinking of my house. The house in Bernardsville was not pretty; but Tony, the nursery, the terrace, my piano (which I played horribly) and books made it home.

If I cried myself to sleep night after night, I always woke up cheerful in the morning. It was a luxurious life. My youth, combined with my healthy curiosity about life, helped to cushion my bitter frustrations. Tony would be brought in by Nana MacGregor while I was having breakfast in bed. I would play with him and then get up and start the day, which usually consisted of reading (I wrote constantly in my diary, beside writing little poems, some articles and book reviews). I would play the piano a bit, lunch with some other young woman, play a round of golf or some tennis and take Tony for a drive in the pony cart or a ride in the car. I had tea with Nana and Tony and then when the five-fifteen train arrived, Dryden and I would usually have a bridge game, ending with cocktails. All of that is quite enough to turn the reader into a communist! Just to gild the lily even more, I had a French maid called Yvonne, who helped me to dress. I adored Yvonne Grimmand. She came from Touraine and was a Gypsy. Every morning after the parlormaid had brought up my breakfast she would stand at the end of my bed and we would talk, I would tell her my dreams and she, reverting to her Gypsy past, would interpret them and predict the future. It was like Act I of *Der Rosenkavalier*. I depended on Yvonne, and she was my real confidante. As Dryden gambled and drank and played around with other women, I took to spending money. I did it instead of eating, as I had done earlier. I wanted to wear the prettiest dress at the Hunt Ball, the smartest dress at the Ritz Roof in summer and the best-cut and latest English suit at the races that took place on Van Schley's estate in Far Hills in the autumn. We overspent our very generous income, but Colonel Kuser always helped us out, probably because all the other young people were living equally extravagantly. Colonel Kuser did say, however, that just because we had checks in the checkbook it did not mean that we had money in the bank. I wonder now at his magnanimity. He got furious, but he always paid up after his "little talks" with us. When I married Vincent Astor, people said to me nicely (and, behind my back, not so nicely,) that it was a great thing for me in that now I could have anything I wanted, and that I should watch out lest it turn my head. I can only say that in fact I lived more extravagantly and luxuriously in Bernardsville than I ever did with Vincent. Vincent had great respect for money and for the responsibility that goes with it; and I, who had spent money so wantonly and been so unhappy while doing so, had no desire to indulge myself.

Rereading these chapters of my early life as I write them now, it all sounds very trivial and egotistical, but then, what can one expect of a young person? I had quite forgotten myself how very self-centered I was, until I started to write it down, but in doing so, it has helped me with my viewpoint of young people today. It is too bad that when one needs wisdom most, one has not yet had the experience. A girl of twenty behaving like a woman of forty would be a horror. Mother used to quote a French proverb, "What is innocence in a girl of eighteen is ignorance in a woman of thirty." I know some women of fifty who seem to have no idea of what life is about, or what makes people tick. It is, I think, a matter of curiosity. Only by being curious and interested in people and learning to give, can one grow.

7

Dryden and I did not spend all our time in Bernardsville. In the winter we rented a house in New York for a few months. After Tony was born, and with Nana MacGregor in charge, I felt that I could safely leave him and go to visit my parents in Haiti for a few weeks. In the summers we went to Maine; but when Dryden and I became estranged, I took Tony, Nana, and Yvonne with me and joined my parents in France. They stayed at hotels, but, except for one summer at St. Lunaire in Brittany, I always took a house: a tiny little house in Étretat (where we went twice) and an even smaller one in Deauville.

Even though I hated leaving Tony, going to stay with my parents in Haiti was like a car having a new battery. I came home re-charged with love and happiness and I think Tony profited by it.

The only way to get to Haiti then was via the Panama Steamship Line, which smelled of rope and sisal and sugarcane and was used mostly by American workers who lived in the Canal Zone. It was a long five days and usually rough around Cape Hatteras, but on the morning of the fifth day we arrived at the Mole St. Nicolas and steamed a hundred miles down the beautiful bay to Port-au-Prince. On our left side were the dry plains of Gonaives, and St. Marc. On the right were the fertile and verdant mountains of Jérémie. At the end of the bay was the city of Port-au-Prince in the folds of the hills that touched the sea. Haiti is

indescribably beautiful. It is said that when General Leclerc returned to Paris to report to Napoleon on Haiti and
Napoleon asked him what the terrain of the country was
like, Leclerc crumpled a piece of paper and threw it on the
table. "Like that, sire," he said. And so it was—wonderful
layer upon layer of mountains rising up against the blue
sky. (The word "Haiti" means mountain land.) The high
spot of my Haitian visit was the moment when I looked
over the ship's rail and saw Father and Mother, vigorous
and smiling, looking up at Dryden and me from the dock.
All was right with them, and the visit was just starting.
Every precious hour was counted from then on.

The architecture of Port-au-Prince was fascinating—
gingerbread gothic houses painted pink and pale green and
blue with white trim. All of them with nineteenth-century
names—such as "Ma Folie," "Mon Désir," "Le Petit Nid,"
etc. My parents' house was called "Le Hasard" and was on
the side of a hill in the town itself with a cobbled driveway up to it and a rose garden all around it. In the back
there was a small latticed swimming pool called a "bassin":
which at that time in most houses was the only bath. At
our house we had a bathroom with a bathtub, but we all
loved the bassin. It was a delight to swim in that little
green latticed swimming pool in the early morning, with
the sun just coming over the hills and the lattice casting a
crenelated reflection on the pool. It was like being inside
an emerald. The only prosaic touch was a primitive
shower which Father had installed. Instead of the scent of
the jasmine which stood by the entrance door of the "bassin," there was an overpowering smell of the carbolic soap
which Father used in the shower.

Father was originally in command of the Marines who
were stationed there. The country was in a rather turbu-
lent state. Roving bands of guerrillas called "Cacos" were
constantly harassing the villages and towns. Even Port-au-

Prince was attacked during one of our visits by a mob of 3,000 Cacos. They were acting under the leadership of their chief, "Charlemagne," who communicated to his lieutenants by the beat of drums and fires on the surrounding hills while he himself was in safe hiding in the mountains. The night that Port-au-Prince was attacked, the Cacos were driven off and fled back into the hills. Eventually Charlemagne was killed and peace restored. When he was shot, he was found to be wearing the skull of a Marine sergeant around his neck on a silver chain. Like his famous predecessor, Christophe, King of Haiti, who had built the extraordinary fortress at Cap Haitien, Charlemagne had fostered the legend that he could only be killed by a silver bullet. Most of his followers thought he could not be killed at all, so his body was put in an open coffin at Cap Haitien for all to see.

Haiti was an extraordinarily interesting place to visit. When Father became High Commissioner (with the rank of Ambassador), Louis Borno was President. Borno was a brilliant and beautifully educated man. He had graduated from the Sorbonne in Paris, wrote music and was included in an anthology of modern French poetry. My parents became great friends of the Bornos and often stayed with them at their private villa in Pétionville. The Bornos, like most presidential families, enjoyed getting away from their huge marshmallow white palace which dominated the Champs de Mars; and their pretty villa in Pétionville was the scene of many attractive informal parties.

President Borno could compose music on classical themes, but in lighter moments he wrote "merengues." A merengue is a typical Haitian ballroom dance—a bit like the samba. He often played them for us at the villa, and everyone danced to these gay tunes. I explicitly say a ballroom dance because there was dancing among the peasants which was distinctly more lusty.

I particularly remember once when we became involved with a robust and rustic dance. We were on our way by car from Port-au-Prince to Cap Haitien. There were three carloads of us, because Mother was entertaining some visiting U. S. Senators and their wives. Father had been kept in Port-au-Prince on business. We started off early in the morning, as the roads were none too good, and we expected to arrive by nightfall and go up the mountain to Christophe's Citadel the next morning. However, it was the start of the rainy season and the rain began coming down in torrents. The roads were inches deep in mud almost at once, and the rivers were flooded. After slithering over the roads for an hour or two, and being pushed across a river by a horde of peasants who were up to their knees in water, we were told by a charming man called Major André of the Haitian Gendarmerie, who was in charge of our party, that we could not possibly get to Cap Haitien that night. Cars and chauffeurs were at the breaking point. The Senators and their wives were not in very good shape or temper, either, and were beginning to look as though they wished that they had never heard of Haiti.

Mother was most concerned. It would not be beneficial to Haiti, to President Borno, or to Father, if the Senators went home disgruntled and voted against any future obligation to the Republic of Haiti. "What will we do?" she asked Major André. "We can't spend the night in the cars." "We are just on the outskirts of a village called Plaisance," replied André. "Half a kilometer beyond Plaisance the Gendarmerie has a small barracks that we sometimes use on maneuvers. It is rough, but clean. There are plenty of cots and I will send someone ahead so that the soldiers on duty can prepare a meal for us. It is not much in the way of comfort or cordon bleu cuisine, but at least we will be dry."

Mother agreed, and told the rest of the party. They

agreed that we all needed a rest and that it would be
madness to forge a stream in darkness. So we jolted along
through the tiny village of a cluster of huts, and then
climbed a short, but precipitous hill to where the little
barracks was strategically placed between two tiny parade
grounds. The house was just as Major André had said—
clean and bare; a couple of cots in each room, a main room
with a bare table, and a dozen rush-bottom chairs; no electricity, just oil lamps, and a combined washroom and lava-
tory in an unheated building outside.

We had some wine, miraculously produced by Major
André, and we sipped it while waiting for our chicken
and rice and fried papaya. I noticed that Mother looked
slightly harassed and glanced from time to time at her
watch. It was only six o'clock and we had a long evening
in front of us. The guests seemed to be revived by the
wine and the relief of being under shelter and showed no
signs of drowsiness. She drew Major André aside and
I—who in those days could hear a pin drop three rooms
away—overheard her say in her very beautiful French,
"What are we going to do after supper? They tell me they
don't play cards, and after twelve hours in the car, I have
exhausted every subject of conversation. Isn't there something we could do? Something that would show them a bit
of Haitian life?" Major André looked thoroughly depressed. "I don't know," he said, but at that moment he
turned and looked out of the window. "Look, Mrs. Russell," he said joyfully, "the rain has stopped, the moon is
out and we are the luckiest people in the world." Major
André was beaming from ear to ear. *"Le Bon Dieu est
Bon,"* he went on. "It just so happens that two of the best
drummers in Haiti are staying in Plaisance tonight. Now
that Le Bon Dieu has stopped the rain, if you are willing
to spend twenty gourdes on rum we can have a dance."
"Where will the people come from?" Mother asked.

"Wait and see," laughed Major André, and he excused himself to go make the arrangements. The rest of us, seven strong, sat down to our supper and made conversation. Mother said only that Major André had had some business to attend to. By now it was just about half past seven, and we were finishing our coffee in a halfhearted way when we suddenly heard the beating of drums and the chanting of voices. Our guests looked rather frightened as they huddled together in the dimly lit room which seemed to be in the middle of nowhere. I must admit that the sound of drums echoing against the hills is not very soothing.

Mother had to explain what it was, and why Major André had not dined with us. She went out onto the parade ground in front of the barracks and we all trooped after her. In the moonlight, the parade ground looked like a large smooth terrace with the land falling sharply away on three sides and just the tops of some palm trees glistening in the moonlight beyond. As we stood there, the throbbing of the drums grew louder. Suddenly, first the faces of the drummers and then gradually their whole figures came up over the edge of the ground. They were followed by a band of a dozen or so women with gay bandanas on their heads and men with ragged trousers and machetes at their waists. Some of the women had on "eye of God" dresses, with gay patches on them designed to attract the eye of God. The theory is that God is so busy that only when something unusual strikes his eye does he stop to listen to a prayer.

This little group, swaying and clapping their hands, followed the music around until the drummers found the spot where they wished to play; then they put down their drums, straddled them, and really began to beat. While this was going on, more and more people came up the steep path, and spilled out onto the parade ground—children of all ages, very old people, flirtatious young people, the whole gamut of human life. In the end, Major André had to station a sergeant at the path to keep more people from coming. We could see the bushes moving as they tried to climb closer. This was obviously going to be the event of the year. Rum was passed around, and as all ages took their fill the dancing became more and more erotic. It was clearly a fertility dance, and the fact that a boy of six was dancing opposite his grandmother seemed to make no difference. Our group began to feel that this was perhaps more than we had bargained for. "I think that we had better stop the rum," said Major André, who was roaring with laughter. "Won't they be furious?" said Mother. "No," he said. "I have an idea. We will see." He had the drummers stop and then he asked the crowd a question in Creole. "What's going on?" inquired one of the Senators. "We are going to listen to a storyteller, Senator," answered André. "Everyone says he is one of the best storytellers in Haiti." And quite certainly he held the attention of his audience, who sat as quiet as mice, seemingly totally forgetful of their frenzied dance of a few minutes before.

The storyteller spoke in a singsong, his voice rising and falling, as he accompanied his words with gestures. He was haughty; he was sly; he was humble; he was elegant. He whirled around singing, then he bent over to play with his feet. (His audience laughed hysterically.) "What is the story?" we asked André. (As it was told in Creole, none of us could understand it.) Major André was laughing so hard that he could hardly translate it for us. "It is a story of a young girl who has lost her mother and who lives with her father and two much older half sisters. These sisters are very very ugly and they hate the girl because she is so pretty. And then one day the pretty girl is invited to a ball at the palace. She dances with the Prince but has to rush away before midnight because her beautiful dress will disappear and her coach will turn into a pumpkin. It was a gift from a fairy." We all recognized this as the tale of Cinderella or Cendrillon. The storyteller had held them completely under his spell. They laughed uproariously at the humiliation of the stepsisters; they clapped with delight when Cinderella had put her foot into the slipper so easily. They ended by chanting and swaying when the Prince finally made her his bride. As the story drew to a close, a tot of rum was handed around. The drummers took up their drums and began to take up their beat again, as they started down the path. The crowd picked up the sleeping children. Walking in single file, they slowly disappeared over the edge of the parade ground, their laughing voices mingling with the drumbeat growing fainter and fainter as they descended, until finally only the faintest beat of the drums came to our ears. We went to bed quite exhilarated by the contrast of the evening.

Haiti in those days had an atmosphere that I have never found in any of the other islands of the Caribbean, and I have visited almost every one of them. What made it different, I think, is that it had been free and a republic since 1804. In spite of their poverty, the peasants in those days seemed contented and happy. They had been a free people so long that there were none of the antagonisms and distrust that are endemic to colonialism. Their lot may have been hard, but as they said, *"Le Bon Dieu est Bon."* Nature was good to them. Mango trees and sugarcane and bananas abounded; one had simply to reach up to pluck a ripe fruit, and the sugarcane could be made into a fiery drink. In the city of Port-au-Prince the shops had mostly French names and imported their wares from France, and there were several very good French restaurants. There were no tourist hotels, only a few little inns. The great iron market in front of the Cathedral was filled on market days with vegetables and fruit. Often the people who sold them had walked all night with their produce in huge baskets on their heads in order to get to the market at opening time. Those who had more money rode into town on skeletal donkeys. The Haitians are very clever with their hands and made furniture and wooden utensils and some pottery. All this was before the great wave of painters and art galleries with which Port-au-Prince is now liberally supplied.

Upper-class society in Port-au-Prince then was mostly mulatto. It was said that there were 110 different shades of color. The fashionable club, Le Cercle Bellevue, had gala soirées once a week with music and dancing. It was very formal. Everyone wore white gloves and the women wore very dressy dresses copied from France. The bookshops were full of the latest French books, which were discussed at lunches at the Cercle Bellevue. If one particularly liked a book, there was a large and flourishing bindery where they could be bound in real leather, gracefully tooled in gold, with end papers imported from France.

In other words, there was a real link with the French past, and lives were ordered by the mode of nineteenth-century France: Mass on Sunday, convent schools, the wives occupied with children, religious fetes, church bazaars, reading the latest novel from France, formal parties and family picnics and, of course, their clothes. The men were primarily interested in politics. The "outs" were always violently against the "ins." They had an active club life, a certain amount of business, and the all-absorbing task of being *père de famille* (head of the family). Port-au-Prince could have been Lyons or Bordeaux. But there was a darker side, fairly close to the surface: voodoo, with all its attendant rites. There was not an upper-class Haitian who would not have been terrified to come out of his house of a morning to find that a "ouanga" had been planted against him at his front door. A ouanga was a curse concocted by a voodoo priest or a "Papaloi." It consisted of items such as the eye of a toad, the tail of a snake, a button, a nail clipping—in fact anything that was handy. No one so singled out could ever return to normal. Often they pined away and died from sheer fright.

There were other manifestations too. Once Father was called down to the Palace at midnight to find President Borno in great distress. Senator King was expected to arrive in Port-au-Prince the next morning on an unofficial visit; and Mr. Borno refused to allow Senator King to set foot on Haitian soil because the Senator had criticized him on the floor of the Senate. He had protested to the United States Government, only to be told that under our Constitution a Senator could say anything he pleased on the floor of the Senate. Father tried to make the President change his mind and suggested that he could be making a mistake. But Borno was adamant, and Senator King never landed on Haitian territory. Senator King always blamed my father for this, and later on he enlisted the powerful Senator Hugo Black (who later became an associate justice of the U. S. Supreme Court) to help in an attempt to destroy my father's career.

The President that night had other things on his mind apart from Senator King. As he and Father were walking to the door he said, "General, I suppose you have heard about the demonstration before the prison." Father said yes he had. It concerned a man called Joliebois, a leader of the opposite political party, who was in prison for his incendiary attacks on Borno. "You have heard the latest development?" said Borno in a low voice. "Nothing except that there was a crowd outside the prison gate clamoring for his release." "Well," said Borno, "during the night it has grown worse. It seems that a bull was being led into the prison to be killed for beef and then to be tanned for leather. And when the bull got to the gate, it refused to go any further, even though the men pushed and pulled with all their force. At the same time"—and the President lowered his voice to a whisper—"it cried Mamaou, mamaou, which, as you know, in Creole means I am your mother—and the mysterious part of it is that Joliebois' mother died last evening and the crowd takes this as a sign that she is pleading for her son's release." The President laughed. "It is rather strange," he added, "but the crowd has grown to over five thousand and is becoming more agitated by the minute." Father urged the President to decide for himself, but said that it would be an act of great magnanimity to set Joliebois free. "It will give you the sympathy of the people and I doubt if Joliebois will cause much more trouble," said Father. So Father returned to his bed. Joliebois was released; and as he walked out the prison gate, the bull walked quietly in. The mob outside burst into song and all was well.

During President Borno's incumbency, roads were built, clinics established, schools built, and the economy prospered. The Carnegie Foundation and the Rockefeller Institute, among other foundations, contributed both men and money to help build up the country. I have not been there in over forty years, and I think that it would make me sad to go. That solid upper class felt a definite commitment to the people, and although the poverty was frightful and diseases such as elephantiasis, leprosy, and syphilis were common, there was laughter throughout the land. The women walking down the verdant hillsides for miles to the markets carried their huge burdens on top of a cushion of brightly colored bandanas and sang in unison as they walked—hips swaying, shoulders back.

I am very proud, too, of what my father did for Haiti. He was trained to be a soldier, not a diplomat; but once he put his mind to something, he could accomplish his end with vigor and tact. During his lifetime he was commended by three secretaries of state and the secretary of the navy. He also received both the Navy Cross and the Distinguished Service Medal, beside the usual campaign medals and some foreign decorations.

Father was in Santo Domingo and Haiti between 1916 and 1930, and here is the rough draft of a letter I found recently, written in his hand from one of those countries (undated) which is so like him that I feel I must include it, although it has nothing to do with Haiti and is only a side-light on my father's character. He was a colonel at the time, and the letter is addressed to General Lejeune, then overseas, so, although undated, it must have been written in late 1917 or early 1918, because it was during World War I.

My dear General—

Knowing that you are frightfully busy now I hesitate to bother you but you have always been such a willing listener to my plaints and have so often helped me by your guidance that I cannot refrain from writing a brief note to you asking your aid.

I am, of course, extremely anxious to go to France or at least anywhere that Marines are sent against the Huns and I am naturally simply eating my heart out down here hoping or expecting that I will have a chance to take part in a war for which I have trained all my life. My ancestors have served through both the Mexican and Civil War while I took part in the Spanish-American War.

So you see from the point of traditions alone I have a sound right to ask to be permitted to do my part and not break the continuity of the chain.

At present I am commanding the 4th Regiment and it is composed most assuredly of a fine body of men. Of course there are not really enough of them to give the power necessary for a decisive blow but they form a nucleus around which in a short time could be built a powerful fighting machine.

Furthermore, this organization has its traditions, or at least the foundation stone of them. Traditions unquestionably increase the moral and fighting efficiency of a unit and cannot be neglected. I am now trying to build up its traditions.

I would, of course, like to go to the front with this regiment which I now command but if it is impossible for me to go with the Fourth I am anxious to go in any way that will get me there and the opportunity offers and if you would put in a good word for me, I would be deeply grateful.

With kindest regards believe me—

Most sincerely,
John H. Russell

Father had a true love of country deeply ingrained in him. I think that much as he adored my mother, his country meant even more to him. His country, the Flag, the President of the United States—these were to be respected, revered and fought for; in fact I think that his country was his religion; he believed in it and he loved it. Woodrow Wilson's slogan of "Too Proud to Fight" struck him as a bit of sophistry and for one moment when it was thought that Charles Evans Hughes had won the election and Wilson had lost, he and Mother waltzed around the drawing room while I, in my nightgown, sat watching and absorbing these grown-up antics. The next day all was gloom when the final vote was counted and Wilson was proclaimed the winner. To my father, the country seemed to have lost its ideals. Father had his regiment all ready to go overseas when the Armistice came. He never got his chance to serve in the war, but went on to many other things including being the father of the Fleet Marine Force, which made the Marines into an amphibious landing force, a unit that was used with great effectiveness in World War II. Still he never quite got over not being able to take his regiment to France. He felt it a stain on his career.

8

Nothing in life ever remains the same. Anyone who refuses to acknowledge or accept that fact is definitely a loser. I remember a couple in Bernardsville so ideally suited in every way that I said to the wife one day, "Oh, how lucky you are to have such a perfect married life." "Yes," she said. "It *is* perfect, but I have had to work at it."

I was astonished. I had never before thought of marriage as something one had to work at. Either one made a good choice and was happy; or one made a bad choice and was miserable. Since then I have come to know how wise she was—nothing, and above all no relationship, should be taken for granted. One must never take for granted a husband, a wife, a lover, one's children, one's friends, or even one's looks. I often hear tales of husbands suddenly announcing to their astonished wives that they are fed up and are leaving. If one has a close relationship, how can one ever be surprised? If someone has once really loved you, and you have loved him, you know when he is irritated or unresponsive, or doesn't laugh with you anymore; or seems very busy away from home. Any wife who has married a man who once was responsive, affectionate and companionable should surely be cognizant of these changes. She should not be taken by surprise when he says he wants out. As the woodsman says, "A woodpecker never attacks a sound tree." A good husband who slowly becomes a boor and a bore is no longer a sound tree, and any rampaging woodpecker can get him. My mother used to say, "Nothing is so dangerous as boredom." It certainly kills marriage and romance. I believe that a marriage between two intelligent and decent human beings can last forever if they both work at it, particularly the wife—not necessarily candlelit dinners, a rosebud every day and a nympho-satyr sex life, but just a little drama, a little excitement, a feeling that there are still questions to be asked, and to have answers that will surprise you. A love affair is harder work; more is expected, particularly when one is young, and most women expect too much. But a love affair, like a marriage, will be happy if both partners work at it. Today though, some of these love affairs are turning into wretched changelings with all of the responsibilities of marriage and none of its rewards. At least in marriage, there are rules. It is in a way easier to get a divorce than break off a love affair. Children should not be taken for granted either. They should be loved, disciplined and made to feel secure, not an easy thing to do. Again, work, work, work. Then there is one's face. "You can keep your face just as it is for thirty years," a dermatologist once said to me. "Don't grow too fat, it will stretch your skin. Don't smoke. Eat and drink in moderation and clean your skin well every morning and night. As for the body, the same thing applies, except that daily exercise is essential. A *very* brisk long walk, bicycling, a swim, tennis, whatever you like—but keep it up 365 days of the year. It keeps the blood circulating."

Finally, and most important, there is the mind, the pilot that steers us through life. The pilot keeps a sharp eye out for shoals and reefs, for stormy seas and tranquil coves. One's pilot—the mind—is an explorer, constantly on the alert, and interested in everything. One should constantly challenge the mind.

Mother tried continually to give me good advice in her letters, but I had not yet realized that she was warning me. Advice usually falls on deaf ears, and it is only by experience that one learns. I had learned how to run the house, how to entertain. But I was certainly not working at my marriage. As for being interested in what Dryden said or thought, I don't think it ever entered my mind; nor did it enter his. Our marriage was a mistake from the start. Granny had said, "How marvelous! You are so young, you will grow up together." Instead of that, we grew more and more apart.

We had dreadful rows that lasted all night. I can't remember what they were about, but I do remember Dryden rushing off in his car at dawn. I never knew where he had gone until he would turn up a couple of days later. This had certain side effects. Though a perfectly healthy young woman, I spent practically a whole winter in bed with a mysterious fever. A trained nurse took me to the doctor twice a week. I caught pleurisy in Newport, where we went for a weekend, and spent a month in the hospital there.

After we had been married seven years, I became resigned to it all and was once again my bouncing self. Our marriage was by that time an "unsound tree" and there were many woodpeckers about. Dryden was engaged in hectic affairs, and I became a flirt. I often had tête-à-tête lunches and dinners in New York, and danced through many nights. I was no longer as simple as when I met Hergesheimer, and I loved exchanging knowing looks and writing provocative letters; sometimes I received, and sometimes I gave, a kiss. The Ritz in New

York was my favorite haunt, particularly in summer. It had an enchanting Japanese garden restaurant, complete with dwarf maple trees, and a stream where baby ducklings swam. There was also the Ritz Roof for dinner and dancing. I remember wearing a very daring black lace dress over a pink chiffon slip and a large black hat with a pink rose tucked under the brim. I was not above playing the neglected wife, a time-worn role which I began to enjoy.

While Dryden was politicking and womanizing, and I was beginning to savor some of the delights I had seen Mother enjoy, poor Colonel Kuser was fighting cancer of the neck. I remember Mrs. Kuser's stricken face when she gave us this news, adding that he only had a few months to live. Even though I had been married almost ten years, I knew nothing of the Kusers' intimate life. My contacts with them for the last few years had been confined to "little talks" held behind closed doors in their upstairs morning room, where they scolded me for absurd things like lunching with Lillian Gish (against whom they could find nothing to say except that she was a movie actress) or demanded to know why I had sent a wedding present to Mrs. Kuser's nephew when she, Mrs. Kuser, was not on speaking terms with her brother.

I always felt as though I were at the dentist's and waiting to have a tooth extracted when I was summoned to the morning room. The Kusers seemed to me cold, hostile, and remote. In their eyes I was a total failure as Dryden's wife, and they had no interest in me at all. I do not remember Mrs. Kuser ever putting her arms around me, or saying something sympathetic, or giving me helpful advice. I do remember her telling me that I should inspect the servants' rooms every Monday morning, including all the bureau drawers, and that I should never give away a coat. ("They always come back into fashion.") I was far too young and frightened to ever do any inspecting, but I have followed her advice about never giving away a coat and have found it to be perfectly correct.

My relationship with them therefore had made me quite unprepared for Mrs. Kuser's agony and desperation. I was too timid to embrace her. When she went on to say that she did not want us to visit them in Palm Beach that winter, I understood. She wanted to be alone with her husband and with their daughter. She wanted no problem-children around during her ordeal. Colonel Kuser died in the early spring, and she brought him back to Faircourt alone in the private car, not wishing even to have Dryden with her. For some reason I can't remember (I think it had to do with getting permission to open the Dryden family vault in the Newark cemetery and having to wrangle with her brother over it), Colonel Kuser lay in a blue suit on his bed at Faircourt for several days, while she kept vigil and had all her meals brought to her.

I had always thought Mrs. Kuser looked like Queen Victoria, and in her grief she behaved in the same passionate way—not even allowing Colonel Kuser's twin brother to come and say a prayer by his bedside.

Dryden and I were in and out of the house, for she kept saying, "You must come and see Father." It was my first view of death, and I felt awkward and dismayed and thought it rather macabre to sit drinking tea at the bedside. But I know now how she felt, and I only wish that I had been more helpful then. I was far from heartless, but when one is young it is hard to believe that old people have emotions. Passion in older people is either absurd or repulsive to a younger generation. It never crossed my mind that the Kusers cared passionately for one another, and I found it ridiculous that they never wanted anyone else around, never entertained, and never went to anyone else's house. They were totally absorbed in each other as they drove endlessly around their property in one of the six electric cars and shared a split of champagne at dinner. I realize now that it was her passion for him that controlled their life. He loved his own lower-class family; and he had confided to me that he had no use for her father, Senator John F. Dryden, but he never told her that. The bond between them was very, very strong, but she was the stronger of the two.

Coming home from Colonel Kuser's burial in Newark, Dryden told me that he wanted a divorce. We were certainly not the ideal couple, but we had been jogging along, and our marriage was not much worse than the marriages of many of our friends. I was not happy, but I was not really unhappy either. I was used to Bernardsville, my friends, my house, and Tony's little friends. It was the only real home that I had; and I had lived there longer than any other place in the world. I never knew why Dryden timed his decision for that moment. I wonder now why I never asked him, but I think that he had at last fallen in love with a woman who was stronger than he was (he had five wives in all) and that he had delayed the announcement because of his father's illness. I think that he was afraid of his father, and that although Colonel Kuser certainly did not dote on me, he would have told Dryden that even an unhappy marriage was better than divorce— probably on the theory that "the devil you know is better than the devil you don't."

Mrs. Kuser at that time was not interested in anything or anyone except her daughter Cynthia. She was totally enveloped in her grief. Dryden wanted a divorce at once. As the lady Dryden wanted to marry was having trouble getting her husband to accept the fact, I decided to go to Reno and get the whole thing over with.

Considering how miserable I had been as Dryden's wife, it seemed absurd to say I was very upset, but I was. I loved Bernardsville. My friends there had taken the place of my parents, and my friendships with them had become the backbone of my life. The older people's kindness to me, the companionship of my younger friends, the church where Tony had been christened, the beagling—all this I hated to leave. It seemed impossible to me that I could make a life of my own. Where would I live? What would I do? I cried a lot, and when Tony and I moved into the Savoy Plaza before going to Reno, I used to look out toward New Jersey at the setting sun and think of all my friends still doing the things they did every day and had done all their lives. Meanwhile, I myself, the lifelong wanderer who thought that she had put down roots at last, was being forced to start all over again.

In those days in order to obtain a divorce, one had to stay three months in Nevada; so, preparing to settle down, I took along not only Tony but Mme. Grumeau, Tony's governess, Yvonne Grimmand, my maid, my Pekingese, Pushkin, and Tony's canary, Goldie. The lawyer out in Reno had engaged a suite for us at the Riverside Hotel; but when we arrived there we found that pets were not welcome, so after two days we moved to a bungalow on the outskirts of town. The lawyer found a cleaning lady and a furnace man—both in their middle fifties, and, of course, also out there for divorce. We were united in our common cause of freedom from our spouses and the little house was full of tales of what *she* said, and what *he* did!

The climate in Reno was magnificent, but extreme— dry and warm in the daytime—one could sit outside in the snow and never feel cold—but at night there was a difference, sometimes of forty degrees; so we were glad to have a handy furnace man. Our first night in the house, I opened a bottle of champagne, and Mme. Grumeau, Yvonne, and I were drinking to my future when there was a knock at the door. We were all rather frightened as there was only one other house near us. The knocking kept on, and when I wanted to go to the door, Mme. Grumeau insisted. "It is better for an old lady," she said, moving bravely toward the door. A man stood there who said, "I live next door and I saw that you moved in today. It is going to be very very cold tonight and I thought I might just look at your furnace." It was a nice voice and I jumped up to say something when I at once recognized him. "Morton," I cried, giving him a hug. "How extraordinary to find you here." He was as surprised as I was and immediately sat down to have some champagne with us. Morton Hoyt was the younger brother of Elinor Wylie, the poet, and I had gone to school with his sister Nancy. At the age of fourteen I had fallen madly in love with him, and I remember once when Mother was out, he had come around to our house and I had read him some of my poems, after which he had exclaimed, "Dear God, you are a remarkable child," and kissed me. As I wrote in my diary: "Dear Diary, Morton kissed me and I nearly swooned." He was extraordinarily good-looking and was supposed to be "wild" as he had left Yale without graduating. The "wildness" made him all the more fascinating to me, particularly as Mother disapproved of him and said he was totally hopeless. Now here he was in Reno, married to Tallulah Bankhead's sister, Baby Bankhead. During the time that I was there, Baby left him once, got a divorce, and went off with some very young man to Honolulu; but she came back and they remarried. Morton was still reading and trying to write, but he was really not making anything out of his life. However, for me, it was a nice beginning to my stay and cozy to have an old friend there.

Reno still had the facade of a frontier town. My lawyer, like the other lawyers, wore chaps, high-heeled boots, a cowboy hat. In fact all the businessmen looked like characters in a "B" movie. To go with these outfits, there was a great deal of talk of "horsewhipping" and "the sheriff is after him" and "he had to leave town." Mme. Grumeau, who in preparation for this Western jaunt had read all of Zane Grey, would whisper to me, "*Il est un vrai Desert Rat* [He is a real Desert Rat]." Mme. Grumeau took to Reno like a duck to water, and I never moved without her. She went with me to the nightclubs, where the main feature was always a huge animal—cat, lion, dog—made of cardboard with a great open mouth which was placed next to the band: the reason being that the band only played for a few minutes at a time, then stopped and would only start up again if the men who were dancing would throw a silver dollar into the animal's yawning mouth. Once in a while a couple who had too much to drink would have a row on the floor when the man would insult his lady friend by refusing to throw in a dollar.

It was at Reno that Mrs. Maurice Wertheim, the mother of Barbara Tuchman, said something very disturbing to me. She said, "Mrs. Kuser, I was thinking about you last night, and I wondered what you would have done in Jerusalem at the time of Christ's crucifixion? Would you have been for him or against him?" I had never really given it a thought. Knowing that I was a believing Christian, I took the fact for granted, but when confronted with this question, I felt most uneasy. Would I have recognized the God in Christ, or would I have been quite oblivious, thinking of him as a rabble-rouser? I could not answer. It would, of course, have depended on who I was at the time and whether I was a Roman or a Jew. I shall never forget that question. Mrs. Wertheim was a very stimulating woman, and I was privileged to have been a friend of hers. She made me read and think in Reno as I might not have done otherwise.

After Reno, I went to Santa Barbara for the spring. I took a cottage at the Miramar Hotel, which at that time was a most attractive place. The hotel was set back a bit from the sea and had a lawn in front, and the cottages were surrounded by huge daisy bushes and hibiscus. I knew quite a lot of people and had a very good trip. I bought a bright yellow two-seater Ford and had great fun visiting all my acquaintances. It had a rumble seat so I could take Mme. Grumeau and all of us together. It was in Santa Barbara that I met a very attractive man who urged me to smoke opium with him. "It slows down one's emotions," he said, "and makes anticipation almost as exciting as the height of pleasure." Everything, he explained, was slow motion, and a person coming toward you in a small room was as if he were approaching you across a vast palace room. I was twenty-four years old, and full of curiosity, but I resisted. I preferred to let nature take its course and be in command of my emotions rather than doing something that was foreign to my nature. Many years later, after Vincent's death, some friends urged me to try LSD, saying that it was a shortcut to God and adding that I might even be able to see Vincent. I was so much older that I had less trouble turning these friends down. If, as they told me, it took nine months for the soul to get beyond this atmosphere and I still had time to catch up with Vincent, if that were true, I still felt it wrong. If Vincent was moving into a new life, I should not interfere. It would be selfish and stupid. He should be allowed peace. In any event, as I had felt in Santa Barbara, I wanted to keep my own wits about me. Life is far too important and interesting to go through it under the influence of drugs. Too much drink amounts to the same thing. If other people find excitement or comfort, or oblivion, all right; but not me.

After Santa Barbara, we came home through the Grand Canyon and arrived safely in New York to stay once more at the Savoy Plaza.

Father and Mother came up from Haiti, and they welcomed the news that I was free. They had grown to dislike both Dryden and the whole Kuser connection, and they were delighted that I was at last free of him. I felt very happy when I was with them, and it was not until I lunched with Mrs. George Post and Mrs. Ledyard Blair, two older ladies from Bernardsville, that I had to face facts. "What are you going to live on?" they asked. "How are you going to educate your child?" Up to then I had not discussed money at all with Dryden; all I had asked for was Tony, and Dryden gave him to me readily. Mrs. Kuser was paying my hotel bill, but otherwise nothing had been said.

Father and Mother were worldly in some ways, but they were now so pleased that Dryden and I were getting a divorce that they never thought to bring up the subject of money. Fortunately my dear older friends were more practical. Mr. Ledyard Blair came to tea with me and said, "Brooke, you must go see Cass Ledyard of Carter, Ledyard and Milburn and get him to help you. Your child must be provided for, and you must have enough money to live decently, and you must do it before you go to Europe."

It was a most inopportune time to discuss money. Colonel Kuser died when the market was way up, and the inheritance tax at that time was based on the estimated fortune on the day of death. Soon after his death the market crashed, and the inheritance tax turned out to be more than the estate. Mrs. Kuser had the fortune which she had inherited from her father, and Cass Ledyard said that she should provide for me and her grandson. This she did, giving us enough to buy a small apartment and an income on which I could live comfortably, but not luxuriously. I took only my books, the wedding presents that had been given to me, and a desk that Mrs. Kuser had given to me on my twenty-first birthday. Having Tony was the most important thing of all. I was also naïve enough to say that if by any remote chance I should marry again, the alimony would go into the bank to accumulate for Tony until his twenty-first birthday. Since then, I have had to do with a great many wives who not only retained their alimony on remarriage but went on getting it from their ex-husbands even when they, the ex-husbands, had gone to their graves.

At that time, though, I was not aware of the prerogatives of the "injured wife." Even if I had been, I would never have asked Dryden for them. It is not in my character. I was furious, and I wanted nothing more to do with Dryden. It was only when older people made me see sense that I realized that I had no means of supporting my child. It never entered my head to take a full-time job, although fourteen years later I did just that. At that time it was rare for a young woman with small children to go to work. Only a few years before, when I first came to New York, life was almost Edwardian. At formal dinners in town houses, a red carpet was laid down from the front door to the curb. If it rained, an awning was put up. The men wore white ties and tails, complete with gleaming white waistcoats and sets of pearl or jeweled studs and cuff links. If they were going on to the theater, men wore *chapeaux mécaniques*, which were folding top hats that could be snapped shut and stuck under the theater seat. Every man carried a cane in the evening, and there were still some who carried a gold-headed cane to indicate to knowledgeable young men that they had a daughter of marriageable age at home. There were axioms such as that a lady should never wear black in her own house, that the calf of her leg should be two inches more in circumference than her ankle, and, above all, that a string of genuine pearls was the supreme sign of elegance. I remember very well that at my marriage to Dryden, Mrs. Perry Belmont came to the reception wearing a fabulous string of perfectly matched pearls. It caused such a sensation that Washington was all agog over it for days to come. Only a New Yorker could afford so princely an ornament!

I was a creature of the age I was living in. I don't think that I was better or worse than anyone else. I was obsessed by the desire to be liked, and I always tried to please everyone. Most of all, I wanted to please older people; but, even above that, I wanted to please Father. He had a tremendous influence over me. He rarely exerted it, but when he did I followed his wishes faithfully.

He used this influence at the most important moment of my life. It so happened that while I was dashing over the Somerset Hills in happy pursuit of the rabbit, I found that a certain fellow beagler often ran the same course as I did. He was an "older man"—twelve years—distinguished, good-looking, very well educated, kind and honest; but, alas, married, albeit not happily. I fell very much in love with him, and we lunched and dined at the Ritz and sat on grassy hillocks in the country while the rabbits and the beagles ran around the meadows below us. I knew that he loved me too, but I also knew that the idea of divorcing his wife never entered his head. He was a firm believer in "for better or worse," particularly where children were involved—and he had two. When I returned from Reno as a divorced woman, my father said to me, "Buddie Marshall is a fine gentleman and I admire him enormously. But now that you are divorced and no longer have the protection of your husband's name"—I thought that remark rather ironical—"I think that you should stop seeing him. You must think of Tony and keep the respect of the people around you."

I took Father's advice, even though it took all the courage and discipline I could muster. Buddie was equally upset, but for almost two years I did not see him or com-

municate with him in any way. It was the first real grief of
my life. However, I never questioned Father's wisdom. It
was, in the end, better both for Bud and for me. But here I
was, with no home of my own and no real deep-seated
affection or truly sympathetic and enhancing relationship.
I had no idea of what my life would be. Of only one thing
I was sure—I would never, never marry again.

PART II _____

Buddie

9

The first summer after my divorce, Tony and I went to Étretat in Normandy. Father and Mother came over from Haiti and went to a charming small hotel there, while I rented a little villa. It belonged to a lady who had a flower shop in Paris and it was *"très coquette."* It had a small pebbled terrace in front and a glassed-in belvedere on the roof from which we got a magnificent view of the tiny beach and the undulating outline of the green-topped chalk cliffs. On the left, we saw the famous bridgelike rock called *"l'aiguille* [the needle]," which has been made famous by Claude Monet, who painted it over and over again; and at the top of the cliff on the right there was a lovely little whitewashed church. It was a fisherman's church, and inside it was crowded with offerings from those who had survived shipwrecks and tributes to those who had died. On Sunday, we could see the fishermen and their wives zigzagging in a long slow line up the grassy cliff to pray for a good week of fishing and a safe return of the men. Étretat in those days pretended to be a summer resort but it was still quite unspoiled. The village people were as numerous as the summer visitors, and on market day the streets were crowded with farmers bringing in their produce, including pigs, sheep and calves, who frolicked happily from street to sidewalk. Apart from Monet and his followers, who had their studios there, there had been also a group of writers who found inspiration in the quietness and remoteness of the little town, so soundly tucked in between the cliffs. Guy de Maupassant was one who spent his summers there.

Étretat had greatly flourished in the nineteenth century and still retained the atmosphere of that time. It was not just one more little seaside resort, but a place of character and charm that said, "Stay if you like, but you must take me as I am." The beach was mostly shale, the water was freezing, but we swam every day—my parents believed that the shock of cold water was excellent for one's circulation.

The James Dunns and their two daughters joined us, and took a flat over the pastry shop. Jimmy Dunn had been with Father in Haiti, but at that time he was first secretary to our Embassy in London, later Head of the Western European Department, and first Assistant Secretary of State under Cordell Hull—the first post-World War II American Ambassador to Italy and finally Ambassador to Paris, Madrid and Buenos Aires. He was a very adroit diplomat, and a charming intelligent man. He and his wife had become great friends of my parents when they were *en poste* in Haiti with them, and I inherited the Dunns as friends. In age they were midway between my parents and me, and we were all immensely congenial and had enormous fun together. The Dunns were the most splendidly happy couple. They enjoyed every minute of their life together, and were never bored for a moment. They were also very, very amusing; and as Mother and my father when on holiday were always ready for whatever anyone wanted to do, this made for an easygoing and agreeable party.

I was welcomed back into the fold with kindness and love, but it had a strange effect on me. I began to feel a reaction from the tension I had been under for so many years. During my marriage, I faced each day as it came, trying to pretend that all was well. Luckily I rarely gave in to self-pity, but sometimes, when I thought how young I was and how long I would have to go on being unhappy, I wondered what would become of me as a person. Would I grow bitter and ill-tempered? I did not like that picture of myself. Looking back, I feel it was a great stroke of luck that Dryden wanted a divorce. I could so easily have become an embittered, frustrated woman, continually in search of a fuller life. As it was, the break happened when I was young enough to start a whole new life. By the end of the summer at Étretat I was quite myself. We were busy from morning to night playing tennis, golf, swimming, or sight-seeing, and in the evening, playing a mild game of chemin de fer or roulette at the unpretentious casino.

It was during that summer that I had the only two paranormal experiences in my life. One was in a dream. I dreamt that I was walking along a street when a gaunt elderly lady came toward me. She looked familiar to me, and I smiled at her, but she returned my smile with a stony stare. We had just passed one another when I suddenly recognized her. It was Granny! I turned quickly and threw my arms around her. "Granny," I cried. "Dear Granny, forgive me. I did not recognize you." She pushed me away from her, and so I said, "I did not recognize you because you have grown so thin." She held me off and looked straight into my eyes. "You know why I am thin," she said slowly and distinctly. "I am thin because the dead feed on the thoughts of the living, and no one is thinking of me." To this day, before I fall asleep, I dash in my mind to the graves of those I have loved, and I say to them, "I love you. I do not forget you."

The other experience was rather different. My bedroom at the villa was on the second floor, with a balcony

overlooking the pebbled terrace. Just below our terrace
was a pebbled path that led to the villa beyond us. I am a
very light sleeper, and soon after we moved in, I began to
be wakened by footsteps that passed slowly by my house in
the middle of the night. When this had occurred several
times, I got out of bed, flung the shutters open, and
stepped out onto the balcony. I saw nothing; but as the
footsteps continued, I supposed that they were on the path
below and heading for the next villa. A few nights later,
Tony woke me up by screaming. I rushed up to his room
on the floor above. Through his sobs, he said that a man
had been shaking his bed. I put it down to a nightmare.
But when it had happened several times, and John Dunn-
Yarker, a very down-to-earth Englishman who was staying with us, heard the steps going up the stairs to the belvedere, I thought that something must have happened in
that house. John had also heard footsteps on the terrace
directly below his bedroom, and he too had opened the
shutters and stepped onto the balcony; but with him, the
steps had continued directly beneath him and he next
heard them going up the stairs. They passed in front of his
bedroom door and went on up to the belvedere. He saw
no one, either on the terrace or in the hallway, but he felt
a slight breeze and heard the footsteps clearly. The strangest thing about it all was that neither John nor I was
frightened. I learned later that the widow who owned the
house had an only son who had shot himself, not at the
villa, but in Paris. The people who told me said that he had
loved the villa and had often stayed there alone even in the
middle of the winter when there was no heat. It seemed to
me that it was where he was happiest. Tormented by some
conflict he was unable to solve, he must have paced up and
down the terrace, tortured by indecision. Today I would
probably look upon these two experiences as a portent,
and would feel a shiver of apprehension of death, as

though someone was calling to me to cross the Styx. But at twenty-four, I felt immortal.

The summer passed, and I returned to New York and my new apartment at One Gracie Square. Billy Baldwin had "decorated" it, and it was very simple, but attractive: simple, because I only had a certain sum to spend, and attractive because, quite apart from Billy's taste, I had scouted through Normandy during the summer and had bought quite a lot of country-type French furniture. It all fitted perfectly, as Billy had sent me the measurements, and I loved every inch of it. There was a fireplace in the drawing room, and directly opposite the fireplace was a long french window looking out on Gracie Square, Hell Gate and the rapid tides of the East River. The only sadness was that I could no longer afford a personal maid, and dear Yvonne had to go. True Gypsy that she was, she predicted that eventually I would marry a very rich man; and she offered to stay with me without any salary until I could repay her. But, alas, my whole way of life was to be quite different. Instead of ten servants, I had three. It sounds rather grand now! There was to be no place for such a delicious luxury. Yvonne cried, and I cried, and three stolid Scandinavians took over the apartment. I still had Mme. Grumeau, Tony's governess, and, believe it or not, she had her bed turned down for her every night, and her nightgown and dressing gown laid out. Tony was entered at Buckley School, and so my new life started.

I am by nature extremely gregarious, and it was not long before, aside from my dear friends from Bernardsville (where I often went for weekends), I acquired a whole new group of friends. I suppose that a young woman with a pretty apartment, enough money to entertain, and an insatiable curiosity about people is bound to have a good time. I had married so young; I had never "come out," as

the saying goes. In other words, my parents had never announced to the world by giving a party that I was old
enough to enter adult society and was of marriageable age.
Now, suddenly, I could have all the fun that I should have
had then, and I took full advantage of it. Eligible and ineli-
gible men seemed to appear from nowhere, and I was soon
savoring the heady experience of being courted. Like my
mother before me, I received flowers, books, letters, and
telegrams every day. I began to think that sex was not as
unattractive as I had supposed, and that after all it might
be a rewarding experiment.

However, Father's advice kept ringing in my ears, and
I felt that if I once hopped into bed that something terrible
might happen to Tony or Father. God would strike them
down in retribution for my sins. So I remained "chaste";
but I could not resist the temptation to be provocative. I
remember well how one angry suitor, after a final refusal
on my luxurious king-sized sofa, got up abruptly, and said,
"You are a dreadful woman. I am leaving at once and am
going off to Anna Swift's." I arose to face him. "Who is
she?" I demanded, rather annoyed and piqued. "The pro-
prietress of a house of assignation," he said as he slipped
into his overcoat. I felt sad to have driven him to such an
extreme. But as I turned out the lights, I hummed to myself and was pleased that I had come out unscathed.

John Dunn-Yarker, my English friend, had come to
New York. He was associated with the London art dealers
Thos. Agnew & Sons, and he came over with the head of
his firm, Colin Agnew, who was a very dear person and an
expert on early Italian painting. It was a very lucky thing
for me that they were my friends, because they opened up
a whole new world to me—not only the world of art, but
the world of the theater. At that time, the New York theater was filled with English actors and English playwrights.
Herbert Marshall and Edna Best were acting in *Jealousy,* a

play in which they were the only two actors, and the only
bit of stage set was a telephone. It was dramatic and beautifully acted. The fact that they were both very good-
looking, charming, and madly in love, though not married,
made them seem particularly romantic to impressionable
me. Noel Coward played in his own play *The Vortex* and
was later to play in *Private Lives* with Gertrude Lawrence.
Dame May Whitty, Ernest Thesiger, doing his "petit point"
in his dressing room, Maurice Evans, Brian Aherne (acting
with Kit Cornell in *The Barretts of Wimpole Street*)—I
found them all fascinating, and I loved going to opening
night, watching my friends on the stage, and turning to
scan the aisle seats to see how the critics—Brooks Atkinson,
John Mason Brown, George Jean Nathan, and Walter
Kerr—were reacting. They usually dashed off just before
the last curtain in order to write their reviews for the
morning papers. The survival of the play depended on
what they would say. We would gather at Sardi's or the
Algonquin or someone's apartment and try to hide our
nervousness by saying Nathan had laughed, or that Atkinson had leaned forward in his seat with rapt attention. We
caught at these straws in the wind, particularly if the
audience had laughed at the wrong time or had coughed
a lot.

Coughing is the actor's nightmare, and it is extremely
contagious. One person starts in the orchestra, it spreads
rapidly through the house, way up to the last row in the
balcony. How I came to dread that first cough! All those
weeks of preparation, those rehearsals when each gesture
was perfected, and then to have it ruined by what seemed
to me just sheer bad manners! It has been an obsession of
mine ever since, and perhaps for that reason I have been
cursed with a cough and have formed the habit of taking a
small flask of water and sipping from it when I feel the
cough coming on. People around me look at me askance as

though to say, "How disgusting it is to see an old girl like
that drinking openly in the theater!" Just recently I did it
at a Horowitz concert and was looked upon by some of
my neighbors with a baleful eye. But I drank on, secure in
my innocence and in my respect for Mr. Horowitz.

Mrs. Nathaniel Bowditch Potter, an older and extremely elegant lady, held court at her small but exquisite
apartment on East Seventy-second Street. It was there that
I met the John Mason Browns (who became lifelong
friends), John Van Druten (*Voice of the Turtle, There's
Always Juliet,* etc.) Somerset Maugham, Osbert Sitwell,
Aldous Huxley, Glenway Wescott, Lynn Fontanne and
Alfred Lunt, the Alfred de Liagres, the Donald Oen-
slagers, John Sargent (Mollie Potter's nephew and now
chairman of the board of Doubleday), Artur Rubinstein,
Kirsten Flagstad, Tullio Carminati, and the beautiful Clare
Boothe Brokaw, at that time Editor of *Vaniy Fair* and not
yet married to Henry Luce. She and I got on splendidly.
The men who liked her never liked me; and the men I
liked quite often did not like her. It worked out very well.

There were also Grace Moore, Henry Bernstein (the
French playwright), and Bernard Boutet de Monvel (the
portrait painter), in fact an exhilarating mixture of the best
and brightest people. I never refused an invitation to Mrs.
Potter's. I enjoyed the people, the delightful look of the
apartment, the delicious food and last but not least, Mrs.
Potter herself, who was always dressed in the "*dernier cri*"
from Paris, marvelously fitted to her beautiful figure with
her shoulder-length and abundant gray hair making a halo
around her face. All this stood for the excitement and the
fun that I had missed by marrying at such an early age. I
loved every minute of it, and of my new-found freedom.

Another friend, Mrs. Samuel Welldon (Julia) was
about the same age as Mollie Potter, and she entertained a
great deal at her house on Thirty-sixth Street opposite the

Pierpont Morgan Library. Julia Welldon, like Mollie, always got her dresses from Paris; but as she had three extremely attractive daughters she was more apt to ask people in after dinner. She gave wonderful waltz parties, and I remember whirling through the two drawing rooms under the crystal chandeliers to the strains of Johann Strauss with Cecil Beaton, who had such long and elegant tails to his evening dress suit that they swept the floor. Raimund von Hofmannsthal was there, and many young Englishmen who were courting the girls. It was there that Edgar Bergen came in after dinner with his not-yet-famous puppet, Charlie McCarthy. I remember following him into the hall after his performance and watching him put Charlie away in his box. Looking down at the absurd, knowing face, I felt a twinge of sadness that he was no longer a person. Edgar Bergen had made him seem so alive and so witty.

Julia also gave little "mixed" luncheons for never more than eight people. Husbands or wives were never asked together. After I had met a very attractive man there several times, I found that he was married to an equally attractive woman. So I asked him and his wife to lunch with me. When Julia came into my drawing room at lunchtime and saw them together, she said, "You have set a bad precedent." Henry Bernstein, the playwright, was as good-looking and attractive as Bernard Boutet de Monvel. Both were over six feet with very good figures, and amusing to talk to.

It was a more relaxed and varied world than the world of Mrs. Stotesbury, and I got a great deal more out of it. I was learning new moves in the game of life, and I also knew I was no longer a young girl who depended on other people. I could stand alone. I was moving in a sophisticated and highly complicated society which stretched my perceptions and filled me—like Kipling's Elephant Child—with "insatiable curiosity." In the midst of this dizzy whirl,

there was my little household of which Tony was the center. I was always home in the afternoons to read to him at
suppertime and listen to his prayers when he went to bed.
At Buckley School, in the first play that he acted in (at
the horrible hour of 8:30 A.M.) he played the part of the
cherry tree that the boy George Washington cut down.
He played his part very well, standing quite still until
George Washington whacked him with the hatchet, and
then he bent quickly over. He was also in the "Knickerbocker Grays," a small regiment of boys who marched
once a week in the Armory at Park Avenue and Sixty-
seventh Street. I never recognized him among the
marchers, but I always told him how splendid he was, and
he would smile and say, "I knew you saw me, Mummy."

That winter drew to a close, and, once again, Tony,
Mme. Grumeau and I set out for France. I took a tiny villa
called "Villa La Brise" on one of the side streets of
Deauville and Father and Mother came to the Hotel Normandy. The summer was uneventful as we spent most of
our time on the beach with occasional side trips to Bayeux,
to see the famous eleventh-century tapestry, and to Rouen,
which we visited twice in the pouring rain. When driving
to Rouen, we complained about the incessant rain there.
The chauffeur shrugged his shoulders, and said, *"Que
voulez-vous? Rouen, c'est le pot de chambre de la France*
[What do you expect? Rouen is the chamber pot of
France]!" It became a family joke with us whenever we
were in a place where it seemed to rain incessantly.

At the end of August, Tony, Madame, and I went up
to Bar Harbor, Maine, to stay with Joe and Liz Pulitzer
(he was the publisher of the St. Louis *Post Dispatch* and
father of the present publisher). Dryden and I had been to
Bar Harbor several times and I loved it. It combined the
sea with pine-covered mountains, and was an invigorating
and health-giving place. I have always loved Maine, and

still go there (but not to Bar Harbor) every summer. The cold water, the smell of the pines, and the rocky walks up the mountains agree with me, and I am always happy even when—as so often is the case—the fog is dense.

Maine during my second summer as a divorcée gave me a wonderful sense of well-being and strength. This was "my home, my native land." Much as I loved the antiquity of Europe, the sense of continuity of life and civilization, nothing could take the place of the simplicity of the white Maine farmhouses, the rock-filled meadows, the brilliant blue skies, and dark pointed firs walking in a straight line toward the shore. Bar Harbor, as I knew it then, was almost totally destroyed in the autumn of 1947 by a terrific fire, but the rest of Mount Desert Island is as wild and verdant as ever. Maine will come into my life often in this sketchy memoir, but this was the first time I really felt its impact on my body and my spirit. I started with a new outlook. I felt that at twenty-six I should begin to take a more serious view of life.

10

In the second winter of my life at One Gracie Square, the apartment was not as pristine and fresh as it had been; and neither was I. My life as an unmarried woman began to seem rather pointless and lacking in substance. I was leading the sybaritic life that most of my contemporaries were leading, but I began to feel restless and unsatisfied. A happy child, a pretty apartment, and a host of delightful friends somehow did not seem enough. I felt that life was rushing by and that I was doing nothing to feed my mind and my spirit. I was living off other people's accomplishments. I remembered Mother saying, "Stretch your mind," and I realized that, instead of doing that, I was becoming very flabby.

So off I went to Columbia University, which in those days had extension courses one could enroll in without a diploma of any sort. Even as a high school drop-out, courses were available to me. I enrolled at Columbia for an afternoon short story course with Helen Hull, who was a very successful short story writer and the author of many books, including *Morning Shows the Day*, *Heat Lightning*, *The Asking Price*, etc. It was a class which seemed to be for people who wanted to be reporters or free-lance journalists and, as a side dish, successful short story writers.

Helen Hull was a teacher who could communicate and stimulate. She read aloud some of our assignments in class (not giving out our names) and asked the class for comments. I often squirmed when she read something of mine, because my efforts were not on the same beam as those of most of my fellow students. After one or two such experiences, I tried to make them as objective and unlike me as possible. As a result of this, they made no statement, came out as a jumble, and were impossibly dull. Nevertheless, Miss Hull encouraged me, and told me that if I really took myself and my writing more seriously I might become a serious creative writer.

Hatcher Hughes, who taught the playwriting class and was the author of the very successful Broadway hit *Hell-Bent for Heaven*, told me the same thing. The playwriting class, because it was a night class, was a true mixture of New York types and was therefore more interesting than Miss Hull's. Everyone in the class worked furiously, hop-

ing that by writing a successful play they would find the
pot of gold at the end of the rainbow and be able to retire
from the monotonous jobs they worked at in the daytime. I
worked as furiously as the rest of them and wrote a three-
act play called *Let Them Eat Cake*, which was never produced. I never tried to place it but talked about it a lot.

My play was what was known as a drawing-room
comedy and showed the influence of Somerset Maugham.
How could anyone have tried to write a suave upper-class
play with a thread of tragedy and not be influenced by
Maugham? I wrote it with an actor friend of mine in
mind. He was extremely nice about it and tried to help me.

The play was not without merit. The dialogue (full of
hidden meanings) was quite bright; but the plot was very
thin, and as I read it now, very dated. When condensed, it
loses whatever merit it had.

Writing plays and short stories was clearly not enough
for me. So I turned to writing a novel. In looking through
the letters I have kept, I found some from a literary friend
who writes about me and my novel. He obviously knew
me for what I was—a young, healthy woman, longing to
be somebody; full of curiosity, but above all, longing to
please and to be whatever the person I was with most
wanted me to be. Here is an excerpt from the letter regarding my great "opus":

> I am so glad that your novel is taking form, that you are
> interested in the characters, and that you are working
> systematically. I really think that it can be made into a
> solid yarn, and that you will gain some praise for your
> efforts. Also, Brooke, it should teach you how to write a
> novel, and next time you may find your picture in all
> the papers. The thought of little Tony sleeping while
> his mother is getting famous in her study below is a
> pleasant one. I wish I were there to share some of those
> studious hours. I could pass you paper, sharpen the

pencils, bring you water and hot coffee and then, when
my presence became an annoyance (as it often has),
steal like a ghost into my chamber and fall into a
snoreless sleep. Isn't that a picture for you? Some time
in August I hope to make part of it true.

Be sure to make use of that line "I let the cook
order the meat because meat isn't interesting." I never
saw it put that way. It is literary and it is true. Your
account of your housekeeping fascinates me. I should
like to see you trudging through the shops with your
little basket, your pink cheeks, your pretty face and
your (to me) enticing figure. Samuel Butler was a
great writer. When you've finished "The Way" read
"Erewhon." A summer on Samuel should greatly improve your literary appearance.

I have kept a few such letters from different people,
and I have some that I wrote myself. I was, it appears, an
inveterate letter writer, keeping the fire warmed, and often
adopting a tone of superior wisdom.

In addition to the two classes at Columbia, I organized
another class at home. Through Ernest Boyd, a member of
the Fabian Society, I met a man, A. R. Orage, whom
Ernest had known in London, who said that he would
come to my apartment and conduct a short story class. I
knew that he was considered one of the most brilliant editors in London, that he and Holbrook Jackson had owned
and run *The New Age* and that Chesterton, Arnold Ben-
nett, Belloc, Shaw, Wells and Katherine Mansfield had
written for them even though they were paid practically
nothing. I also knew that he was very much under the
influence of the Russian mathematician and philosopher
P. D. Ouspensky and of Georges Gurdjieff. It has been said
that Ouspensky sought the truth through esoteric study
while Gurdjieff claimed that he had found it! I was not
aware of all this at the time, but Orage made a deep im-

pression on me. There were just four young women in the class, and it was a unique experience. Nothing could ever prepare one for Orage. He was in New York working for, and raising money for, the Institute that Gurdjieff had opened in New York.

Orage was a born teacher: a pied piper who played a tune that still echoes to me down through the years. I suppose that he taught our little class in order to make a bit of money, either for himself or for the Institute, but I don't think that any of us realized at the time what a very rare teacher we had. First of all, it was not a short story class in the ordinary meaning of those words. Each of us put down on paper a single experience that gave us a feeling of heightened awareness. I remember writing about being lost in the Maine woods during a deep fog. The stillness was almost intolerable, and the trees seemed to reach out their branches to embrace me not with tenderness, but in animosity. They resented that I was up there on the mountainside, intruding on their fog-bound privacy when I should have been with other humans, comfortably settled indoors by the fire. I was frightened, and ran frantically hither and thither over what was normally a familiar mountain walk.

I remember also writing about standing in a hospital corridor near a window, full of agony that someone close to me was near death just down the hall. My heart seemed to stop beating as I thought what life would be after such a loss. Then suddenly I felt the warm sun on my back and reacted to it like a lizard, luxuriating in the warmth; at the same time I felt guilty that I should react in such a way and be so glad to be alive when behind a closed door someone dear to me was struggling to live. I felt that I was betraying a trust, and most certainly betraying myself. How could I take such a sensual joy in my enjoyment of the sun? Were I and the moment all that mattered?

These two efforts were written in answer to some of Orage's questions. In Orage's essays on consciousness, re-published recently in paperback, I find much in the chapters on animal consciousness and the description of plant and universal consciousness that has haunted me ever since without my remembering where they came from. How much does a tree suffer in a storm? Through what eyes and with what feeling does an animal view the world? Orage instilled an eternal questing in us.

What a joy it is to read all that again and to see in my mind's eye Orage sitting quietly relaxed, talking to us so many years ago at One Gracie Square. He said one thing that I remember very well. It was on time and our relation to it—a simple version of P. D. Ouspensky—*nothing exists but the present*. Time is like a train. The past is up close to the engine. The future is behind us, yet to come. We are at *this* spot, *this* moment, and that is all we know. We can only see out of the window at the present, and the morning, when afternoon comes, is already as far away as the very beginning of time. I used to think of the train as a European wagon-lit, crossing Siberia. I longed to jump out of my compartment and run up ahead to talk to Christ and Socrates and Voltaire and Mme. de Staël. As for the future, I hadn't any desire to explore that. I might open Pandora's box! On looking back, I hope that we gave something to Orage. Life had not been too good to him.

It was that winter that I met Arthur Krock, managing editor of the New York *Times*, who became a lifelong friend. What a thrill it was to go down to the Times Building after dinner and see the great presses rolling! Through Arthur I met Herbert Bayard Swope, the last editor of the *World* and inventor of the Op-Ed Page. Herbert and Maggie Swope kept open house on Long Island and had two separate staffs so that they could have a full course meal at any hour of the day or night. I also met

Ralph Pulitzer, the Publisher of the *World*, and his wife, Margaret (Peggy) Leech, the writer. She wrote several best sellers, among them *Reveille in Washington, McKinley* and *Tin Wedding*. She was a brilliant woman with a very penetrating and witty turn of mind. She also became a lifelong and devoted friend.

Ralph Pulitzer was a dreamer and a poet—an enchanting person. We used to lunch often at Robert's, which is now La Caravelle, and I always think of him and his charming old world manner when I lunch there now. I also met Walter Lippmann, who had been on the *World*. His "Preface to Morals" was practically my Bible. He, and his second wife, Helen, also became lifelong friends. Also, I met Franklin P. Adams (F.P.A.), whose column "The Conning Tower" appeared in the *World*. He was a somber-looking man but immensely witty. I knew him only casually but one could not forget him. The editorial staff of the *World* made a "world of their own." They had an immense esprit de corps and they made the demise of the *World* seem like the death of a dearly loved friend.

These people all influenced me tremendously. They were *workers*. They enjoyed the luxuries of life, but before anything else, they were people who worked endlessly and were perfectionists in their fields. Arthur Krock, three times a Pulitzer Prize winner, was a magnificent reporter. Walter was au fond a philosopher, a beautifully educated *gentleman*, a writer of great quality with a kindness and sensitivity that set him quite apart from the crowd. At the time I was enchanted to know these men and appreciated their qualities; and I now realize what a standard they set. They could not have tolerated the bad English and the political drivel that is written today. Arthur and Walter were rivals in their field, but they respected each other's integrity and ability.

Through this group I met Robert and Madeleine Sherwood: Madeleine was so pretty and so deadpan funny, as was Bob, singing, "When the red red robin comes bob, bob bobbing along," and doing a sort of buck-and-wing dance. He was always modest, in spite of his tremendous success with his plays and books. There was also Ernest Boyd, an Irishman, a Fabian who wrote a very good biography of Guy de Maupassant. Ernest had brown hair, a brown beard, and—what was rather eccentric at that time— wore a brown dinner jacket. He frequently came to One Gracie Square. Unfortunately, he had one failing: He had to go to the "loo" often. Somehow he could never find his way to the loo which connected with my small library, but always took a shortcut through Mme. Grumeau's room to the bathroom that connected with Tony's room. I did not know about this nocturnal happening until one day Mme. Grumeau came to me and said that she would have to leave Tony and me. I was overcome! Life without Mme. Grumeau would be terrible. "Why, why?" I asked. "How could you possibly abandon us?" "Because the situation has become intolerable," she said. "At least once a week you have a bearded guest who seeks out my room. I feel sure at the back of his mind he means to end up by raping me." After that I made sure that he went in the right direction, although I think that Mme. Grumeau secretly missed his visits. His manners and his French were both impeccable, and I am sure that he paid appropriate compliments to the old lady, swathed in a long-sleeved bed jacket with a shawl over her head (to protect her from a night wind), whom he only saw in the light from a half-opened door.

Ernest had a job that was unique. He spoke and read French and German as well as he did English. These were great assets, but translating was not always available; in Herman Oelrichs he found the answer to his dilemma. Herman should have been born in the Italian cinquecento or in nineteenth-century England. He was born to be a patron, and—meager as the field was in the twentieth century —he became one. He paid Ernest a yearly fee to read all the most interesting new books in English, French and German and make a digest of them with an evaluation of his own by way of supplementary comment.

Ernest did this superbly, never losing a nuance of the original and adding his own salty and analytical remarks. He was a one-man *Reader's Digest*. When I first met Hermie Oelrichs, I marveled at his erudition. It seemed incredible that a man who spent so much time in Newport and in traveling could have read and digested so many books. I was filled with admiration and envy. When I found out about Ernest I marveled even more that Hermie was so mentally agile that he remembered all those digests and could discuss what he read with anyone. It was a great contribution that Herman Oelrichs made to all of us. He seemed to have intelligently devoured so many books that he put me on my mettle to do likewise. Herman had a little flat (which he called his office) over a shop on Fifty-second Street and there, surrounded by books, he received his friends. I often dropped in late in the afternoon and found people like George Jean Nathan, H. L. Mencken, Padraic Colum, Alexander Woollcott and Monty Woolley.

Ernest was a real friend of mine until his death. Hermie Oelrichs and his wife, "Dumpie," were also intimate friends of mine and of Buddie Marshall's, as was George Jean Nathan—so these people all became a part of my life. Lillian Gish is a dear and lifelong friend, a generous spirit, a woman deeply sincere, full of heart and integrity. I have been lucky to have known such people. What endeared so many of them to me is that they had the qualities my parents considered important: intelligence, humor, honesty.

It was in the middle of the winter that I got a letter

from Buddie Marshall asking if he could come to see me. On Father's instructions I had not seen Buddie for almost two years. During that time I had seen a great many other men and had had several proposals of marriage. More than one of them I might have accepted, but each time I wondered if I were cut out for the life that they offered me, and if I really loved them as much as I had Buddie. I knew that it was hopeless to think of marrying Buddie, but I never forgot his dearness and kindness and understanding when I was so alone and unhappy with Dryden. I felt that it was better to be alone and unhappy than to marry someone and perhaps make him unhappy.

When I got Buddie's letter I called up Father and said, "What shall I do?" and Father said, "See him." So Buddie came to One Gracie Square and told me that he had been totally miserable, that he could stand his life no longer, that he had decided on divorce, that his wife had finally agreed, and that he wanted to marry me. He also said that he had given up his children. They were to live with Alice and visit us.

When confronted with Buddie's seriousness, I felt frightened. Buddie was in my eyes an "older man." That he would decide to do this, to walk out of his home, leaving his children, leaving everything: furniture, pictures, objects, his horses, taking only his father's books, seemed a terrible responsibility for me to assume. I was exhilarated but afraid. I rushed down to Quantico to see my parents and begged them to tell me what to do. I felt quite inadequate to take on so much responsibility. Buddie's whole life and his children! I was no tough *femme fatale*. I had not seen Buddie in two years. My ideas had changed. I could never again live in a closed community. I might fail Buddie, and that I could not bear to do.

I told my family of this, and Father said, "If a man of the character of Buddie Marshall has decided to take this step, you are a very lucky girl. I could die happy knowing that you were married to such a man." Mother said, "I think you have had quite enough of being by yourself. If you stay out in the rain, you will get wet." I thought her dreadfully cynical, but I suppose she was right. Buddie Marshall had all the qualities that go in the making of a great gentleman. He was intelligent, sensitive, had natural good manners with everyone, was a good "shot," an excellent fisherman, and a "man's man," but with an enormous appreciation of women. He was one of the most loved men I have ever known. He had a rare low-keyed charm that was irresistible.

To add to this, he was good-looking, loved to read, had a great sense of humor, and was a person of enormous discipline. I knew that he must have come to his decision after a great conflict within himself, and in spite of my family's advice, I hesitated. Knowing my own shortcomings, I wondered if I could live up to such a man. But he had made up his mind and had no misgivings. Finally, knowing that I loved him, I felt that his confidence in me would make me into what he wanted me to be. He had not been happy. I wanted to do everything in my power to deserve his love and trust. I wanted to be more than myself. I wanted to become the perfect wife. Of course, no one can be perfect, and I am among the frail ones in life. But because of Buddie's faith in me, and because I knew what he unconsciously expected of me, I had twenty of the happiest years that anyone could possible have.

11

Buddie and I were married at six o'clock on a late April day in front of the long window of my drawing room overlooking Gracie Square. We could not get an Episcopal clergyman to marry us, as we were both divorced, but we found a very responsive Presbyterian who read the same marriage service and presented us with a white leather book which contained the whole service and our names. I had the florist put up a little prie-dieu, so that Buddie and I could kneel, and the entire window in front of us was outlined by branches of apple blossoms. It was quite different from my wedding at St. John's Church on an equally beautiful April day ten years before. This time there were just Buddie and me. But there were also Father and Mother, Buddie's sister Evie Marshall Field (who had just divorced Marshall Field), Buddie's cousin, Arthur Butler, Jimmy and Mary Dunn, Tony, Mme. Grumeau, and my cook, waitress, and housemaid.

After the ceremony, we had champagne, then supper, with toasts and kisses and happy tears; and then the Dunns, my family, Evie, and Arthur Butler, all came down to the *Bremen* to see us off. We had a splendid cabin and sitting room and a room for Ingrid, my housemaid, whom I was taking along as a personal maid. There was a great deal of champagne drinking and eating of caviar until a steward went through the corridors beating a gong and crying, "All ashore who's going ashore." We bid our little group farewell and listened until we heard the deep blast of the ship's foghorn and knew that we had pushed off from the dock and were heading out past the Statue of Liberty to Ambrose Light, where we would drop the pilot before finally confronting the Atlantic Ocean.

I felt suddenly very shy and uncertain. Father, Mother, Tony—all were left behind. Here I was, leaving them all and staking everything on one person. No matter what happened, I could never from now on leave Buddie. He, I knew, would never leave me. All my fears came back to me as we sat in the salon waiting for Ingrid to finish unpacking. We talked about the wedding and Tony's teeth (he was going to an orthodontist) and Buddie's children. Finally Ingrid opened the door and said, smiling, "Good night, Mr. Marshall, Mrs. Marshall." So it was true. I was no longer Mrs. Kuser. I gave Buddie an enormous hug and kiss, and we walked into our bedroom, where Ingrid had made my berth up with my own pink crepe de chine lace-trimmed sheets (a relic of my extravagant days). Buddie was a bit shocked by this mad luxury, but he soon forgot it, especially as he was very pleased when he saw me putting shoe trees in my shoes and hanging up my dress and putting all my underclothes neatly away. "You are divine," he said, "I never expected you to be so tidy."

The trip was marvelous—a smooth sea all the way, and we ate in the special restaurant on the top deck which was all windows and we could see every ship on the horizon and every porpoise and every cloud. The days passed like a dream, and we were soon at Cherbourg and on the train rushing to Paris through the Normandy countryside with the fields of poppies on either side of us and the white Charolais cattle browsing among them. In Paris, Buddie had engaged a suite at the Hôtel Georges V. We did touristy things like dining in Montmartre at Nini's, and then walking down the stairs by moonlight to the boule-

vards. We walked all over Paris and drove to Versailles
and lunched at the Pavillon Henri IV at St. Germain. We
went to Fontainebleau and into the forest to lunch at a little inn called La Vanne Rouge, which stood by a lock on a
canal. We also went to nightclubs, including the now ven-
erable Crazy Horse.

We dined one night with the Cole Porters at their
beautiful house at 11 rue Monsieur on the Left Bank. Cole
had been in Buddie's class at Yale and at twenty-six years
old had married the ravishingly lovely Linda Thomas, who
was fourteen years older than he was. She was about fifty-
six when I met her (I thought that a very old person) but
was still extraordinarily beautiful and extremely *raffinée*
and elegant. The house reflected her taste as she was able
to make the eighteenth-century rooms comfortable and inviting without losing the original dignity of the eighteenth
century and its architectural statement.

Cole was a small man with eyes like brown marbles.
He never stood still a moment, and talked in quick jerky
sentences. Howard Sturges was there, among others. He
was a charming dilettante who at that time was a very
close and dependable companion of Cole's and Linda's but
in the end became more a friend of Linda's. Louis
Bromfield, the novelist, and his wife, Mary, were there,
too. They had bought an old mill outside of Paris which
they were enchanted with and had no intention of ever
leaving. (Later they went to live on a farm in the Middle
West and Louis became an authority on the rotation of
crops.) When we saw them in Paris, Louis had already received the Pulitzer Prize for his novel *Early Autumn*.
Mary Bromfield was a relative of Mrs. George Post of Bernardsville, so I already knew the Bromfields, but I did not
know the other people. Buddie was devoted to Cole, and
Cole to him; they had been Whiffenpoofs at Yale, and
Cole, of course, had written the Yale song "Boola Boola."

At the time that we dined with him, he had already had an enormous success in writing the words and music of quite a few hits, including *Anything Goes* and *Red, Hot and Blue*.

The guests at dinner all asked us to lunch or dine, but we were leaving Paris for Italy because I had a special project in mind. When Buddie and I had talked over our honeymoon trip, I had been reading a book called *The Enchanted April* by Elizabeth Russell (also known as Countess von Arnim—writer of *Elizabeth and her German Garden*). It was the story of a small castle that some English people had read about in an advertisement in the London *Times* and had taken sight unseen for the month of April. It was a delightful book. The description of the castle and its surroundings was charming and Elizabeth described the life there vividly and with a sense of humor. The castle dominated the little port of Portofino on an arm of the Mediterranean called the Gulf of Tigullio and was eighteen miles from Genoa. We read up on it in the guidebook and had booked a room at the Imperiale Hotel in Santa Margherita, which the guidebook said was the best hotel in the neighborhood. We were tempted to stay in Paris, but thank heavens we did not, for our life would not have been the same if we had!

We set off on the night train, the Rome Express, and arrived at Santa Margherita in the morning. It was very chilly when we drove to the hotel in pouring rain. The Imperiale Hotel was on a hillside and we had a large balcony, but there was no thought of stepping out on it in the downpour. The hotel itself was rather dreary, with only two or three other tables taken in the dining room. We felt shut-in. In the afternoon we put on our raincoats and got out our umbrellas and tried walking about the town. In the piazza we found some open carriages that took people to Portofino (no cars were allowed between Santa Marghe-

rita and Portofino then). The cabbies said that the
weather was too bad and they were going home. A man
came along who spoke English and told us that there was a
bus that went to Portofino twice a day. We thanked him
and found the bus, but it was already jammed to overflow-
ing. So, soaking wet in spite of our raincoats, we returned
to the hotel and had some hot tea in our garishly decorated
bedroom. "Let's go to Portofino tomorrow," we said. "It
will surely clear up by then." But it didn't. So, frustrated
in our quest, we left for Florence and went to the Grand
Hotel on the Arno. The weather there, though cool, was
sunny and beautiful. We started out on a round of sight-
seeing. The superb tomb of the Medici with its
magnificent Michelangelo statues of Dawn and Dusk; the
Loggia dei Lanzi with its exquisite statue of Perseus by
Benvenuto Cellini; the glorious Ghiberti north door of the
Baptistry, called "The Door of Paradise," by Michelangelo. We walked around with our noses in our guidebooks,
trying to memorize every object.

Fortunately, Buddie had called Mrs. George Keppel,
who was a friend of his mother's, and she had asked us to
lunch with her at her house, the Villa L'Ombrellino. We
went there the next day. It was only a family party, Colonel Keppel, Mrs. Keppel, and her two daughters, Sonia
Cubitt and Violet Trefusis. Mrs. Keppel had been a famous beauty and was the last attachment of Edward VII,
who was madly in love with her. She had behaved so perfectly during this liaison that when King Edward was
dying Queen Alexandra asked Mrs. Keppel to come to his
bedside for a last farewell. Born a Miss Edmonstone, Mrs.
Keppel was Scottish. After King Edward's death, she and
her brother Sir Archibald Edmonstone had come to Peking and had stayed with us at the temple in the Western
Hills. I was only a little girl, but I had never forgotten
her lovely voice and charming presence, even though she

had asked my Amah to unbind her tiny "lotus feet" and show them to us. I had never seen Amah's feet and had always thought them pretty as they were only about three inches long and were covered with gleaming white socks and little black satin slippers.

When the white socks were off and I saw them, I was profoundly shocked. Little girls in China up until the first decades of this century had their feet broken and bound in very early childhood. The toes touched the heel and the foot only grew up into an arch. It was considered seductive to totter and sway on these tiny feet. I had often run away from Amah when she wanted to brush my hair or make me take my bath, but I never did it again after I saw her sad deformed feet. I felt sure that it must have hurt her to run after me.

Mrs. Keppel remembered this and she particularly remembered my mother. It was another link with Buddie that both our mothers knew Mrs. Keppel and were friends of hers. Violet Trefusis, of course, became a well-known writer and a person around whom there was much gossip and controversy. I disliked her on the spot, particularly as I sensed that she was writing me off as a person not worth even the bother of a few polite words. Sonia, on the other hand, was utterly charming and most *sympathique*. I feel that we have been friends ever since, although I have seen very little of her. She wrote a book about her childhood and her mother which was extremely well written and had a great success. Colonel Keppel was a fine-looking man with the upright bearing of a real soldier. He had a ruddy complexion and snow white hair and a white mustache. It seemed that he had written a guidebook to Florence, so he took us under his wing and we had three glorious days of sight-seeing with him. He knew every stick and stone; and though I have been to Florence many times since, no visit has been quite like that, because of his enthusiasm and pure enjoyment of every statue and arch, every bridge and tiny piazza and viale.

After those three days we went back, as we had planned, to Portofino. This time we piled ourselves and our luggage into two fiacres and drove to Portofino to stay at the Hotel Splendid. It is only a five-mile drive, the road winding precipitously at the foot of the hillside along the coast, constantly rounding a curve in order to discover a new view of the rocks ahead and across the Ligurian Sea to the mountains. At that time of year, the hillsides were covered with golden broom and aromatic plants which, mingling with the tang of sea air, were almost intoxicating. Clop, clop, clop—along we went through the tiny beach resort of Paraggi, which consisted only of a pensione and some beach cabanas.

At last we rounded the final curve with the driver cracking his whip to spur on his nag. We saw on our left the castèllo crowning the promontory across the tiny harbor, with two huge pine trees rising from the battlements like feathers in a hat. The hillside on which the castle stood consisted entirely of silvery olive trees rising on terraces and pierced here and there by an enormous dark cypress. It was an enchanting sight as the terraces on their rocky base seemed to spring up from the deep blue of the water. I drank it all in. It was like a fairy tale. "We must go and see it closely directly after lunch," I said to Buddie, and he agreed heartily.

The room at the hotel was clean and airy, with a nice balcony, and we had our lunch on a vine-covered terrace facing the castèllo. Of course, we had to have our siesta, but as the church clock struck four, we were on our way, walking across the piazza of the little port.

Portofino has become a tourist's haven now, with boutiques and bars and discotheques; and the people have changed with it. It is in the Province of Genoa, and the

Genoese are noted for their hardheaded business ability and their close attention to the value of every penny; so the Portofinese are not letting the chance to increase their incomes slip and they are cashing in on the postcard picturesqueness of their village, at the same time adapting themselves to the changing times. Who wants peace and natural beauty anymore? Instead of a group of young people singing together on the rocks at the entrance to the harbor; or a fisherman's voice drifting back as he turns his boat toward the sea, one hears the very latest in punk rock turned on to the highest decibel. Never mind: The beauty of Portofino can never really be destroyed, nor the equanimity of the people. The fishermen still dry their nets on the piazza and the women click their bobbins as they make lace; and at night, the lamparas on the fishing boats twinkle on the dark sea. They are lit to attract the fish into nets.

When Buddie and I first came down the hill and crossed the main road onto the piazza, the people were just waking up after their siesta. The old women were putting out their stiff-backed chairs at their open doors and starting on their lacemaking. The men at the two cafés were lounging indoors waiting for the afternoon bus to arrive and bring them some customers. The children were playing, fighting, and shouting, and were occasionally scolded or called to by an irate parent at an open window. The countless cats were waiting near the water for the fishermen to return with their catch, and the dogs were snapping at flies as they lay near the butcher shop.

The harbor is shaped like a U, with the restaurants and cafés in the middle and houses built up along the quayside on the left. On the right, the land of the castèllo came right down to a gate at the end of the U, with only the Ristorante Delfino near the piazza. Behind the Delfino there was a cobbled path which led up toward the castèllo.

It was a path made originally for donkeys and mules and was rather rough on the feet. During the eight summers we spent at the castèllo, I used to sprint up and down that path numerous times every day and thought nothing of it. I grew to know all the lacemakers sitting on their chairs in the doors of their houses, and I learned, too, of every problem they had and of the inevitable vendettas that occurred between rival fishermen and rival café owners. I loved every stick and stone of that village, and I was a friend of the village priest, the postmistress, the café owners, the *contadini* who lived on the hillsides and kept their cows locked up in sheds for fear they might break a leg on the terraces (that part I did not like). All these people became a real part of my life, even to an ancient ginger bobtailed cat who was ferocious and the king of all the ever hungry cats who thronged the piazza.

However, on that day we knew no one. Not speaking a word of Italian, we simply smiled and they smiled back. We were holding hands and they took us for lovers, which indeed we were. Finally we reached a grilled iron gate, and peering through it, we could see a path that led past a greenhouse and on our left the bastion of the castle. I longed to enter, but we were both very law-abiding, and other people's property was sacred. So we were just about to continue up the path to the end of the promontory, where the lighthouse was, when an Italian woman in the black dress of a maid with a little white apron came walking toward us from around the bend of the castèllo path. "You like see castèllo?" she asked, grinning broadly. We looked at each other and hesitated. "It's rented to Americans," she said, "but they have gone to Rome."

We hesitated no longer. We were not intruding on Italians and it did not even belong to the Americans. We followed her up the path, getting a breathtaking view of the sea before the path turned and we found ourselves

climbing the steep stone steps inside the castle walls to arrive at a grill door that opened onto a wide, stone-paved
hall. The hall led straight out onto what had been originally a parade ground but had been turned into a terrace.
The terrace had a higher level on the village side, and that
was where the two enormous pine trees grew. On both
ends of the terrace were little walled lookouts, a smaller
one on the village side and on the gulf side one large
enough for a table for six to have dinner. The dining room
gave out onto the terrace and also had long windows looking right down into the sea. There was a guest bedroom on
that floor and a kitchen and maid's rooms. On the next
floor there were three bedrooms on the sea side, and three
on the village side, and one bathroom. The two sitting
rooms were small round rooms in the tower. One was on
the bedroom floor, the *salotto*. The other, called *il biliardo*,
or billiard room, was above it and was surrounded by a
parapet and stone guardhouse. It was really a miniature
fortress, perfect in every way, even to a cannonball imbed-
ded in the staircase. Needless to say, we fell in love with it.
The view on all sides was absolutely breathtaking.
"Wouldn't it be marvelous to live here?" I said. "Think of
waking up in the morning and flinging open the shutters.
Imagine seeing that huge cypress right under your window with the brilliant blue sea behind it and the silvery
olive trees on either side. What a joy it would be."

We went back to the terrace and looked down at the
little port encircled by its pink and yellow houses. The
voices of the children rose up to us, and the song of a boatman rowing out toward the sea. With the village on one
side in full activity, there was nothing remote about the
castèllo. It was a friendly and happy place. Again, I
repeated how wonderful it would be to live there, and
Teresa (that was her name) said we should call the lawyer
in Genoa and rent it for the next year. And that is just

what we did. Teresa escorted us down to the post office, where there was a telephone. Buddie spoke to the lawyer (who fortunately spoke English). To our chagrin, it was rented for the next summer, but we could have it for the summer after. I was depressed about not getting it at once, but we went back to the castèllo, took measurements (for comfortable chairs, etc.), decided how we could all fit in, and the next day drove into Genoa to see the lawyer.

By that time were so in love with the castèllo that we could think of nothing else; and when the lawyer suggested that we could have it all year round and on a long lease if we wanted, we eagerly signed up for ten years. Ten years in an enchanted castle! We never gave a thought to the travel involved or how we would have to adjust our lives. Business, children's schools, and vacations, other ties and responsibilities—they never entered our heads as we lay on long chairs on the terrace of the Splendid, watching the moon rising and outlining the valiant sturdy little castle. We only thought of our extraordinary luck in being together and being able to start our new life in this beautiful place.

The next day we set off for London, where life took on quite a different tempo. We were greeted by Buddie's mother's chauffeur at Waterloo Station, who led us to a smart small Rolls Royce limousine. It was dark blue, had a crest on the door and was outfitted inside with rosewood and ivory accessories. "It seems Mrs. Marshall has a fine new car, Herring," said Buddie. "It is not Mrs. Marshall's, sir," answered Herring. "It is a present to you and Mrs. Marshall."

Buddie and I were both astounded, but we should not have been. It was just the first evidence of Mrs. Marshall's thoughtfulness in welcoming us. I had wondered if she would be upset at Buddie's divorce and remarriage, be-

Le Hazard. Father and Mother's official residence in Haiti.

Father and Mother with Charles Lindbergh.

Mother in 1931—
Melvin Sykes.

Father as Commandant
of the Marine Corps.

Dryden and me in Venice when I was seventeen!

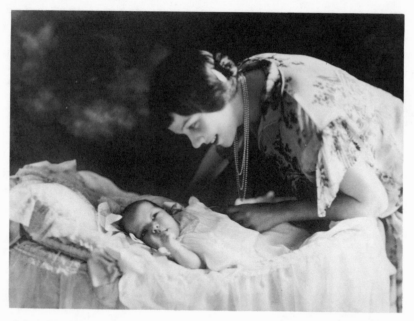

Tony in his christening dress.

Tony is a year and a half.
I was twenty.

On the lake trail at Palm Beach.

Tony and Buddie and me at the field trials in Virginia.

The Castello in Portofino.

View from my window at the Castello.

Miln House in the Tyringham Valley.

Buddie and me in the Victory Garden at Tyringham.

With Florabell and Hamlet.

Christening the destroyer U.S.S. Russell *in memory of my grandfather. My step-daughter Peggy is on my left. The wife of Admiral Bellinger is on my right.*

cause she did not know me at all and Alice was the mother of her grandchildren. Brooke Kuser was not a familiar name to her (although she had lunched and dined with me in Bernardsville), whereas Alice was the sister of Vincent Astor's first wife, Helen. This first gesture meant a great deal to me. It was, however, one of the first of many acts of affection and understanding from Mrs. Marshall. I grew to love her and admire her, and it was one of the first deep losses in my life when she died of cancer only two and a half years later. But that first day in London there was no cloud in the sky, and we arrived at 6 Grosvenor Square to find Mrs. Marshall having tea with Lady Cunard. They were in the upstairs drawing room discussing the Prince of Wales and Mrs. Simpson. Emerald Cunard was extremely derogatory in her remarks about the Prince, and I was horrified by her frankness. As she was an American, I felt that it was none of her business and quite out of order. Her house was next to Mrs. Marshall's on the corner, and she left soon after we arrived as she was going to a concert that Sir Thomas Beecham was conducting. He was apparently her *cavaliere servente*, and Buddie and I would lean out of our bedroom window and see Sir Thomas Beecham's car parked at her front door at three in the morning. Very, very racy!

Mrs. Marshall gave a dinner dance for Her Royal Highness Princess Mary and her husband, Lord Harewood, while we were there. It was a very attractive party and I remember two things especially. One was that during one dance the ladies were given green flashlights and the men red ones. The overhead lights were turned off and we danced while flashing our lights. The other thing was that it was the first and only time that I wore a tiara. It was really a sort of diamond bandeau made of "old mine" diamonds in a rose pattern. Mrs. Marshall's maid fastened it securely in a circle on top of my head, and I danced sedately, trying to hold my head up and my chin in. Later I had it made into a large double clip, which unfortunately I lost.

There was another great moment when at Covent Garden during the intermission, Mrs. Marshall took us into the Royal Box, where I shook hands with Prince Arthur of Connaught, the son of Queen Victoria and Prince Albert and the godson of the Duke of Wellington (the Iron Duke). I felt a tremendous link with history as I shook his hand and made my curtsey. Napoleon and the Battle of Waterloo seemed only yesterday to me at that moment. Mrs. Marshall also took us out to visit Lord Berners at his country place. He was one of those gentlemen-eccentrics that only thrive in England. I had read his book *First Childhood*, which is one of the most delightful of early memories, and *The Camel*, an amusing fable. At the time I met him, he was composing music for a ballet on the subject of Max Beerbohm's *The Happy Hypocrite*. When I became Feature Editor of *House and Garden*, our English correspondent did a feature on him which included a photo of him writing in a very disheveled bed with a lampshade on his head.

As a sideline, I remember Ingrid, my Norwegian maid, being totally bewildered by the staff life at Mrs. Marshall's 6 Grosvenor Square establishment. Ingrid was called Mademoiselle and took her meals in a special dining room with Mrs. Marshall's maid, the cook, the head housemaid, and the butler; and sometimes this group had tea with the housekeeper in her sitting room. The footmen (some of whom slept on mattresses in the pantry), the housemen, the various degrees of maids, assistant cooks and scullery maids, and laundresses all ate together. Ingrid was overcome not only by being called Mademoiselle but by the fact that when she passed through the halls, young maids with starched collars and caps and crisp striped pink uniforms scuttled out of the way. Apparently it was not proper for them to be seen around. They were the unseen hands who kept everything orderly.

This wonderful first visit ended and we were on the *Europa*, sister ship of the *Bremen*, turned toward home. I think that I got Ingrid away just in time, and I hope that TV has penetrated to the tip of Norway where she now lives in retirement, and that she was able to see "Upstairs, Downstairs." If she did, it must have brought back memories.

As I write, I stir the pot of my own memory and wish, as I have many times during the years, that Mrs. Marshall could have lived longer. She was a beautiful example of the type of American that fascinated Henry James. She took to London society as a duck to water, and I gather that London took to her. Mr. Marshall had died many years before, but even before his death she had come to London alone—always renting a house and entertaining and being entertained. Mr. Marshall, who was quite a bit older, stayed at home surrounded by his books. In the Franco-Prussian War of 1870, he had been head of the French Relief Society. In return for his assistance, the Comte de Paris, Pretender to the throne of France, sent him his four-volume *Histoire de la Guerre Civile en Amérique* with a dedication in each volume and an interesting collection of letters.

As we sailed across the Atlantic we became more and more serious with each day's run. The marvelous "impossible dream" holiday had come to an end. I knew that it had been as wonderful for Buddie as it had been for me. I also knew that with his strong sense of duty and discipline he would never live a totally carefree life. In other words, *we* never could. Thanks to Buddie, I learned self-discipline and the responsibility that a person of means has toward those less fortunate. "Give of money or of time," said Bud.

"If you have both, give of both." I think of him so often now that I work in the Vincent Astor Foundation, and it lifts my heart.

These rather sobering thoughts entered into our Paradise for Two. "Does the road wind uphill all the way?" asks Christina Rossetti. "Yes, to the very end." But at the end of our hill was the castèllo. What luck to have given in to that impulse!

12

We settled down uneasily in my apartment at One Gracie Square. It was charming for a woman alone, but with a man in it, it seemed to shrink and become overcrowded and uncomfortable. In the first place, my bedroom was only large enough for a small single french bed, so Buddie had to sleep in the library down the hall past the domain of Mme. Grumeau and Tony. This was a most unsatisfactory arrangement. Mme. Grumeau claimed to be the world's lightest sleeper, so we had to tiptoe past her room, usually to the accompaniment of her snores. We had rented a house at Hull's Cove, Mount Desert Island, Maine, for August but Buddie decided that he could not stay at One Gracie Square even until then. So he rented a house at Westbury, Long Island, for two months. We moved out there and put my apartment up for sale, having at the same time decided to buy the south penthouse at Ten Gracie Square.

During all this, Buddie confided to me that there was

one more change to be made. Mme. Grumeau must go. He said that he simply could not stand her another month. Mme. Grumeau, I may say, was not an easy person to be fond of. First of all, she was an egomaniac. Every happening, every single subject mentioned, reminded her of something in her own life and started her off on an interminable tale of what *she* had done and how she was able to show every one else up. She was as vain as a peacock, and as jealous of her prerogatives as a squirrel of his nuts.

In spite of all this I was devoted to her. She had been with me during the most unhappy period of my life. She had been the confidante of all my troubles and fears and had been my support and chaperone during the trying time in Reno. In short, she had taken on the role of an older relative and I was very dependent on her. When Buddie became my husband, everything changed. I no longer referred to her. I no longer needed her. I turned to Buddie with my problems (actually I did not seem to have any). Now, looking back, I can see why this change brought out the beast in poor Mme. Grumeau. She must have felt it terribly and took it out by being rude and sulking and putting Tony up to asking absurd questions. I tried to pretend that I did not notice this new behavior, but of course I did; and when Buddie said that she was not only trying to rule me, but spoiling Tony, I knew that he was right. It was a dreadful decision to have to make—there were tears and scenes and I almost weakened. But I knew, even after such a short time as Bud's wife, that he never acted on impulse, but always spoke from reason. In the end we parted amicably. Madame found a much nicer (more lucrative) position with a French family who divided their time between New York and Normandy. She was supplanted in our house by a Scottish nursery governess, and all was calm again.

Life on Long Island was much more sophisticated and

more suburban than in Bernardsville. It was not really my cup of tea, nor was it Bud's, although he was away all day at his office on Wall Street. Weekends we played golf and tennis at the Piping Rock Club, went to Jones Beach with Tony, went to the polo games at Meadow Brook, and dined out constantly—mostly either to play bridge or dance. It was a stopgap for us. We dreamed of the castèllo, at the same time rushing into town to superintend the decoration of our penthouse on Gracie Square. I saw a side of life that summer that I have never entered into since. It seemed to me then, and still does, a sort of Hollywood existence. Women playing bridge by a pool, while a manicurist and a pedicurist and a hairdresser worked on them, or just lying around all afternoon gossiping and talking about clothes and diets and men. I never fitted into that world, even though I tried to. I still felt a bit like the sixteen-year-old at the Princeton prom. I felt awkward and out of it. Their idea of the good life was not mine, and I had not yet achieved confidence or any sense of my own value.

Actually it was not until I was forty that I was able to go into a room and say to myself, "What do I think of these people?" Before that, I had always thought, "What do these people think of me?" When I became forty, I said to myself, "You are either a whole person now, or you never will be. Believe in yourself." But by that time I had been married to Buddie for fourteen years. That made all the difference. I constantly think how lucky I have been to have had such a love in my life. To have a perfect relationship in every way with a man who loves you deeply—a man whom you, in your turn, love and respect—is truly a beautiful and satisfying thing. It makes a woman blossom and grow. It brings out all that is best in her character, and it is the fine and filtered essence of being feminine, without in any way denying that many thousands of women are stronger and happier today because of women's liberation. I must admit that never in my whole life have I ever thought for a moment that being a woman was frustrating or would keep me from doing what I wanted. If I wanted to be a lawyer, a teacher, a newspaper reporter, I felt that I could become one. Actually, I eventually became an editor and this without even a college education! (Board of Ed.—I hope you read this!) It was because of my curiosity and my desire to achieve. I do not pretend to be in any way extraordinary.

I feel that if I could do it, any other woman can too. The main thing is to set your mind on what you want and then make a success of it by hard work. However, it is not always easy to find out what one wants and, of course, one wants different things at different times in one's life. I have found out if you enjoy your work and are intelligent, you will quite naturally be successful. To work at something you don't like and don't understand must be very unsatisfying. Luckily, I have never had to do that. I will shock all feminists by saying that one of the things that I have enjoyed most in my long life has been to be an *éminence grise*—a power behind the throne. In my case, of course, the power behind a man. I do not mean power in the sense of control, but more of being a "backup"—someone that a man can come to when he is worried and upset and full of problems. If he can unload them, and be comforted and helped and made to feel that what he is doing is important, useful, that you understand what he is aiming for in life and that you admire him for doing it, that is really a fun job. I have done it all my life (except with Dryden, and even there I tried, in politics). I find it enormously satisfying. It makes the person you love happier and more confident and it gives you pleasure to be able to give useful support.

That fall, we moved into our penthouse at Ten Gracie

Square. The stockmarket had been doing very well, and Buddie, who was a rather frugal person, felt that we could indulge ourselves in making it attractive. It turned out to be a really outstanding and livable place, one of the nicest I have ever lived in. It was full of sunshine and with a glorious view of the East River and the Hell Gate Point of what was then called Welfare Island. We built a room for Tony on the roof like a ship's cabin with a bunk and large portholes for windows. He loved it; and during the years we lived there, he cheerfully survived measles, German measles, mumps, chicken pox, whooping cough, and appendicitis in that cabin with its ship's bell clock and shiny brass portholes!

Our living room had very high ceilings and was thirty-eight feet long. It had a fireplace and three long windows. It was a good place for people to be in and so we organized our friends to come in after dinner to play "the game," which was a craze then. We divided up into teams, and a member of the team had to act out a word or phrase given by the opposing team while standing in front of his own team. The teams were timed, and if the team could not guess it in the allotted time, then the other team could choose a member of the losing team to come over to their side. I remember acting out "The Holland Tunnel"—a difficult and awkward assignment—and "Sacred and Profane Love." The Ralph Pulitzers, the Tom Finletters, the Bob Littells, Marc Connelly, the John Mason Browns, Harry Bull, Arthur Krock, the Bob Sherwoods, Stuart Preston—were all aficionados of these games.

Then there was "Shedding Light," where you described a person. Usually you tried to find an obscure one and when someone recognized whom you were talking about they joined in adding extra details. Pietro Aretino was one of my standbys to try out on new players. There were many other games including one called Guggenheim, which was our favorite for a pen and pencil game. One chose a four-letter word like HOME, then had categories down the side, each one beginning with one of the letters of the word. We marked ourselves "10" if we were the only one to have a certain name or object, "0" if more than two others had it. So, as in "Shedding Light," the obscure was important. We had terrific arguments, and books of reference abounded.

We also organized chamber music concerts. We invited fifty couples to pay fifty dollars for three concerts and had different quartets come to play and then had supper afterward. I had only candlelight for the parties, even putting candles on the old music stands. I thought it very elegant and civilized and loved arranging the room for the party as though it were a stage set. Actually, for those parties, we opened up the doors into the dining room and I had nothing but comfortable chairs and sofas—stripping all the other rooms of the apartment of everything with legs!

To prove to Buddie what a good housekeeper I was, I drove to market every day in our wedding-present Rolls and kept an account book. It makes fascinating reading—for a household of eight, the bills were seldom over four dollars a day and when we had parties, indulging in such extravagances as hindquarter of baby lamb ($2.98 for one large enough for ten people!), the bills might soar to almost forty dollars for the week. Liver was nineteen cents a pound, and one got two heads of lettuce for five cents. If anyone doubts me, I have my neat little book to prove it! A top cook was paid sixty dollars a month and a chauffeur, seventy dollars.

That is forty years ago, so one cannot even say that they were "the good old days." The good old days were supposed to have been before World War I. Anyway, I found them good. I was living a happy, civilized, and certainly luxurious life, though not in the extravagant way

I had lived in Bernardsville. That had been a nightmare of the "Poor Little Rich Girl" who seemed to have everything and in reality had nothing. As I say, Buddie was frugal. We lived within our income and had a good time doing it.

During that winter, and because Harry Bull, our friend, was editor of *Town and Country*, I became a contributor to the magazine. I wrote an article on "Hello, London," just after the transatlantic telephone was installed; one called "Messagerie Maritime," a take-off on people who take world cruises and never know where they have been or what they see; one about Christmas presents—what one gives a bachelor, married couples, etc.—and one about an opening night at a theater. I kept the money I made in a special account so that I could sometimes buy more flowers than Buddie thought I should, or an extra bottle or two of champagne for a party. Buddie kept a list of what each guest cost a head, whereas until then I had thought that if you entertained at home it cost you nothing. I soon began to realize that it was not so.

Buddie was certainly not stingy, and at that time he was extremely well off; but he had a thrifty nature and he tried to teach me to respect the value of money and to think twice before I bought whatever pleased me. To watch over the housekeeping bills was fun that first year, but I found out that for me to do all the ordering did not exactly please the cook. As the choice was between keeping a good cook and spending a few more dollars, I gave it up and took up Italian lessons instead. La Signorina Innocenti came to me three mornings a week and she compared me to Ruth Draper's skit *The Italian Lesson* because I so often had to break off in the middle of a sentence to answer the telephone, speak to the cook, or talk to Miss McBride, Tony's governess. Talking to the cook was an excellent thing because the signorina (a lady of uncertain age, but great humor) made me repeat everything in Italian and write it down in a copybook. In this way I learned exactly what I needed when I finally had to have my sessions with Angela, the cook at the castèllo. I had an Italian friend, Guido Colonna, and I practiced my new talent on him. Learning Italian made all the difference in life at the castèllo, and I wanted at least to be able to carry on a simple conversation with ordinary people. I did not aim to excel in persiflage or impress the intelligentsia. Basic needs were my aim, and I achieved them.

During that winter we started a custom that continued during all of our years together in New York. Every New Year's Eve we were asked for a soirée with champagne and oysters on the half shell at the Hamilton Fish Armstrongs' house on Tenth Street. Ham Armstrong was the editor of *Foreign Affairs*, a quarterly. He was an extremely intelligent and perceptive man, and the house where the parties were held was the house in which he was born. We usually either gave a dinner beforehand, or went to someone's house, and we only missed one of these events if we were ill. In the beginning of our going to these parties, starting with Anne O'Hare McCormick, the New York *Times* ace correspondent, we saw down through the years: the Charles Merzes, the John Gunthers, Edna Ferber, Harold Nicolson, Anita Loos, Lillian Gish, the Bob Sherwoods, Ambassadors, Cabinet officers, writers, actors, journalists—they were all there crowded around the oyster bar, champagne glasses in hand, and looking around to see who was, or was not, there. The Lion of the Hour was always there, roaring in the center.

Speaking of lions, it was at Ham's that I saw Buddie put on an act. We had just arrived and were standing together looking around the room to see which group we would join when a well-known reporter-journalist came up to us. This man was an outstanding writer, but a real lion-hunter and snob. We knew that Mr. and Mrs. Charles Henry Marshall meant nothing to him for, though we had been at the same parties many times, he had always ignored us. Now, suddenly, he was most obsequious and addressed Buddie as "Mr. Ambassador." I expected Bud to say that he was making a mistake. Instead of that, Bud nodded his head in formal recognition. "What do you think of the situation, Excellency?" continued our friend. "I think we have it well in hand," responded Buddie, "but if you will excuse me, I must join a colleague of mine," and he walked off, leaving me to follow. When we got home that night, I asked Buddie why he had not told our friend of his mistake. "I did not want to humiliate him," said Buddie. "He is so proud of always being right."

That shows what good manners Buddie had . . . the good manners that Mother said came from a kind heart. Of course we did make a family joke of this little contretemps, particularly, as when we saw that man again he never paid the slightest attention to us. Who he thought Buddie was that night, we never knew. It was only after Bud's death, and when I became Mrs. Vincent Astor, that he noticed me again. I bore him no rancor. If one can laugh, one recognizes silliness for what it is, and as Bud and I had laughed about it so many times, I enjoyed having him play up to me as Mrs. Vincent Astor and thought how Bud would have savored it with me.

During those years together in New York, we had very varied acquaintances. The Winthrop Aldriches (he was later Ambassador to the Court of St. James), the William Woodwards in their superb French house on Ninety-sixth Street by architect Charles Codman, the Sheldon Whitehouses, who gave a marvelous "last ball" at their house on West Fifty-eighth Street before it was torn down to make way for Bergdorf Goodman. The Whitehouses were very good friends, and we went shooting with them near Tallahassee in the winters as we did with the William Moores, who had an enchanting old house nearby with a beautiful camellia garden. Both these couples had lovely houses and large plantations. The men went out early to shoot, and the women joined them in the fields for a picnic lunch, riding out across the country on ponies. Life was easy and relaxed, and rather like the Old South must have been—with a wagon drawn by mules filled with the hunting dogs following the hunters. When a dog got tired, he was put in the wagon, and a yelping fresh dog was let in. To watch a dog pointing toward the unseen game, one paw up, tail straight in line with nose, is a joyful sight.

We usually went shooting with the Gerry Chadwicks each winter. They had a pre-Civil War house called "The Wedge" on a rice plantation near Charleston, South Carolina. When I say "we," I mean Buddie shot. I have never even held a gun in my hand. I remember only too well Father saying, "A gun is most dangerous when it is unloaded." By that he meant when one *thought* it was unloaded. Buddie was extremely careful as he had shot all his life, and a couple of Augusts when we were in Portofino we went shooting in Scotland, once at Duntreath near Glasgow, where Charlie Edmonstone, Mrs. Keppel's nephew, lived (he had married Gwen Field, who was the sister of Marshall Field, who was Bud's brother-in-law—all very complicated). Duntreath, a Victorian castle, was very much a Scottish home, with the piper piping us in to dinner and marvelous picnic lunches on the moors with Ben Lomond in the distance.

Another year, with some American friends, we took a moor called Ranagullion in Perthshire near the Spital of Glenshee. I love the soft damp air of Scotland, the heather-covered moors, waiting in the butt, a sort of trench, listening to the cries of the beaters and then seeing the birds suddenly come flying overhead. I would not like it today as I cannot bear to see anything killed, but in those days I thought that anything Buddie did was all right. Besides, the Scots claimed that if the grouse were not shot, they would overpopulate and become diseased, which is apparently what happened during the war, when no grouse shooting took place.

Looking back, I do not think that I led a useful life. But happiness is money in the bank and can be drawn on in times of sorrow. I needed those wonderful years later on when the light went out; but even during my happiness, I did not take it for granted. I thanked God every morning and every night and told him how grateful I was.

In those years I had seats on Thursday afternoons at the Philharmonic, and on Friday afternoons at the Opera. In order to get the most out of these musical days, I got together a small group to form a "musical appreciation" class. Samuel Chotzinoff, a friend, who was Toscanini's right-hand man, used to play through the program of the concert we were going to hear on the piano and tell us about it. He was a fine teacher and we all looked forward to our mornings with him once a week. Once when he was in Europe, we had Olga Samaroff, the pianist, for several sessions. Deems Taylor, the musical critic, was also a friend, and he taught me all that I know about opera. After Buddie's death, I somehow could not bear to listen to classical music and I have hardly entered a concert hall since.

In the spring, Evie Field (Bud's sister) and I went to Italy to refurbish the castèllo. She had said that she would like to have it in August and so she was going to share the expense of redoing it. We went first to London, where we ordered some things, and then to Italy. Genoa, we discovered, was a wonderful place to shop. We bought cotton brocades for window seats—there were a lot of window seats as the walls were so thick. We re-covered the sofas in the salotto (they had been made to fit the curved walls of the tower). We removed the billiard table in the billiard room. It was a relic of the British Consul in Genoa, Mr. Brown, who had originally bought the castèllo. In those days, every Englishman felt that a billiard table was part of being "a gentleman."

Mr. Brown was the father of Francis Yeats-Brown, who wrote *Lives of a Bengal Lancer*. When we had been in the castèllo a year or so, we got to know Francis Yeats-Brown and his Russian wife, and they visited us several times. He was a mystic and a great practitioner of yoga. One day a week he never spoke all day and such was his control of his whole system that he was able to drink a quart of water and have it flow immediately through his system in order to purify himself. I must confess I never saw him do it, but I took his word for it. He sounds like a bore, but he wasn't. He was gay, full of stories of India, had a great sense of fun, and was knowledgeable on any subject one could think of. He was a tremendous walker and Buddie and I walked for hours on the hills behind Portofino with him, listening to his tales of India and the philosophy of yoga.

We bought long chairs and a swing and a dining table for the terrace, and I had ordered from Hammacher Schlemmer a huge double chaise longue with an awning top which was the *pièce de résistance*. Evie, who had a passion for everything to be spick and span, got Cecil Pinsent, a well-known English landscape architect who lived in Florence, to come up to look at our terrace and advise on planting. The view was so beautiful and the pine trees so magnificent that there was not much to do, but he planted flower beds and ordered dozens of huge terracotta pots from Florence that were eventually to be filled with daisy bushes and hydrangeas. He also planted daisy bushes at the foot of the castle wall on the path that led down through the olive terraces to the sea. When Evie and I left, everything was ready for our return in the summer. I could hardly wait.

13

In all, we spent seven years at the castèllo, supposedly only for the summers. But as we had no country home in the United States, and only the apartment in New York, I often stayed from May through the *vendémmia* (grape harvest), which occurred in late September or early October. Buddie usually came over with me—then would go back to New York and return in July or August. This being before World War II we came by ship, taking the Italian Line (either the *Conte di Savoia* or the *Rex*) directly from New York to Genoa. The car was put on in New York loaded with all our luggage, so we got off at Genoa and drove to Portofino, which at that time had only one garage for two cars, of which ours was one.

Looking back on those years, I think that they were just about as perfect as life can be. The contrast with my miserable marriage to Dryden made me realize just how unhappy I had been and how dreary life had been with the wrong companion. It was a revelation to me that life could change from complete chaos to order and serenity. I knew how lucky I was, but it took the quiet days at the castèllo, the peace, and the beauty, to bring me to full realization of what had been given me. First, there was Buddie, older,

wiser, a rock to lean on, and who was at the same time loving, intelligent, understanding. There was Tony, who
looked upon Buddie as a father and was already being
influenced by Buddie's strength of character. And last of
all there was the romantic and dramatic castèllo, a unique
place in which to live, with its sturdy gray stone walls, its
battlements and defiant position on the hilltop.

To make living in the castèllo a real fairy-tale existence
we had, to look after us and to tend to our every want, the
Balma family, who presided over the house. There was
Teresa, the eldest sister, the "majordomo" of the castèllo,
who ran the entire group, and who now, at the age of
eighty-two, is still alive and alert in Santa Margherita.
Then there were the other sisters. Luigia, Luisa, and Isabella. In the tradition of Genoa they were a group of
"*testa dura*"—hardheaded people with a *mafioso* spirit, but
incredibly diligent and hard-working. They were up at
dawn polishing the stone floors with rags wrapped around
their feet, waxing the furniture, mending the linen, press-
ing our clothes, and doing our laundry.

Last, but certainly not least, there was Angela, their
aunt, who presided over the kitchen with its charcoal stove
and copper pots, and from which emerged food that was
fit for the gods: homemade pasta. *Al pesto*—a Genoese
speciality—was our favorite. It is served with a well-
pounded basil and cheese sauce. Next to that came her
soufflés, which stood a foot high and never fell. Because
her soufflés were made only of egg whites, the day after
the soufflé we always had zabaglione, in order to use up
the egg yolks. There were also fried zucchini flowers and
lupo di mare (a sort of bass) cooked in a paper bag with
herbs. As I hung over the castle wall I could see Angela
walking slowly up the path coming back from the market.
She should have been painted by Rembrandt—her oval,
brown, wrinkled face, her smooth graying hair parted in

the middle, wearing always a dark gray dress, a black shawl around her shoulders, heavy black cotton stockings on her sturdy legs, and those black felt slippers on her feet which seemed to be the hallmark of the European peasant. Angela led a motley band of village youths who carried on their heads, or in wheelbarrows, the morning purchases for her larder. Angela herself carried a black string bag in which reposed some special delicacy—white truffles or tiny squids, or just-ripened figs. I could not help but notice that our neighbors' cooks never had more than one follower, whereas Angela had five or six. The Balma family were connected with half of Portofino, and I decided not to inquire into how many sat at our table each day.

The other half of Portofino were relations of Beppo, our ancient gardener, and his son Guido. They belonged to the Guardini family, and were mortal enemies of the Balmas. At first Buddie and I took it seriously. When Teresa told us that Guido was ordering three times the amount of manure that was needed for the garden and was selling the rest, we felt worried, and wondered what to do about it. Then when Beppo told us that Angela was seen buying the entire catch from a cousin fisherman and that only two fish found their way up to the castèllo, we decided not to interfere at all. The cost of living was very low, the wages we paid were nothing compared to America, so we let things slide. We laughed it all off and grew to enjoy the horrendous tales that were told us by both sides. Beppo died one winter, and Guido took over. There was a frightful scene that spring. Teresa claimed Guido was a lazy good-for-nothing, while a brilliant nephew of hers trained in the garden of the Baronessa Mumm (who lived below us) just happened to be free, and could come to us. "He will transform the garden into a Paradise," exclaimed Teresa, "and having been trained by my sister with the 'standards' of the Balma family, and

also by the Baronessa Mumm, he will never buy more manure than is needed." This made our decision very easy—
we kept Guido, who eventually, after the war, became cus-
todian of the castèllo when it was bought by the National
Trust. There was also Mario, our boatman, but he kept to
himself—smiling a little at the shortcomings of others.

This domestic life was like a never ending comic opera,
and the recurring scenes were a small price to pay for the
affectionate and interested service that we got from both
the Balmas and the Guardinis.

There were, of course, moments of irritation, annoyance, anxiety and concern. The first summer, for instance, when Buddie's children came to stay with us, we
had a minor irritation. The children were dear. There was
his daughter, Peggy, who was fifteen and a darling girl
whom I grew extremely fond of; her brother, Peter, four
years younger, also a dear, was a delicate boy, and so had
with him an old Irish nanny, whose good manners left
much to be desired. Through some misguided idea of loyalty—I suppose to Alice (who incidentally had remarried)
—she refused to shake my hand or speak to me during the
entire visit. Buddie had never liked her and wanted to send
her home at once; but the boy would have had to go too,
and I certainly did not want to start my life with Buddie
by having a row with Alice over the children. So we ignored her sulks and rudeness. We weathered the summer
but she never came to us again. Peggy came many times
and was a joy.

On a more serious level, Tony had a terrible accident
and almost died. It happened this way.

After a couple of summers at Portofino away from
other American children and ruling over the apartment in
New York, I decided that Tony was getting spoiled and
should go to boarding school, where he would not have
everything his own way. I remember so well how I first

spoke to Buddie about this. We were swimming at Paraggi when I said, "Buddie, I think that Tony should go to boarding school." Buddie lost a stroke or two, and when he recovered said, "I never thought you would come to that conclusion. I have been wondering about it, but as Tony is your boy, it was up to you to make the decision." "When do you want him to go?" "*Now*," I answered, "and as you are leaving for New York next week, you must find the school."

By consulting Buddie, I had given him the "green light" so that from then on, he was not just a "father figure," but a real father—correcting Tony—stern at times —and showing plainly that he was disappointed in or disapproved of what Tony was doing, but at the same time, affectionate, understanding and always there when Tony needed help.

Buddie found a school that took boys from eight to twelve, called The Harvey School at Hawthorne in Westchester County, New York. I went home early to get Tony ready, and off he was sent. He came home for the Christmas holidays. When we left him at the school, he and I cried a bit, but I knew that he was as happy as a sheltered small boy could be away from home, and I felt that it was a character builder. Buddie and I went down to stay with the Will Moores in Florida for ten days' shooting right after Christmas, satisfied that all was well with Tony.

It was a bitter cold, icy winter, and we were glad to have some time away. A few days after we arrived, I was called to the phone to speak to the headmaster of the school. "I am afraid that I have some bad news for you, Mrs. Marshall," he said. "There has been an accident. Tony ran into a tree on his sled and we don't know how badly hurt he is. He is in the hospital at White Plains waiting to have x-rays." We did not give ourselves time to think about it—while our hosts telephoned Jacksonville about planes and ordered a taxi for us, I packed rapidly and within an hour we were on our way. The drive to Jacksonville seemed interminable as we rattled over the roads in the one local taxi. The plane flight through the night suspended us in limbo while I held on tightly to Bud's hand. We arrived at Newark airport just as the sun came up to touch the snowy landscape with a rosy pink, and I prayed that it was a good omen. Friedland, our chauffeur, was waiting for us in the "wedding-present Rolls" and drove us off to the hospital in White Plains.

I shall never forget being led into Tony's room and seeing him lying there so pale and wan, his poor little tummy as distended as a pregnant woman's and tubes suspended from bottles attached to him on both sides. He murmured, "Mummy, I am glad you are here," then drifted off. Dr. Kingery, who was the Doctor-in-Charge, told me sotto voce that it was hard to tell exactly what was wrong because the blood clots made it impossible to take a clear x-ray. He explained to us that he felt that an exploratory operation should be performed and that he thought it was the kidney that had been damaged. Buddie and his sister, Evie Field, who had joined us, felt that we should have another opinion, and so did I. Bud got one of the foremost urologists in New York to come out to White Plains. He arrived and I took an instant dislike to him. He was fat and unctuous, stuffed into striped trousers and morning coat (it was Sunday) and obviously only came because Buddie's sister was Mrs. Marshall Field and visions of sugarplums danced through his head.

I followed him into Tony's room, where, after touching Tony's tummy for a moment, he declared in a loud voice that the boy should be operated on at once or he would probably die. I went out of the room followed by Buddie, who said that the great specialist would stay and operate if I wished it. I knew that the decision was up to me; fortunately at that moment I remembered that another boy at Harvey School the year before had had a football accident which had damaged his kidney and that a doctor at the same hospital had operated on him successfully. As luck would have it, Dr. Kingery came into the waiting room at that moment, and I asked him the name of the doctor who had operated on the Condon boy the year before. "I did," he answered. "Then," I said, "I want you to operate on Tony." Somehow I had had total confidence in Dr. Kingery from the very first moment I saw him.

My confidence was well rewarded. He performed a most extraordinarily delicate operation on Tony. Both the kidney and the spleen had been damaged and had hemorrhaged. He took them out, cleaned them off, and put them back! Tony was cut almost entirely around the middle of his body, and for a week we were not sure if he would pull through. Transfusions in those days were given from fresh blood, and if the donor had eaten meat recently, the patient got a protein rash. As I saw the parade of burly policemen, fire fighters, and truck drivers who appeared as blood donors, I realized that poor Tony was going to itch from head to foot for days. In any event, that wonderful doctor pulled him through with the help of the dedicated nursing of the nuns. The operation itself was written up in the medical journals, and sad to say Dr. Kingery died only a few years later at an early age. I never saw the Great Specialist again, but I did get a bill from him within twenty-four hours, which made my hair stand on end. I think that the name Marshall Field was too much for him, although it was I who paid the bill. Tony, naturally, could not return to school, or take any exercise, so we thought it best to engage a tutor to keep him up on his lessons and to go to Portofino.

I was not political-minded in those days, and so when

one of my Italian friends on the ship going over said to me very seriously that I should not have Albert S. as a tutor for Tony because he was a Communist, I laughed in his face. "Don't worry," I said. "My son is a natural born capitalist." But as the summer wore on, and the *Daily Worker* was delivered to us, and I listened to Albert's comments on life, I began to think about Communism as it was shown in the habits of the tutor. He was constantly telling me and my friends at the table (this was before Bud came over) how wonderful it was that the factory workers in France were staging a sit-down strike and how vile it was that employers cared nothing about their underpaid, underfed, and overworked employees. But despite these sympathies he spent much of his time with his finger on the bell in his room, making Luigia and Luisa or Isabella answer his call and asking why his shirts had not already been washed or his trousers cleaned and pressed. The maids complained that his room was such a mess that they spent an enormous amount of time tidying up after him. I felt that his brand of Communism was to throw us out of the castèllo and live there himself. He gazed upon every big yacht that came into the harbor with envy mingled with hatred, and nothing ever struck him as funny or made him laugh. He took himself very, very seriously. I often think of him, and when I meet a so-called Communist, or someone whom my parents used to call a "parlor pink," I am grateful to Albert S. for showing me that a lack of a sense of humor often characterizes the self-styled "man of the people."

In my mind people who take themselves so seriously are dangerous. They are usually egomaniacs and unreliable. Tony, thank God, thought Albert a bore, and if he learned very little from him during their lessons, he at least was not influenced by him. That whole summer might have been spoiled if it had not been for the magic of the castèllo. Buddie, of course, knew how to steer the conversation away from Albert's one field of interest: the iniquity of bloated employers.

Quite selfishly we led a life on our own schedule. Up at six o'clock for a long walk over the hills, back at eight o'clock for family breakfast on the terrace, reading, writing, opening mail, talking with the family and servants until ten-thirty; then all of us for a swim, either out on Mario's little fishing boat, or off our own rocks, where we had built a sunbathing platform, or to Paraggi and its beach. Twelve-thirty lunch, then the siesta. Up again at four for a long, long walk, or tennis or golf at Rapallo, tea or a drink at a café in the piazza, and dinner out under the stars around eight-thirty on whichever parapet gave us the best view of the rising moon. It was restful, it was beautiful, it was again another deposit in the bank of life to be used later on.

We had another and quite a different ordeal that summer. A trusted member of Buddie's firm defaulted for a very large sum of money. This hit Bud very hard, not only because of the money, but because it was a blow to him personally. The man had been a good friend, and a trusted colleague. I was at the castèllo when the defalcation was discovered and our telephone bills were enormous. I wanted to return to New York but Buddie said no, and so I stayed on. After the children had gone back to school and when he came over, we had a marvelous October alone together at the castèllo. We walked over the hills in the beautiful autumn sunshine and sat by the fire at night. Buddie was there for the *vendémmia*, and we picked our wretched grapes (the Portofino wine is practically undrinkable) and ate lunch on trestle tables under the grape arbor. The village priest came to bless our harvest, pinned up his cassock, and set to with a vengeance to pick the grapes. What with the laughter of the peasants, the kindness of the priest, and the entire calm routine of our life, Buddie was able to regain his objectivity and courage.

It was in Portofino that I began to believe more and more in the healing quality of nature. I learned too that the gift of appreciating nature has to be acquired by stopping in a busy life to observe and absorb. I think that John Hall Wheelock in his poem "Sea Horizons" says just what I am trying to say:

> As bread that for my daily fare is broken
> the eternal loveliness before me spread
> Unalterable gesture—word unspoken
> In the proud silences forever said!

It was the priests in the Western Hills who taught me this, and it has never failed me. Portofino in those days was a fantastic blend of unspoiled nature and unspoiled picturesqueness created by man. It was the most delightful of transitions to turn from the sparkling sea and distant hills to the little group of gaily painted houses that clustered together in the cove that was the port. It was like going in one step from the infinite to the cozy, and I suppose that was one of the reasons I loved it. I am not someone who could live on a lonely mountaintop communing with myself. I want those moments of solitude, but I need companionship, and at the castèllo the laughter of children, the barking of dogs, and the chatter of women rising from the piazza kept me from ever being lonely.

In August Buddie's sister Evie usually came over for her stay at the castèllo, and then Buddie and Tony, Fafner, our dachshund, and I would jump into the car and be off. We spent several Augusts at St. Gilgen on the St. Wolfgang See in the Tyrol, just outside Salzburg. Buddie and Tony immediately got out lederhosen and Tyrolean hats, while I put on my dirndl and apron.

The freshness of the mountain air, the stillness of the lake after the restless sea, and the sound of the cowbells far up in the hills made a change in our summer life. We became even more active physically, less active intellectually. Our one intellectual gesture was to go into Salzburg for the Opera and concerts and to see *Everyman* acted in the square.

In the early years, when friends were with us and could stay with Tony, Bud and I would start out with our rucksacks on our backs and head for a few days in the mountains. We usually walked between ten and fifteen miles a day, making a circuit of the mountains back to St. Gilgen so that we need not retrace our steps. The walk up to the mountaintop was usually tough, and I often felt that I could not take another step or my heart would burst. But Buddie led the way and kept on until we reached a ridge and our first night's destination. Our destination was a *balmhütte*, or rest cabin, which we would find supplied with clean straw on the floor, candles and matches, and a small box where we left the few schillings that it cost us. Although I have always been a poor sleeper, I used to sleep as though drugged and would only awake at dawn to the sound of the distant cowbells. The villagers drove their herds to the upper pastures in the summer, so the cowherds and the cows were our friends on these jaunts. We often stopped to pick wild strawberries as we walked, and covered them with creamy milk straight from the cow.

I loved those walks. They were not climbs—no ropes, or pickaxes, etc.—but very long hard walks. Later I was to feel that they were too strenuous for Buddie, who was much older than I, and who spent all winter without a bit of exercise. However, at the time it was such fun I never thought of illness and death. It made us feel very superior to our friends who were moving around like sluggish ants a mile below us. It was romantic, too. We never found a *balmhütte* with anyone else in it, and to be all alone in the cool mountain air, cut off from everyone else, just the two of us lying on the sweet-smelling straw, was truly delicious. I recommend it highly!

During those years we took many other trips, too. We drove through Trieste and Ljubljana to Budapest on a ten-day trip. We had letters to several people in Budapest, but we had such a good time that we never used them. We had trouble getting to Budapest. We lost our way and had a flat tire, which Bud mended with difficulty, and we could not find the border. So at long last we arrived at the Duna-Pelota Hotel on the Danube around eleven-thirty at night. We had eaten nothing since breakfast, so Buddie rather timidly rang for room service and asked for a sandwich.

"Just a sandwich?" said the waiter in French. "Monsieur does not want dinner?" Well, of course we did, and Buddie started off by asking for two double martinis. When they came, beautifully iced, he brought me mine as I lay in a steaming bath! It was the first and only time I have had a martini in my bath but it was then, and always will be, a memorable event. It started us off in a gala mood. We had our dinner in our dressing gowns on the balcony of our room, which overlooked the Danube. As we ate the delicious fish from Lake Balaton and drank the Tokay wine, we heard Gypsy music floating up to us from the street below. From then on we went every night to a different restaurant to hear the Gypsy violins and the boys' chorus, never even thinking of the letters of introduction that our thoughtful friends had given us. During the day we went sight-seeing—the Palace, filled with mementos of Empress Elizabeth and Franz Joseph; museums, etc., then on to St. Margaret's Island, where we lay in the radioactive water and floated on the artificial waves.

Every summer we took time off from Portofino to go to the Palio in Siena. The "Palio" is a prize banner which is paraded around the piazza in front of the fourteenth-century town hall, drawn by a bullock cart. The Palio, or prize, goes to the winner of a horse race held at six o'clock in the afternoon—the horses are entered from the different districts of the town, each is paraded with their special banners—"The Goose," "The Wolf," "The Ox," etc. During the entire race the bell of the city hall is tolled, as apparently during the fifteenth century, Siena was besieged, and as a gesture of defiance the Sienese held the race and tolled the bell. Since then it has been held twice every year on July 4 and August 22. An amusing feature is that in each district the horse who is to race is led into the parish church to be blessed. If, while standing before the altar, he urinates, it is a sign that he is a winner, and the church rings with applause. Another reason for the charm of the Palio is that all the young men of Siena want to be connected with the race and with that great moment of their historic past. So they let their hair grow to a page boy style and on that day wear medieval clothes and end by looking as though they had walked out of a painting by Buoninsegna. The cathedral in Siena is one of my favorites with its mosaic floor of sibyls.

The whole town remains in an uproar for twenty-four hours. There is never any service in the hotel as all the personnel are out placing bets on the horse from their own district. The little inconvenience of unmade beds and sketchy meals is well worthwhile because suddenly the wonderful medieval town with its winding streets and cream-colored towers and palaces becomes filled with people who are all back in a cinquecento painting. We watched the race leaning out the windows of the palazzo of Prince Chigi, our arms resting on red velvet cushions with Prince Chigi's banners hanging below. The noise was tremendous, the people shouted, the horses snorted, the bells rang, and the hundreds of swallows darted in and out of the tower windows. For sheer excitement it was hard to beat.

The year that Mrs. Marshall died, Evie, Buddie and I took a Mediterranean cruise and visited the even more ancient civilization of Egypt. We went down the Nile, only as far as Luxor, but the sense of infinity in the desert, the huge monuments rising out of the sand—the Colossus of Memnon, the Tombs of the Kings, the Tomb of Tutankhamen, the Temple of Karnak—all these ancient ruins with at the same time the very primitive life of the bedouins made the ancient times seem very near. It was an incongruous sight in the twentieth century to see a blindfolded donkey and a blindfolded camel drawing water from a well by going around and around it to pull up the water buckets. We also took with us a snake charmer; when with only a loincloth on, he sat down and played his flute, snakes began poking up through the sand and weaving drunkenly toward him. We only went down the Nile a short way in a felucca, but we promised ourselves to return and take a houseboat on an extended trip another year, which, alas, I have not done to this day. I was happy years later to have been slightly involved in getting the Temple of Dendur for the Metropolitan Museum of Art.

Egypt and the Middle East have an appeal that no other place has. So primitive and yet so civilized. Istanbul, Persepolis, Baalbek, Byblos, Anatolia—I have visited them all many times. Also, the Sea of Galilee, the Plains of Esdraelon, Haifa, but, unfortunately, never Jerusalem. One of the happiest visits of my life was much later when I went to Turkey and Lebanon with Tony after his divorce; we visited a *Yalla*, or villa, belonging to friends of Tony's on the shores of the Bosporus and the Kahriye Cami with its frescoes and mosaics and Santa Sophia and the Topkapi Sarayi. Another time on a visit to Iran with the Dunns we went from Persepolis and Isfahan to the

Caspian Sea over the Elburz Mountains—that was particularly beautiful as we drove between fields of wild white iris along one side of the Caspian and on the other, snow-capped mountains. Walking through the ruins of Persepolis by moonlight, just the three of us—visiting the Sassanian Tombs, and the simple but elegant tomb of Cyrus the Great were glories never to be forgotten. I have a constant memory of this trip when I see the beautiful late fourth- or early fifth-century A.D. Sassanian silver sculpture of a king from northwestern Iran that we have at the Metropolitan Museum. I am on the Acquisitions Committee and when the Sassanian head came up for purchase, I had fortunately just come from Iran, where I had had the benefit of learning a bit from top scholars; so I was able to vote for it with confidence and persuade some of my colleagues to do likewise.

When I go to an airport these days and am pushed about by the crowds and find myself cursing them and thinking, "What a nuisance it is to have to always travel in the midst of a horde," I stop to think what a really snobbish approach, and I have to acknowledge that it is a marvelous thing that so many people can travel inexpensively and see the "Wonders of the World" that used to be available only to a privileged few. The more contact between races and nations, the better their understanding of each other's problems. Albert S., Tony's tutor, I hope is pleased that the average person, although not in a yacht or private plane, has a good chance of seeing some other part of the world apart from his own little corner at least once in a lifetime. No experience is really rewarding unless one understands the lines written over the main entrance to the Union Station in Washington. "He who would bring home the wealth of the Indies, must carry the wealth of the Indies with him."

14

When we spent our first summer in the castèllo, Mussolini had already been Dictator for four years—having formed the Fascist Corporate State in 1928. His sayings, signed *Il Duce*, were written on every available house and wall spreading the Fascist philosophy—"*Sèmpre Avanti*"—"Always Forward"—which meant always forward to Imperialism, to making the Mediterranean "*Mare Nostrum*"—"Our Sea." Libya was already a colony, and I remember going into Genoa to watch people embarking on ships which were to take them to a new life in Libya. It was to be the promised land, with a house for everyone, pasta in the larder, a donkey in the stable, a piece of land to be sowed and cultivated. Over 20,000 people poured into these ships cheering themselves with patriotic songs as they staggered aboard laden down with all their worldly possessions.

In addition to this enterprise, Il Duce had the railroads running on time, the mail delivered promptly, and the Pontine Marshes drained. On the humanitarian side, one thing he was praised for was that all underprivileged children who lived by the sea were sent to the mountains in the summer, and vice versa. Most of my Italian friends, though not exactly Party members, were pro-Mussolini during the early years. They felt that, even if they disliked him, he was doing much to further Italy's interest. They also applauded the Lateran Treaty with the Vatican, which finally solved the problems between the Vatican and the state. These had existed since 1871, when the state had seized all papal possessions, and the Pope thereafter had looked upon himself as a prisoner. According to the Lateran Treaty, the Vatican became a sovereign and independent state, called Vatican City, and the Italian Government guaranteed the Pope's inviolability. This was a very special point in Mussolini's favor among our friends.

Our great friend Prince Potenziani was the first mayor (*podestà*) of Rome under Mussolini's regime. Gino Potenziani was a real patrician, cultivated, intelligent and patriotic, in the true sense of the word. He was a Senator and President of the Agricultural Society, among many other positions. When he took on the job of being mayor of Rome, he very shortly became disillusioned and resigned. Gino was no yes-man, and as time went on he became so outspoken in his views that we used to say to him, "Hush, you really should not say that publicly." A favorite joke of his during the late thirties was—"Mussolini is carrying an umbrella today." "Why is that? It is a fine day in Rome." "Yes, but it's raining in Berlin."

Gino not only had a beautiful country place in Rieti, north of Rome, and a small palazzo in Rome, but also a very pretty little flat on the quayside of Portofino. It was through him we met members of the great and ancient Roman families: the Colonnas, the Pallavicinis, the Aldobrandinis, the Sermonetas—to name a few of our many friends. We also met Dino Grandi, who was to be Italian Ambassador to the Court of St. James when Italy entered the war. A truly patrotic man, he was dreadfully torn between loyalty to his King and country and despair at seeing it headed toward a fatal alliance with Germany. He was enormously liked in England, and when he went back to London after the war, not knowing how he would be received, he was overcome by the warm welcome he got.

His exchange of letters with Winston Churchill, which have been published in F. W. Deakin's book *The Brutal Friendship*, show clearly what a sad time it was for so many Italians, and how frustrated they felt. We also knew Air Marshal Badoglio, who completed the conquest of Ethiopia, signed the armistice with the Western democracies, and became premier in 1943. Another friend was Italo Balbo, who was Governor of Libya and often came to the United States before the war.

I remember a dinner party in a great palazzo, where in the entrance hall hung the coat of arms and hat of a relative who had been a Cardinal. There were sixty people for dinner in the vast dining room, and I sat between Balbo and Badoglio; the table was glittering with a gold service, golden candelabra and a battery of wine glasses at each plate embossed with the family crest in gold. Behind every other chair stood a footman in the family livery, swiftly changing the plates with his white-gloved hands. The occasion for this party was that we were to go on to the Palazzo Venezia afterward, where Mussolini was giving a reception for Von Neurath, at that time German Foreign Minister. We entered the Palazzo Venezia by a huge door, and walked up an immense stone staircase. On every other step stood a Fascist guard in a black shirt, immobile as a statue, looking straight ahead with his hand raised in the Fascist salute.

At the top of the stairs there was a long gallery, where quite a group of people had already gathered. We milled about talking to the people we knew, taking in the chic dresses of the ladies and eyeing the men, who, whether in uniform or civilian clothes, were covered with medals and had sashes across their chests and crosses hanging from broad ribbons around their necks. It was a glamorous sight, and reminded me of the pictures of Napoleon's Court. After we had been there a half an hour or so, and more people had come, there was suddenly a stir and a murmur throughout the crowd. It seemed that the official party—headed by Mussolini, Von Neurath, Ciano, his wife, Edda, (Mussolini's daughter), the Ambassadors of the two countries, air marshals and generals—had slipped into the gallery through a hidden door, and were now starting to lead us slowly through the galleries and salons of the palazzo.

After we had gone through a couple of salons, the procession stopped. Those in front, who knew the protocol, formed a semicircle, leaving an open space. Before us we could see, leaning against a fireplace, Mussolini and Von Neurath, in white tie and tails, much taller, bending his head to engage in what seemed a most merry exchange of talk. They stood there chatting, while the Chef de Protocol after a nod or a glance from Ciano, singled out guests from the circle and brought them up to exchange a few brief words with the two statesmen.

It was very royal indeed and went on in almost eighteenth-century fashion as we progressed from salon to salon. In some we stopped and had a glass of champagne and a small sandwich; in others, there was a muted orchestra. Edda Ciano moved languorously around, smelling a long-stemmed pink rose. When she accidentally dropped the rose, several high-born ladies jumped forward in order to have the honor of retrieving it.

As we progressed, I became more and more interested in the guests. Those who had finally pushed themselves into the front row of the semicircle were obviously hoping to gain the attention of Mussolini. Gray-haired generals, diplomats, pretty women—all hoped by the force of their glances to attract attention and looked enviously at those who had the good fortune to be summoned. There was one, though, who aroused a murmur of surprise when he was escorted up. He was a young man in an Air Force captain's uniform, and was received in a particularly cordial manner by Mussolini, who patted him on the back in fatherly fashion as he presented him to Von Neurath. *"Incredìbile,"* whispered people in the crowd. *"Còsa fantàstica!"*

Wondering just what was so surprising, I waited until I found someone I knew, and then asked who the young captain was. It appeared that he was an avid card player and gambler. Five years before, being heavily in debt, he was discovered one day cheating at the Caccia Club, whereupon his fellow players said that they would not press charges but that he must resign immediately from the club and exile himself from Rome. He resigned at once, but remained in Rome, going out only at night, and was never seen by any of his friends. When the war against Ethiopia started, he at once signed up and joined the air force. He did so well that he was ordered to the Ethiopian front. Once there, he apparently distinguished himself on his many bombing attacks and he was recommended to Air Marshall Badoglio for promotion, and his name was brought to the attention of Mussolini. That night at the Palazzo Venezia was the first time in five years that any of his friends had seen or heard of him. It was quite a drama and outshone Mussolini himself as an attraction. It frightened me, as it should. How hysterical and unlike themselves the people were becoming. In Portofino, life had gone on much the same, but that night showed us what an unnatural turn things were taking. Eventually the procession ended up in the gallery where we had first assembled. It made me realize why there are so many salons in the great palaces of the world. Those great abodes were built for crowds to stream through, jostling for a look at royalty.

We not only had Italian friends, but quite a few English and American ones. At the Rapallo Tennis and Golf Club, we played tennis with Ezra Pound. I was dismayed to find that this fine poet was an extremely uncouth man with bright red hair and an enormous stomach. He drew attention to this unattractive feature of his body by wearing only a pair of trousers, and no top, thereby showing his stomach protruding boldly over his low-slung belt. As everyone else was dressed in spotless white, which included a Lacoste shirt, his nudity caused quite a sensation. He swore at the ball boys, both in English and Italian, causing them to run across the court like frightened birds. We only played with him because the tennis pro arranged the matches. He was not a good player, but neither was I, which is why, I suppose, I so often had to endure his rudeness.

On quite the other side of the coin was Max Beerbohm, who with his American wife lived in a charming small villa, high on a hill, looking straight out over the rooftops of Rapallo to the sea. The first time I went to tea he was seated in a canvas garden chair, his feet on a low footstool, and a glass of orange sherbet in his hand. He was dressed in immaculate white from head to foot, and under his thatch of white hair his eyes were as blue as the sea behind him. Opening onto the terrace was his workroom, just as neat as he was, with its large drawing board and a table beside it on which, in various-sized containers, were the pencils, pens, and brushes with which he drew his famous caricatures. It was like the calligraphy room of a Chinese emperor. The walls of that room were a dark blue, and the ceiling white. I went to visit him in a spirit of awe and reverence. His delicious novellas *Zuleika Dobson* and *The Happy Hypocrite* were and still are two of my favorite books. He did not disappoint me, for he was as amusing and witty and original as his works. His wife obviously adored him, and as we drank our tea she kept refilling his sherbet glass. When she saw that he was getting tired, or perhaps a bit bored, she got up to show us the garden.

Gerald Kelly, the English portrait painter, was another friend. He was a great friend of Somerset Maugham, and his portrait of Maugham, called "A Glass of Sherry," was Maugham's favorite of all the portraits that had been done of him. Francis Toye and his wife, Nina, were our very special friends, and it was at their house that Gerald Kelly, who was Francis' cousin, stayed. Geoffrey Toye, who was Managing Director of Covent Garden from 1934 to 1936, was Francis' brother, and came there often too.

Francis Toye was a music critic and an excellent writer. His lives of Rossini and Verdi were best sellers. His *Verdi* was considered to be the most complete and comprehensive biography in English of that great composer. Francis also was an authority on Gilbert and Sullivan, and many is the night we sang from the famous Gilbert and Sullivan operettas while Francis played madly on his upright piano in his villa on the other side of the hill from Portofino. Buddie having been a Whiffenpoof at Yale was particularly good at solos. Francis was a tremendous walker, and the three of us roamed the hills from Portofino to Zoagli across the bay. I remember how once when Francis and I, walking alone, had reached the summit of a small hill looking out to sea, Francis turned to me and said, "Last week I christened this hill 'Brooke.'" I thanked him profusely—knowing of course that the hill did not belong to him—but after that, whenever I would not do exactly what he wanted—and he was *most* demanding—he would say, "How dare you treat me in this way! Didn't I name a hill after you?"

His villa was perched precariously on a steep hillside upon whose terraces grew the most acid and dreadful grapes. Francis made a tremendous thing of opening his own wine, which we swallowed politely, as it took a lethal course down our gullets. He also considered that the food in his house was the best in the world. "Tonight," he would say, "we are having something very very special," and indeed it *was* special. I remember one casserole that as I peered into it seemed to be filled with small goldfish and seaweed. It was only for love of Francis that I choked it down. He was really a dear, adorable person—so funny, so full of odd mannerisms, all totally unaffected—they were just Francis being natural.

Many years later, I wanted very much to do something for Francis—something that I would do in his lifetime, but would be in Francis' memory. I discussed it with my dear friend Jimmie Smith, who was at that time on the board of Covent Garden and also of the Royal College of Music and Sadler's Wells. I wanted to know what would be the most appropriate. We came to the conclusion that the best thing was to set aside a sum of money for young singers at Covent Garden who wanted to specialize in Italian opera and would need a season of study in Italy to perfect their accent. This, we felt, would combine Francis' two loves, Italy and Italian music. Having agreed on this, I asked Francis to come to dine with me at the Connaught. I was waiting for him in the lobby when he came in, carrying a vast and evil-looking walking stick. "Have just walked two miles across London to come to dine with you," he said gruffly as I led him into the grill room.

We had a delicious dinner. Francis got through a whole grouse, an entire bottle of burgundy, and finnan haddock as a savory. As he was drinking his *filtre* and sipping his brandy, I timidly broached the subject of the Francis Toye Scholarship. "Can't be done," he said, biting at the end of his cigar. "They hate the name Toye at Covent Garden. Geoffrey wasn't popular." "But I have spoken to *them*," I reassured him. "They are delighted." He shook his head, then, lighting his cigar and looking away from me—a habit he had when he wished to put over a point—"How much?" "How much?" I echoed. "How much what?" "Money," he answered. I told him the sum that Jimmie, always optimistic and conservative, had settled on. "Pounds or dollars?" demanded Francis. "Dollars." Francis rolled his eyes. "Impossible. It's not half enough. Even that in pounds wouldn't do it." I *did* change it, and it is now the Francis Toye Scholarship at the Royal Academy of Music.

The Herberts had a large villa just below us called "Alta Chiara," the Italian version of the name of their house in England, "Highclare," which belonged to the Carnarvon family (the family name of the Carnarvons is Herbert). We only knew the mother, Mary Herbert, the son Auberon, and the daughter, Laura, who married Evelyn Waugh. We did not know Mrs. Herbert and Auberon well, but it was the fashion in Portofino in those days for the people on the promontory (where the castèllo was) to invite each other once or twice a year for a seated tea, and we in our turn always did this.

The German baroness who lived just below us came. She wore, even on the hottest days, a small fake fur across her shoulders (she was an animal conservationist and only wore canvas shoes, even in Berlin), a huge hat on her head and silk crocheted gloves on her hands. She had six women gardeners from Germany and never allowed even the tiniest dead leaf or flower to be left in her garden. Her hydrangeas were as big as Halloween pumpkins, and were the envy of the rest of us, and the glory of the promontory. Augustus John and one of his daughters, Poppy, stayed with Sylvia Harrison just above us. Poppy and Sylvia came to tea wearing Liberty prints and Italian sandals. Mrs. Herbert came in a plain linen dress and tennis shoes. Pol, a Dutch painter, who also stayed with Sylvia, always came. Alas, although I saw Augustus John often, he never came to these teas, nor did I ever really have a chance to talk to him. I would have liked it, as I admired his work so

much. I only saw him in his pink shirt and floppy straw
hat which almost reached to his beard, struggling up the
steep path to the castèllo.

Evelyn Waugh came to Alta Chiara on his honeymoon. He was very pleasant and friendly then, and not as
difficult and rude as I found him to be when I met him
later on in life. He and his wife lunched with Buddie and
me several times in New York, and I crossed the continent
on the train with the Waughs when they were going out
to Hollywood. We had a merry trip, as Evelyn was fond
of brandy and found some congenial men on board who
shared the same taste. His wit grew keener as the evening
wore on, but I felt that it was wasted on some of his companions.

I shall never forget when he got off at Pasadena. I was
going on to Los Angeles, and was standing on the platform
between the cars to wave them good-by. From the look on
Evelyn's face, I felt the Hollywood visit was sure to be a
disaster. It was a brilliant sunny day with a temperature
over ninety degrees, and Evelyn was dressed for a north-
ernmost clime. He had on a tweed suit about an inch thick,
a striped shirt with a stiff collar, wool socks, brogues,
pigskin gloves, and a bowler hat. He had an umbrella in his
hand, and a heavy raincoat over his arm. As he advanced
toward the Welcoming Committee, his furled umbrella
half raised as though to fend off these aggressive greeters, a
feeling of intense disgust and annoyance emanated from
him. I felt that to him the scenery and the people seemed
totally unreal and preposterous. Untutored public relations
were no match for Evelyn's mordant wit and sly ego. Out
of that visit came *The Loved One*, the ironical and brilliant commentary on our American "way of death." Only
Waugh could have written it.

Just before the war Rex and Lilli Palmer Harrison
rented and then bought a house above the Hotel Splendid.

Since then a whole new group of interesting people have moved into Portofino. I am sure they love it as much as we did, but then I cannot help feeling that those pre-war years were very special. Life is so much the same everywhere now. Life in Portofino then was entirely different from our life at home—new viewpoints, new friends, a new curiosity about what went on around us. There was also a feeling that we were approaching the end of an era. The ships laden with Italians setting off to colonize in Africa, the constantly changing political scene in Italy, the rantings of Hitler on the radio—all tended to give us a sense of foreboding. Things had changed greatly after our first carefree years. Our Italian friends would say to us in the autumn, when we left the castèllo, "How lucky you are to be returning to America, how lucky to be an American!" They had turned to Mussolini in time of chaos and confusion and they found themselves worse off than ever.

Even *we* had annoyances. The Carabinieri in their nineteenth-century uniforms of cocked hats, tail coats and swords would walk up to the castèllo more and more frequently with orders that a foreigner could not have a bathing platform on the rocks or that our grapes were to be taxed double, etc., etc. None of this was very important, but it was irritating. Then, too, the Germans were flooding the place, climbing all over our peaceful mountains, carrying mammoth and very expensive photographic equipment to take pictures of every nook and cranny, shouting to each other, "*Ein schöner Blick*," (a beautiful view) while in reality, as we learned after the war, they were preparing Portofino to be used as a submarine base.

In September 1938, instead of the ravings of Hitler over the radio, we heard the calm English voice of Neville Chamberlain, who told us from London that at last a pact had been signed which would insure "Peace in Our Time." We set off at once to celebrate on a motor trip with Sylvia

Harrison and Pol to the Brenner Pass to our favorite village of Vipiteno, or Sterzing. The only sign of Germans was a lone officer playing Chopin in the twilight of the inn's upstairs guest parlor. We felt it was his way of expressing his own relief.

When we stopped off in London on our way home, we found quite a different mood there. Most of our friends were anti-Chamberlain. After the joy in Italy, it was quite a shock, but certainly more realistic. In Italy, the people were trying to buoy themselves up with any glimmer of hope for peace.

Strange as it may seem, life in New York went on as usual. Tony was at boarding school, and Buddie and I continued our normal life. When spring came around, we embarked once more on the *Conte di Savoia*, looking forward as usual to one long uneventful summer—the summer of 1939: June and July were quite peaceful, except for a visit to an American friend of ours who had married a Hungarian and was living in a schloss in the Tyrol. The wife was a dear old friend from my Bernardsville days, an absolutely charming woman, and a true romantic. It was this streak of romanticism in her that had made her marry the Hungarian. He had a very small waist (Hungarian officers all wore corsets), broad shoulders and knew how to please women. At the same time, he had a terrible temper. They had stayed with us first, and then we all motored up to their schloss in the Bavarian Alps. I shall never forget the impression their homecoming made on me. We drove through the gate into the cobbled courtyard, which was surrounded on three sides by an eighteenth-century stucco house painted in that lovely soft yellow that one finds all over Austria. A footman in a baize apron was standing by the stone steps to the main entrance door to take our luggage, and a very pleasant-looking gentleman in Austrian costume came out to greet us, followed by a maid and another manservant. Our host, who had been away for six weeks, ignored them completely. Instead of shaking the hand of the man who was obviously expecting a greeting of some sort, he only barked out a few orders, which I gathered were about our rooms, as I heard the word *Zimmer*. Later I asked who it was that had come out to greet us at the door. I also ventured to say that I thought he looked sad. Our host told me that he was Count X—a Jew—and that he looked sad because his father had hanged himself a few days before in Vienna.

"How terrible!" I said. My host shrugged his shoulders. "He ought to look cheerful because I still employ him," he retorted. "What difference does it make—one Jew more or less? To kill a Jew is no more important than killing a chicken." After this conversation, Bud and I were ready to leave at once. However, our hostess was a dearly loved friend, and she was looking so stricken and subdued that for her sake we stayed for two days, having originally intended to stay a week. During those days we realized that "Peace in Our Time" was more of a catch phrase than a fact. Soldiers were everywhere, rumbling by on tanks or driving trucks, or caissons, or in motorcycle groups. Officers sped past in large touring cars with the tops down. "No German officer ever drives in a closed car, no matter how bad the weather," said our host. "It is a good example to the soldiers." "There seem to be troops everywhere," said Bud. "Summer maneuvers," said our host, smiling. When he showed us gently rolling hills covered with grass and daisies, he explained that they were bomb shelters or anti-aircraft gun emplacements. "A country should always be prepared for attack," he told us. "That's what Roosevelt believes," said Bud. Our host looked surprised. (I was surprised too, as I knew Bud was not for Roosevelt.) "You are a Republican," he said, "and I thought all Republicans were against Roosevelt." "Not any more," declared Bud firmly. "The whole country is behind him." I cheered silently and felt that Bud's remarks made our rather sudden departure easier.

There was one thing that was particularly horrendous. In our host's bedroom was a shelf on which stood a large picture of a smiling Hitler, with legs outspread and small children bearing bouquets standing between his legs and crowded all around his knees. On the shelf beside the picture were a vigil candle and a small bouquet. Though our excuses were very flimsy, and I know that my dear friend found them so, she gave me a very special hug as I left, and we both had tears in our eyes. I never saw her until after the war. She came home then, and got a divorce. Subsequently she remarried. We never spoke of those war years, and she regained her gaiety and self-confidence.

All of this was in mid-July of 1939. We returned to Portofino, leaving as usual around August first—this time going to Switzerland and moving around from one hamlet to another. We ended up at Grindelwald, a simple mountain resort above Interlaken with a wonderful view of the Bernese Alps and the Eiger and its glacier. The hotel was crowded as usual with Germans and English, all true hikers in sensible no-nonsense outfits. All, to a man, were united in a fierce territorial obsession as to which chair was theirs in the lobby for that brief but important moment of extravagance when they indulged themselves in an after-dinner demitasse, an item not included in the table d'hôte of the pension. Rather than wear ourselves out in this absurd competition, we poured our coffee into a thermos and drank it out of collapsible plastic cups on our balcony.

That visit ended in a way which I will never forget. One fine morning we set off for a particularly long day's walk on the slopes of the Eiger—Buddie, Tony and I, and Fafner. (Fafner, in spite of being a small dachshund, was a fine walker, though sometimes he would get tired; then we

would have to take turns carrying him in our rucksacks.)
Well, off we started, leaving the hotel filled with guests
and the streets of the village crowded. After a glorious day
up on the edge of the Eiger glacier, we returned to Grindelwald to find the streets deserted and the hotel empty of
all except the personnel. It was as though a plague had
struck, and it was eerie and frightening. "Germany is
about to invade Poland," said the manager, who looked
distraught. "It came over the radio, and everyone left.
They wanted to return to their homeland."

So did we, but we had to spend the night, so we ate
dinner in the deserted dining room; and went to bed down
a darkened corridor. The next morning we were up at
dawn, stowing our luggage away in the car for the long
trip over the Alps and into Italy. We only stayed a night
at the castèllo, packing a few things frenziedly amid tears
from the for once united Balmas and Guardinis. We were
in such a rush that we did not dwell on the fact that we
might never sleep another night in our beloved castèllo,
nor could I believe that I was never to fling open my bedroom shutters again in order to say "good morning" to my
cypress tree.

We were lucky to get reservations on the Rome–Paris
express, which was crowded, and we arrived in Paris on
the morning of September 2, 1939. Buddie went immediately to a travel agent, and found that the only passage
that we could get at once was on an English ship, the S.S.
Arandora Star. Most Americans were trying wildly to
procure space on American ships, and as we were quite far
down on the list it might have taken us months to get accommodations. Buddie wanted to get home as quickly as
possible. We were able to get a cabin for ourselves and a
berth for Tony. The ship was to sail on September 4. On
the afternoon of the third we were sitting having tea and
drinks at the Café de la Paix on the corner of the boulevard

des Capucines and the Avenue de l'Opéra, when we noticed
that all traffic on the streets had stopped. We were wondering what had happened when a waiter rushed out to tell
us that France had declared war on Germany. Suddenly,
as if by magic, trucks loaded with young men began to
pass our corner, a band came by, and some marching soldiers. People passed, stretched out arm in arm, walking
down the middle of the street singing the "Marseillaise." In
a few hours, it seemed, France was on the move—
exhilarated and united.

The next day when we left, Paris was already a city at
war. We had to get a bus to take us to the station as there
were no taxicabs about. As we drove, we saw once again
truck after truck filled with young men. Girls ran out to
touch their hands as they passed, or to hand them a flower.
It was a blessing that we could not look into the future.
We were sad enough as it was!

The first morning on the *Arandora Star* the steward
came in with my breakfast to tell us that the S.S. *Athenia*—
a British ship—had been torpedoed and sunk just fifty miles
away from us. From then on, our course was most erratic.
The captain zigzagged across the Atlantic and brought us
safely into New York Harbor nine days later, having
avoided the nineteen different submarines which at various
times had tried to catch us.

When we sailed into the harbor, on the morning of
September 14, 1939, we were sailing into a world that was
going to be quite different—a world that was going to
challenge all we had heretofore taken for granted.

15

The first change in our lives was economic. We found that we could no longer afford to live in our large apartment at Ten Gracie Square with its live-in staff; nor could we keep on having a chauffeur. The question was, should we live in town or in the country? Buddie thought the country was a good idea, and we began thinking of the so-called "bed-room communities" of New York, but our choice was limited. Neither of us wanted to return to Bernardsville; nor did we care for Long Island. This narrowed our choice to Connecticut. So when, in looking through the New York *Times* ads, we saw a renovated schoolhouse for rent for the winter in Wilton, Connecticut, we went out to see it and rented it with the idea of using it as a base for winter weekends. By doing this we could go house-hunting each weekend. House-hunting is a marvelous pastime. We saw an enormous number of houses as we scampered about each weekend with genial real-estate people who were equipped with rose-colored glasses. Each house apparently had some special feature—an ever running stream, an eight-eenth-century fireplace, a pine-paneled library, a lake, a completely modern kitchen—we dashed from one to the other in the eager expectation that *this* would be our future home. We wandered through cornfields in the snow and trudged through woods to see a never failing spring or a house built in 1690 (and never touched since). We saw converted churches and schoolhouses and split-level bun-

galows and fake cantilevered Frank Lloyd Wrights. We
were indefatigable.

Eventually, we began to go farther afield and found
ourselves up in Massachusetts, in the Berkshires. We had
many friends in Lenox and Stockbridge, and there was one
place in that area that particularly struck our fancy. This
was the Tyringham Valley—a lovely, unspoiled bit of real
country. There was a house there on the eastern side of
the valley, with a beautiful view of a hill, called a "cobble," which terminated a higher range of tree-covered
hills. A "cobble" is a special sort of upside-down hill, like a
green dumpling with no trees. I adored the view, but I
thought the house hideous. It was a dirty gray stucco with
a Hansel-and-Gretel roof and a long stone porch on one
side with ugly stucco columns. Inside, there was one large
room with a staircase in it, a small dingy room opening off
it on one side, and, on the other, a dining room. The
kitchen and pantry were 1900 and quite hopeless. The
sight of a herd of cattle wandering up the "cobble" and
the sound of the stream outside the dining room were enticing and poetic, but I felt the house was dreary. Even
with my most vivid imagination, I saw no future in it.

Fortunately, soon after we saw this house, we spent a
weekend with Linda and Cole Porter in their home in
Williamstown, Massachusetts. On the outside, theirs was
an old-fashioned rough-stone monstrosity, about the same
vintage as the Tyringham house; but inside, with her extraordinary flair for decorating and assembling the
beautiful furniture and objects brought over from the
Paris house, Linda had made it outstandingly attractive. I
thought how lucky they were to have found it, and it was
only when we were back in New York that I woke up in
the middle of the night thinking of the Tyringham house.
In my mind's eye, I waved a wand over it. I could hardly

wait until Bud woke up to tell him that I felt that I had solved the problem.

He was as astonished as I was. The house, aside from being unattractive, was totally impractical. It was over three hours from New York with no possibility of commuting; but it did have something about it that appealed to us both—the lovely unspoiled valley with only a scattering of houses—some of them old Shaker houses—and the village of Tyringham itself, which was picturesque in a real Grandma Moses way. It consisted of a general store/post office and a church with a steep white spire and two or three neat white houses. Across from it rose the luscious green cobble with its herd of grazing cattle. It was really idyllic.

We went back to look at the house and noticed more features—the large meadow below the house, the driveway shaded by huge white pines, the stream (which sometimes failed us, we learned later), and beyond the stream, an inviting wood with, beyond that, another meadow directly above the village. All in all, about thirty-five acres to be bought for the sum of $18,000—so we bought it and began coming out every weekend with a picnic basket, going over and over the house, making our plans for its renovation. We had no architect, only a contractor, so it was truly *our* house, and we created something that was livable, pretty, and easy to keep up.

We blocked up the stairway so that we had an enclosed living room which you stepped down two steps to enter. The staircase rose directly on the left from the very small entrance hall and, fortunately, had a landing halfway up with a large window. We took out the paneling from our library at Ten Gracie Square. With a few alterations, it fitted beautifully into the room off the living room. We did over the kitchen and pantry. We painted the outside of the house a soft yellow, like an Austrian schloss, the

woodwork white, and the shutters gray. It stood out beautifully against the pine-clad hills which rose behind it and
reminded us of a Tyrolean scene. In the spring of 1941, all
of this was just in the planning stage; so, as we had taken
what we wanted out of the apartment, we decided to go
out to Coronado, California, where my parents were living.

Father had retired as High Commissioner to Haiti several years before. A committee headed by Cameron
Forbes, ex-Governor of the Philippines, and including such
prestigious people as William Allen White, Editor of the
Kansas City *Emporia Gazette*, and Senator Medill McCormick of Illinois had decided to withdraw the Marines from
Haiti and to have an ambassador instead of a high commissioner. Norman Armour, a very distinguished career diplomat, became the first ambassador after Father left.

Father, of course, had returned to the Marines immediately after Haiti. Even in Haiti, he had been serving two
masters—the U. S. Marine Corps and the State Department
—so, in effect, he had never really left the Marines. His
record in Haiti was commended by both the Marine Corps
and the State Department, and it is only because I do not
wish this to become too lengthy that I do not quote from
the letters in my possession in which he was commended
by three secretaries of state and the marine commandant.
When he came back to the United States, he was first ordered to San Diego and then to Quantico. Finally, in 1934,
he was recommended by the Corps to become commandant and moved into the commandant's house in the Marine barracks. He was a brigadier general at that time. In
order to remain commandant, he had to be promoted to
major general (later the marine commandant became a full
general). This promotion had to come before the Senate in
order to be confirmed, and there it was challenged by Senator Hugo Black of Alabama (later to become associate

justice of the U. S. Supreme Court), who—among other reasons for his opposing the confirmation—was an intimate friend of Senator King, of Utah, who had been refused permission to land in Haiti by President Borno.

It just so happened that when Franklin Roosevelt became President, he had issued an order that in all the services, men who had not been promoted since World War I should come up before a Selection Board. The Board would review their records and find out if they had simply stayed in the service because of lack of ambition or initiative. If this was the case, they were to be "plucked out."

This had never been done in the Marine Corps, but in 1934 the secretary of the navy had decided to introduce it there, and chose Father to be the Chairman of the Board. Naturally it was a most unpopular board among those who had for many years led an easy and undemanding life. They cited their years of "service" and saw no reason for new and ambitious young officers to take their places. They had benefited from a policy that was clogging up promotions and killing incentive in the service. Father, as chairman, received the full fury of their wrath, and they wrote their Congressmen and Senators, complaining bitterly that as Father was a Naval Academy graduate, he was plucking out those who had risen from the ranks.

As handmaiden to Senator Black, there was Brigadier General Smedley Butler, who was the other contender for commandant and a very active and competitive man with a keen sense of politics and a ready access to the media. General Butler found it convenient to take up the cudgels in defense of those who had been removed, and pictured Father as a tyrant who was totally insensitive to the feelings of others. He also accused Father of being a coward, citing an incident in Mexico in 1917, when Father and the Marines were guarding some waterworks at El Tejar outside of Vera Cruz. He said that Father had claimed to be

besieged by a large force of Mexicans when in fact there
were only one or two. He called this affair "Russell's
Run."

All of this appeared in the Washington papers day
after day. Butler gave constant interviews, and so did Senator Black. I knew nothing of this, but when Father was
talking to me on the telephone one day I knew from the
tone of his voice that all was not well. When I told him
that I thought something was wrong with him and that I
wanted to know what it was, he told me all about these accusations. I was absolutely furious, and I reminded Father
how often he had told me that "when you are a second
lieutenant, the whole Corps is your friend, but when you
are a general, you can count your friends on one hand."
Father laughed. "I never realized I was such a prophet," he
said.

I was glad to hear him laugh, but when I hung up, I
felt desperate. *What* could I do? I knew in my heart that
all these accusations were untrue. Then, my luck held. My
mind, which is a veritable attic, produced a little gem from
obscurity. I remembered a spring day in Washington
when I was a girl. The windows were open in our upstairs
sitting room in the De Sales Street house, and I suddenly
heard a newsboy coming down the street shouting, "Extry,
Extry—all about the trouble in Vera Cruz." Mother, who
was downstairs, sent a maid rushing out to the garden gate to
buy a paper; and there was Father's name. It was true that
he had turned his back on an insolent, mounted Mexican
captain who had demanded his surrender, but only after
he had said, "I'll see you in Hell first," and turned his
back abruptly. "Major Russell Defies Mexican," said the
headlines.

I remembered how Mother and I had hugged and
kissed one another and how proud we were. Grandfather
and Uncle Charlie had rushed over to see us and they all

had sherry, even allowing me a sip. And now, seventeen
years later, this was all being distorted. I wondered what I
could do and what advice I should seek. As he was a good
friend of mine, I called Arthur Krock (who at that time
was the New York *Times* correspondent in Washington)
and told him the circumstances. "When exactly was it?"
he asked. "I think it must have been May 1917," I said,
"but I remember that it was spring." "Well, go down to
the New York Public Library," directed Arthur, "and ask
for all the newspapers of that spring including May. If
you find the article, have a copy mimeographed and send
it down to me."

I lost no time in jumping into a taxi and rushing down
to the library. When I explained what I wanted, I soon
found myself surrounded by yellowing newspapers, and
set to work. And, oh, glorious moment, I found it—the
headlines almost exactly as I remembered them. As the
hearing was just about to come up before the Senate, I
took the next train in the morning down to Washington
with all my mimeographed copies and handed them over
to Arthur at lunch at the Mayflower. "These certainly
prove that the charges are lies," he exclaimed. "Good
work, Brooke. I think that Millard Tydings and Peter
Gerry, both fine men, are going to speak for your father."
It was a happy lunch, and I felt then, as I still do, forever
in Arthur's debt.

Father felt it undignified to lobby for himself, so it had
been up to me. "It is all in my record," he had said. "I am
not going to blow my own horn." He was very pleased,
though, when after lunch I went down to the commandant's house and told him what Arthur had said. Mother
was away on a trip with Mary Dunn, and I had told Buddie that I was going to stay with Father until the hearing
was over; so we had lots of time to talk it all over. We had
dinner alone that night in the dignified and handsome La-

trobe house, which is the commandant's residence in the
Marine barracks. It was saved from burning in 1812, when
the British sacked Washington, because the British officers
found it a pleasant place to be quartered in; and although
generations of marine commandants have tried to alter it
to their taste (one even willed it to his relations), it has
remained fundamentally as it was. In fact the whole compound has remained in outline almost as originally planned
—the commandant's house at the end, the officers' quarters
(separate houses) on the right, the Marine Band quarters
on the left, and the enlisted men's down at the end. In the
middle is the Parade Ground, where even today on Thursday nights from June through September, the Marines go
through a snappy close-order drill, which is open to the
public (first come, first served). At the end of the parade,
the troops fade slowly from the Parade Ground in the
darkness, and above the gate in the middle of the building
on the left of the commandant's house, a floodlight is
turned on the flagpole, and slowly, slowly the flag is lowered as three Marines resplendent in full dress—blue trousers with red stripes down the side, blue coat with a tight
white belt with a shiny brass buckle, white cap with the
U. S. Marine Corps insignia on it—stand with their bugles
to their lips sounding "taps." It is a marvelously moving
and stirring sight. Remember, any Thursday night (at nine
o'clock), free, in the summer months, this beautiful patriotic ritual is there for you and your family to enjoy. I urge
you to go—it is very worthwhile.

Father and I sat in the commandant's house on the afternoon after my arrival in Washington, talking of this
and that. Father had left his office near the State Department early in order to be available for the good or bad
news. I could see that, dearly as he loved me, his mind was
far away. I looked out the window, and seeing the dome
of the Capitol in the distance, I got an inspiration. "Why

wait here?" I said. "Let's go up to the Senate Gallery and see for ourselves what they are doing." Father was hesitant. He felt it bad taste, but I saw a gleam in his eye. "Why not?" he said after a pause. "I'll order the car." So off we went to the Capitol and the Senate Gallery. It was certainly far better for our nerves than hanging around waiting.

When we walked down the steps of the gallery to seat ourselves in the front row overlooking the floor of the Senate, every head was turned toward us. Once seated, Father, after a smile and a nod or two, kept his eyes glued to the senators; I had no such qualms about dignity, and I gave a good look around and saw many who had come to gloat if Father were not confirmed. There were several whom I had never trusted, although they pretended to be my father's friends. Now they gave me a shifty glance and an embarrassed smile. After giving them the "cool look" I turned my attention to the floor, where Senator Black was holding forth against Father—reading bits of a long letter from an indignant man who had not met the requirements of the Selection Board and had been "plucked." Senator Black also blamed Father for the incident in Haiti. He called Father a tyrant and recited Butler's accusations that Father had been a coward on the occasion at El Tejar, which had been laughingly called "Russell's Run."

It was not very pleasant to sit there and hear this, and I was torn between impotent fury and despair. Father gave no sign of emotion even when we heard something like smothered applause behind us from time to time. But relief was in sight. Senator Tydings of Maryland and later Senator Gerry of Rhode Island took up Father's defense. They refuted every point that Senator Black had made, although he constantly asked them to yield and very skillfully pursued Father's destruction. He was long-winded but had a very shrewd legal mind. Just as Senator Black began to launch an especially lethal attack on Father, Senator Huey Long, of Louisiana, appeared on the floor and asked the senator from Alabama to yield, which Senator Black did. Thereupon Huey Long began a complicated and sometimes rather funny attack against General Johnson of NRA, Bernard Baruch, and sundry other people connected with them. I thought it funny, because they were not my relations! It was a filibuster but it came at a lucky time for us.

Finally, the presiding officer (the vice-president) rapped his gavel, silencing Senator Long, and the Senate resumed the consideration of the nomination of Richard P. Williams, to be Brigadier General, U. S. Marine Corps—who was confirmed. Then Father's name was brought up. "The question now is will the Senate advise and consent to the nomination of John H. Russell to be Major General in the Marine Corps?"

Senator Black: "I move that the nomination be recommitted to the Committee on Naval Affairs for further and more complete investigation."

The presiding officer: "The question is on the motion of the Senator from Alabama."

Senator Trammell (chairman of the Committee on Naval Affairs): "Mr. President. I have to oppose the motion in view of the fact that for some three or four weeks at different hearings the criticisms which have been made in the Senate were investigated as best they could be investigated by the Committee, and there was practically no evidence whatever to substantiate the criticisms and allegations which have been made here and which in large degree were also made before the Committee. I will not weary the Senate, etc. etc.—I will quote only a few excerpts. General Russell stated that he did not try to dominate the Board, and no one has intimated that he did. There is nothing to suggest to a fair mind that he was try-

ing to pack the Board and there is no evidence to that
effect." Senator Trammell also said that as far as the Haitian incident was concerned, "The State Department had
advised the Minister of Haiti that while they preferred
that the action to exclude the Senator not be taken, yet
Haiti was a Sovereign State and had control over its inter-
nal affairs and the United States should not interfere with
its control of the situation. President Borno issued an
order. The record would indicate that prior to that time
General Russell had tried to persuade him not to do it."
Senator Trammell went on to speak of certain articles of
the Treaty, in which the President of Haiti could do as he
wished as to control of the Army. Senator Trammell, after
vindicating Father in Haiti, then took up the subject of
"Russell's Run" at El Tejar, where he again vindicated Father.

The question was then put: Will the Senate advise and
consent to the nomination of General Russell? The "ayes"
had it. There were eighty-eight Senators present. That was
March 5, 1935. I can remember my emotion even after all
these years, but I have quoted the senators from the *Con-
gressional Record* of that day as I cannot trust my memory to be accurate on this subject. It was, however, one of
the great days of my life. It was not only that Father was
confirmed, but it was also something even more fundamental than that. After listening all afternoon to those four
Senators—the one against, the three for Father—I was reassured in the workings of democracy. Everything was out
in the open, and fair-minded men had made the decision.
Father had always had implicit faith in the government of
his country, but I often had a heavy heart and misgivings.
The wheeling and dealing that I had witnessed even when
Dryden was running for the Assembly, and then for the
state senate, in New Jersey, had firmly established in my
mind that the almighty dollar and its fellow traveler

cronyism are very strong factors in American politics. On that great day, March 5, 1935, when Father and I went back to the commandant's house, I felt that I had seen more than a personal victory. I had witnessed a triumph of justice.

16

Father was Commandant of the Marine Corps from 1934 through 1936, when he reached the retirement age of sixty-two. Anticipating the retirement, Mother had found and bought an early nineteenth-century house in Alexandria, Virginia. She was very enthusiastic about it as it had an old-fashioned double drawing room with two fireplaces (really a front and back parlor) and a good-sized garden in the back filled with syringa and lilac bushes. It reminded her of her childhood house at 1800 G Street, N.W., in Washington.

When the time came to start modernizing it, Father found that he could not reconcile himself to it. He actually began to hate the idea of it. As it was so close to Arlington Cemetery, "It should be called 'Villa Muffled Drums,'" he said. "I will be in constant demand as a pallbearer." He imagined people saying, "Look at poor old Johnny Russell, he will surely be the next." They were staying at a hotel in Washington while fixing up the house when, as luck would have it, they met Colonel and Mrs. Ira Copley. Colonel (Colonel, like Colonel Kuser, a courtesy title) Copley was Publisher and owner of the Copley Press. The home base of the publication was in Elmira, Illinois, but Colonel Copley also owned the San Diego *Union*, a morning paper in San Diego, California, and had a large house in Coronado. My family struck up an instant friendship with the Copleys—Father with Colonel Copley and Mother with Chloe, the colonel's much younger wife. They met at that moment in world affairs when military commentators were much in evidence and the San Diego *Union* needed one. Hanson Baldwin of the New York *Times* was the Dean of the Corps and there were many other minor ones. Colonel Copley suggested to Father that he come to San Diego and try out writing a weekly column on military subjects for the *Union*.

The idea appealed to Father and Mother. They knew San Diego well, as they had been stationed there. Also they were used to moving around all their lives, so they found no difficulty in pulling up stakes again and accepting the offer. "Villa Muffled Drums" was quickly sold to Frances Parkinson Keyes, the authoress; and once more, and for the last time, the Russell lares and penates made the long journey across the continent by train while my parents sailed in great luxury through the Panama Canal aboard the Copley yacht *Dias Allegras*. On arriving in California, they rented a house in Coronado (at that time an island—no bridge) and later built a house there. It was a charming quiet backwater then, as the ferry deterred the tourists, and consisted of pretty little houses on tree-lined streets dominated by the Hotel Del Coronado, an old-fashioned resort hotel. Buddie and I spent the summers of 1940 and 1941 in Coronado, renting a very small Spanish-style house near my family.

Coronado was, and still is, a naval base, and even then, though we were not yet at war, it was teeming with naval personnel. They seemed very gay and carefree, as though sensing that the good times were growing short and that

the summer might be the last spent in such security. I had
had my misgivings at Father's throwing down the sword
to take up the pen. Up to that time he had only written
reports, and I was not sure if he knew how to condense a
subject and make it interesting. He was totally unversed in
the technique of writing.

I need not have feared. At first, of course, his column
was perfectly passable but not tremendously new or strong
in viewpoint; but as time went on he grew better and better and when the war finally came, his articles were really
little masterpieces. All the officers of the Pacific fleet were
friends of his, and when they touched base in Coronado,
they told him many things. Naturally, he never divulged
what he heard, and it was a difficult tightrope to walk—to
be *au courant* without betraying a confidence. As Father
had been in Naval Intelligence, an instructor at the Naval
War College at Newport, and the founder of the Fleet
Marine Force, he was well-versed in military tactics and
knew when to keep his mouth shut.

Toward the end of the summer of 1941, the dozens of
Japanese gardeners, who kept the gardens of the houses in
Coronado beautiful, began to disappear. No longer did one
see their pickups filled with rakes and lawn mowers and
weed killers. "They are all admirals in disguise," said the
Navy people, half believing it. "They are on their way
back to Nippon to report just how many destroyers and
sub-chasers and aircraft carriers we have here."

The summer passed swiftly, as most summers seem to
when one is drenched in sun and yet impatient to pick up
one's life again. With all the activity around us, we felt a
bit out of it. Buddie wanted to get back to his office; I, to
see about our new home. Only Tony was reluctant to return. He was a wretched scholar and disliked school. After
his accident, he had gone to Groton School for a term, but
as he was the only boy in the school who could not exer-

cise—because of his accident—and as there was a great emphasis on sports there, he was absolutely miserable. Bud was disappointed, as he had gone to Groton and had loved every moment of it. Dr. Peabody, the Rector, suggested that Tony go to Brooks School, which, in a way, was an offshoot of Groton. Tony was happier there, but he still would have preferred to be at home. In those days, though, it was "the thing" to send boys away to school—supposedly to get them away from the temptations of the city and to toughen them up. Looking back, I am afraid that it was a misconception.

When we returned to New York we signed all the contracts on the Tyringham house. Work was to start on December 8, 1941. We did not expect it to be "ready for Christmas," but for the summer. We drove out almost every weekend to measure the rooms for our furniture and to gaze endlessly at our view and our driveway of huge white pines. It was all ours—the trees, the house, the view—the first bit of land we had ever owned together. An apartment is all very well, but to own land is something different entirely. It is home in the way a slice of building in which many other people are living can never be. Buddie and I both found a sense of security and peace in, at long last, making a real home.

It was lucky we had it, because on December 7, 1941, our world suddenly came to a stop, as it did for every other American. Buddie had gone to Arkansas duck shooting with Joe Pulitzer, and I was in Bernardsville visiting friends. I had lunched with one friend and was going back to the house where I was staying, driving my own car, when I happened to turn on the car radio. I had expected the Philharmonic; instead, I heard the news of the Japanese attack on Pearl Harbor. At first I could not believe it. I thought it might be a broadcast like the one in which Orson Welles described an imaginary attack on the earth by Martians. But that comforting thought was soon dispelled when more and more detailed accounts named ships that I had been on as having been sunk and I heard the voices of men I had met at my parents' house in Coronado. By the time I had reached my destination, I realized only too well the magnitude of the attack. I walked into the house as the telephone was ringing and it was Buddie saying that he was returning at once from Arkansas and that Joe Pulitzer was going back to St. Louis.

The next day, when he returned, we both felt shaken and terribly worried. We spoke to Father, who gave us an even more depressing picture of the damage done to the Fleet. So many men Father knew had gone down with their ships. It was a catastrophe: The whole of Pearl Harbor was choked with wrecks.

Buddie's younger partners went off at once to join up. Buddie wanted to go, too, although he was over age, but he had to stay home and look after the firm so that there would be something for his partners to return to. I went first to the USO at 99 Park Avenue and signed up there. Mrs. Julius Ochs Adler (Babs) was already running a very efficient center there, arranging everything for servicemen coming to New York—from free theater tickets and museum tours and dances to calling their families back home and helping them with every conceivable problem. She had recruited a fine group of volunteers and I enjoyed enormously working there, but as America got more and more involved in the war, I felt that I wanted a different type of work. I told Babs Adler what I was going to do and parted from her with great regret.

I joined a Red Cross class and became a Gray Lady, and then asked if I could work in a hospital library. St. Albans, the naval hospital, refused to have any volunteers, so I went to the army hospital, Halloran, on Staten Island and worked there five days a week until late October

1945. It was a fascinating and rewarding job. We were living at 4 Sutton Place then and so I usually left the house around 7 A.M. and took the Third Avenue "El" down to the Staten Island ferry. I tried to catch the eight o'clock ferry as that was always met by a Red Cross car. Sometimes I was lucky enough to get in a Red Cross car that was going down to the ferry and straight on to the hospital.

Halloran was a huge compound of ugly red brick buildings connected by paths and roads above ground, and tunnels underground. Every sort of wounded were brought there, including those in need of psychiatric care, but Halloran's "speciality" were paraplegics. My job sounds very dull and unglamorous, but I loved it. I am in no sense qualified to be a Florence Nightingale. I don't have the patience or dedication that one must have to be a nurse; so I took what I knew I could do. I had a library cart which I wheeled through the wards, bringing books and magazines to the men. As I love people, it did not take me long to find out what the different patients wanted; and each morning I filled up my cart in the main library, trying to get the books and periodicals that the patients had asked for or that I had told them about. Then I started off pushing the cart down the ramps and through the tunnels. We went to certain buildings and certain floors on certain days. Each of us had a different route and a different routine. We wore gray linen dresses with white collars and cuffs and a gray veil that was attached to a starched white bandeau. It was very becoming and very practical. Sometimes, the weather was extremely cold and snowy. When I volunteered to meet the men just landing from overseas, I wore a huge gray coat with a red cross on its sleeve, a gray cap with a visor, and high rubber boots. I must have looked a bit overdressed, because as one man passed by in a litter, he burst out laughing when he saw me and said, "Oh, boy, I haven't seen anything like that since Eisenhower."

As Halloran was the largest Army hospital in the New York area, we received an enormous amount of seriously wounded men from the European theater. The ships usually arrived late at night, as I imagine the authorities thought it caused less publicity. Sometimes I would not get off the El until three o'clock in the morning and would take the Fifty-ninth Street crosstown bus to Sutton Place and walk the two blocks home. At that hour of the night, there were many homeless men, some sleeping, some just drunk, who rode all night on the El from the Bronx to the Staten Island Ferry terminal and back; but somehow I was not afraid of them. As I jumped off the bus and walked down the darkened street to Sutton Place, I felt invisible and invulnerable.

We had German prisoners at Halloran too, but the volunteers were forbidden to speak to them or to give them any kind of service—only servicemen and Army nurses could do that; so they received books, papers, etc., from regular Army personnel. They were an elite group, Rommel's men, and were quite rude if one met them in the tunnel or crossing the road. They would deliberately block the way and look as arrogant as possible. This was when they were "trusties" and were on their own. But what used to make me both amused and irritated was when a squad of prisoners would march briskly by, followed by a lackadaisical U.S. soldier holding his gun any which way and just slouching along waving his hand at the Red Cross workers and giving a wolf whistle if a very pretty girl passed by. It was a triumph of democracy, but I sometimes wished our men looked a little snappier.

However, when I was in the wards, my opinion of our men soared. They were optimistic, cheerful, and grateful to be alive. I got to know them very well as I wheeled my cart through the wards, stopping at any bed that looked as if the man in it were anxious to get something to read or just to chat. Some of them wanted to be alone with themselves, others had their own reading matter, but for the most part they were anxious for contact with a nonprofessional person. They read omnivorously: everything from comic books to *Studs Lonigan* and Shakespeare. I grew to know their tastes, and would squirrel away books from the library in order to bring "my clients" what they wanted. The paraplegics were great readers. They had to be flat on their backs, then were turned over to lie flat on their stomachs. Their beds were hard, straight cots and when they lay on their stomachs, there was a piece of the cot cut out so that their face was out, not pressed against the cot. Their hands were free, so lying face down they could hold a book in their hands and read. Usually they were totally immobile from the waist down, and the smell of urine from the bottles by their beds was overpowering.

I remember one boy in his early 20's who was smiling from ear to ear when I came up to speak to him one day. "Hi there," he said. "Guess what?" "What?" I said. "Gimme your hand," he said, and when I put my hand in his, he took one of my fingers, pressed the nail against his stomach as though I were scratching him. "Ouch," he cried loudly. "I certainly feel *that*." It was wonderful. I don't know how much he really felt, but he had been totally without any sensation for months from his chest down and even a tiny tingle was a joy to him. I rejoiced with him and wished with all my heart that his hope would become a reality.

The whole experience at Halloran was so moving. There were moments of joy and moments of great despair. The visiting days were the worst for the very young men who had married hurriedly before going overseas. Their wives' visits were often disillusioning and depressing. The girls were young and usually quite incapable of thinking about anyone but themselves. They had married a strong man, a lover, who had gone forth to fight, and now they had a broken invalid on their hands who might never again be able to take his place in life. They saw a bleak future before them and they could not resist feeling sorry for themselves. The women in charge of the volunteers always asked us to stay on after visiting hours, if we could, because the men so often needed cheering up. I felt desperately sorry for these young people. It was not their fault. It was the fault of history and of the decisions of old men. As time went on, some of the men grew very bitter. The euphoria of having survived fell away as they learned from their visitors how hard it was to find a good job.

There was one rule at Halloran that I thought was rather demoralizing. This was that even the most active convalescents were required to wear pajamas and bathrobe. Only officers were permitted to wear their uniforms. To see men walking around everywhere in those dark red bathrobes and bedroom slippers made them sloppy both mentally and physically. They did not shave as often as they should have. They left their bathrobes open, not bothering to tie the sashes, and spent more and more of their time playing cards and cursing the hospital. Of course, there was a lot of entertainment. Theatrical people are very generous with their time and I organized writing classes and got authors to come out and talk and magazine publishers to say what type of story would appeal to them. It was quite a success in its small way—but small it had to be, since everyone does not want to write.

In December 1942, things had changed for me. Tony came home from Brooks School for the Christmas holidays and went off one day, ostensibly to visit a schoolmate. Buddie and I were sitting by the fire that evening when Tony came into the room and said, "I have just enlisted in

the Marine Corps." We couldn't believe our ears. "But
you are under age," Buddie said. "You are only seventeen." "I said that I was eighteen," said Tony, "and they
believed me." He then went on to say that he felt that people on the streets were looking at him with a scowl, that he
looked old enough to join up, and it made him uncomfortable. He also said that he knew that my father would
be pleased, as it was a family tradition, and that he couldn't
visit them in Coronado, surrounded by young sailors and
Marines the same age as he, without feeling like a shirker.
We were struck dumb, and it was then that he delivered his
greatest shock. "I enlisted under the name of Marshall," he
said. "Anthony Dryden Marshall. I explained to the re-
cruiting officer that Kuser was my last name, but that I
wanted to be called Marshall because Buddie has been a
father to me. So I am now legally A. D. Marshall for the
rest of my life and have the papers to prove it." You can
imagine how I felt. I jumped up and gave him a hug. It was
almost more than I could bear. Buddie gave him a hug too
and we both had tears in our eyes. "I am not going back to
Brooks," announced Tony. "I am going to boot camp at
Parris Island."

One has to remember that this was not an unpopular
war like Vietnam; Americans were fighting in the Pacific
because other Americans had been killed in a sneak attack.
Young men and women all over the country wanted to
participate in the making of history. It seemed a miracle
how quickly the country prepared. In the Pacific, it was a
naval war. Carriers, destroyers, battleships, cruisers, submarines, PT boats, Landing Ship Tanks, airplanes, tanks—
all began appearing as if by magic. San Diego, being a
naval base, and also the home of aircraft manufacturers,
was heavily covered with camouflage, with nets overhead
and houses and rooftops painted. Tony's feeling of not
wanting to visit there again in mufti was perfectly reasona-

ble. So on December 15, 1942, he became a private in the
U. S. Marine Corps Reserve. In March 1943, he was
selected for officer training. We were all very pleased. But,
alas, Tony had not graduated from Brooks and so had no
high school diploma. Without a diploma he was not eligible for officer's training. When we spoke to Frank Ashburn, the Headmaster of Brooks, about this, he refused to
give a diploma as he said that Tony had been such a
wretched student and probably would never have graduated.

Buddie and I were absolutely sunk. But Father, without telling us, wrote a strong letter to Ashburn, mincing
no words, and said that as Brooks School had never inspired Tony or brought out the potential in him, they
should not play dog in the manger now. "The Marine
Corps is making him ambitious and has given him the
desire to succeed," declared Father. "Will you ruin this
boy's life by depriving him of the chance to prove himself?" I never saw the letter but I knew that Father could
be extremely tough if the occasion warranted it. It was not
until much later that we even knew about the letter. We
were simply surprised at Frank Ashburn's change of mind
when a diploma appeared in the mail.

Father was right. Tony not only eventually became a
captain in the Marine Corps Reserve, but he has also been
three times an ambassador to important and interesting
posts. What would his life have been if, at seventeen, he
had been made to feel that there was no future for him? It
taught me a lesson, too. I had always been nagging him to
do better and was furious when he would shrug his shoulders and say, "Well, at least I am not at the bottom of my
class—there is one boy below me." I realize now that nagging him had been the wrong approach—and that he had to
find his own way.

17

Tony was assigned to active duty attached to the Third Battalion Twenty-first Regiment, as a second lieutenant, and was sent to Guam. The winter passed, with me very busy at Halloran and Buddie working overtime at his office. We tried to get up to Tyringham, but with gasoline rationing, it was too far, and the trains were so over-crowded and stopped so often that it sometimes took over four hours, which hardly seemed worth it for a weekend.

We had to go up at least once a month, though, as we had started a pig farm with the idea of providing ourselves with meat and soap. It turned out to be a great mistake. I got so fond of the pigs that I simply could not bear to have one killed. Flora and Hamlet were the standard-bearers, and their progeny were named alphabetically. The first lit-ter, as I remember, were called Acapanthus, Azalea, Aster, Acorn, etc. The second, Bluebell, Bacon, Buttercup, etc. Then Camelia, Castor, Carnation and finally we got down to poor little "Umbie." He was a fragile piglet who was not quite as savvy as his brothers and sisters. Instead of running immediately after birth to the heated shelter of a small overhanging shelf where he would be safe, he stood uncertainly, still tied by the umbilical cord, and was given a sharp push with his mother's foot. It was three o'clock on a Saturday morning and I was the midwife. I picked the piglet up and put him under the protective shelf, hoping for the best. Then I went wearily to bed. Later in the

morning, when Buddie and I went down to inspect the
new family, all the little piglets were busy feeding except
the poor little fellow who was forlornly lying in the straw,
his umbilical cord hanging behind him like a piece of dried
spaghetti.

We telephoned the vet, who gave us advice on what to
do, so we put him in a cardboard box and took him up to
the house. By this time we had about thirty pigs and they
really lived in style. We had two cement pools for them,
one for ladies, one for gents, and they disported themselves
in them every day during the summer. Contrary to what
most people think, pigs like to be clean. After their bath, I
used to wait by the fence with a long-handled brush to
scrub their backs. They loved it, and would try to run
after me as I departed. Umbie came to be quite a pet. I had
pulled several of the pigs through illness, but he really
touched my heart. It did not take long for him to grow big
and healthy and when that was accomplished, Buddie said
that he felt that we had really had enough of raising pigs
and he was going to take them into Great Barrington and
sell them.

I knew what that meant. Death for those happy useless
creatures. I could not resist letting a tear run down my
cheek; and Buddie said that Lucian, our man of all work,
would take them to Great Barrington when we were in
New York and that he thought it might be a good idea if
we got away from everything for a while and went out to
Coronado to visit my family. It was sad leaving early on
that Monday morning and seeing the dear pigs with their
upturned snouts (they were Berkshires) lined up along the
fence craving a bit of affection. We hurried past them, but
they remained always in our memory as part of our
Tyringham life—like the square dances in the village, the
walks over the mountains, the gathering of sticks, for kin-

dling wood, and the day we took the first dip in our new swimming pool beneath the pine trees.

California was all sunshine and flowers and the family's sweet lemon tree was in full bloom and the family's house so attractive and cozy. Coronado was humming with activity—Navy men on leave, the Secretary of the Navy James Forrestal coming out to inspect, amphibious landings being practiced, and Father engaged in conversation behind closed doors. We were staying only two weeks and had our compartment on "The Chief" booked for February 20, 1945. The marines landed on Iwo Jima on February 19 and from then on, we were glued to the radio. "Mount Suribachi should be called Mount Plasma," said one broadcaster. "Men are dying by the hundreds, cut down by the cross fire of the Japanese mortars; there is no shelter on the beaches." It was on the nineteenth that we heard, "The Third Battalion of the Twenty-first Regiment is attempting to land amid tremendous resistance." We sat stunned. Our Tony, aged twenty, was out there as a second lieutenant in command of men. He had to lead, he had to have guts. Even if he was terrified, he had to appear calm. In my mind he was cannon fodder. Father kept calling people he knew and getting reports, but there was not much news, and very little to encourage us. The next day we left, and for that long journey across the continent, I only had a tiny radio, which I kept to my ear, only giving it up to Buddie, who was as anxious as I was.

The apartment seemed so unbelievably empty when we walked into it. To make it even more poignant, Buddie received a letter from Tony which meant so much to him that it was in his safe-deposit box when he died. In the letter, Tony told him what his influence had meant to him and he recounted his memories to Buddie—Buddie reading a book by the fire in Tyringham, Buddie working in the

garden, Buddie chopping wood, Buddie walking in Austria, and he thanked him for everything and ended with, "I
adore you, Buddie—Father." It was almost more than we
could bear. Tony had obviously written it knowing that
he was going into combat. From then on I never spent so
much time in a church in all my life. St. James Church at
Madison Avenue and Seventy-first Street was my church,
and although it was far from Sutton Place I went there
constantly. Buddie went into Trinity Church every morning when he came up out of the subway at Wall Street.

I was deeply moved when I read that James Forrestal,
the Secretary of the Navy, had flown to Iwo Jima. I wrote
him a letter telling him what it meant to me that he, the
secretary of the navy, had gone out to the battlefield and
that I was sure that it had lifted the morale of the mothers
of the Marines who were there to know that he had taken
such a great personal interest in the welfare of their sons,
and I received a very nice letter in reply.

I cannot remember now just how long the battle for
Iwo Jima lasted, but I do remember one evening when we
were dining with the John Elliotts at their house on Sixty-
second Street. Charlie Merz, the managing editor of the
New York *Times*, and his wife, Evie, were there. Just as
we were having our coffee in the drawing room, Charlie
was called to the telephone. We knew it was something
important and we tried to talk, but our hearts and minds
were not in it. When Charlie came back, he was beaming.
He came up to me and gave me a kiss. "The Japanese mortar fire on Iwo Jima has ceased," he said happily. What a
moment that was! Our prayers had been answered and
God—so I thought—had arranged that we should know it
as quickly as possible.

After that wonderful evening, we still heard nothing
from Tony. Three weeks passed, and one afternoon quite

late, when I was alone in the apartment making myself some tea, I suddenly picked up the telephone and called the Casualty Department at the Marine Corps Headquarters in Washington. "Marshall you say?" said the man who answered. "Rank, first name, and regiment, please." I recited them and after saying, "Hold on," he left me. I stood there in the pantry, the floor seeming to float away from under my feet. The voice on the other end of the phone said, "John? Alfred? George? Jackson?" "No," I answered. "Well, that's all we have under Marshall," he reported. "Thank you," I said. "I am so sorry to have taken up so much of your time." "No trouble at all," he said briskly. I almost felt that he was going to add "It's been a pleasure" as he hung up. Well, at least Tony was alive. A few days later we got a telegram printed as an Easter greeting with a cross on it in which Tony said, "I am in the land of the living and all right. Love, Tony." Buddie and I drank old-fashioneds in those days. That night we swallowed down quite a few.

It was soon after that that I left Halloran. I hated to leave, but Buddie felt that I had done enough and that we should start resuming a normal life. I did not want to leave Halloran, because almost everyone else had left. The show business people who had been so wonderful during the war stopped coming, the volunteer ranks grew thinner every week and patients were few, because so many had been moved to hospitals nearer their homes. Some wards were closed and others were half empty; mostly men from New York and the adjacent suburbs were left, and some very ill paraplegics.

The mood of the men was bitter and depressing. When I trundled my cart through the wards, my gray veil flying out behind me, they would say, "Go away. We don't want you here. The Red Cross stinks." They were still in the same old bathrobes and spent the days gambling. Discipline had totally disappeared and some of the personnel were not a very healing or decent influence. For all of those reasons, I wanted to stay. I felt that I was really needed more than ever as a morale builder. But first things, as they say, come first, and my life with Buddie was more important to me than anything else. The Red Cross uniforms were packed away in boxes and put up in the attic in Tyringham.

Tony stayed on in the Pacific as an adjutant with the rank of captain and came home in 1947. He was very thin and drawn, had nightmares, and spent his time contacting the families of the enlisted men who had been under his command. This was a sad and exhausting job as he had to relive the experience continually and somehow try to be manly and calm. There had been 250 of them, and the casualties had been enormous. He talked very little about it, but he did tell us how seasick they had all been as they waited before dawn in their small boats in a rough sea. Then finally at a signal they jumped into the water with their guns and grenades in their hands and dashed up the steep sides of "Blue Beach." It was only when we heard him cry out in his sleep that we knew how deep the scar went.

At first Tony thought that he might stay in the Marine Corps. Then he changed his mind and thought of going directly into business. He figured that as he had held down the very complicated and meticulous job of adjutant, he could be equally efficient in an office. He soon found out, however, that without a college degree he could not get any worthwhile job. The market was flooded with job seekers like himself. It was difficult at that time to get into college, as he had returned home later than most; but with the help of a friend who was a Trustee he got into Brown University in Providence, Rhode Island, and graduated three years later.

Before I go on to 1947, I would like to skip back to the autumn of 1946 for a little vignette of Europe after the war. Jimmy Dunn was appointed as the first U.S. ambassador to Rome after the war. He and his wife, Mary, asked us to come to pay them a visit, and we accepted at once as we longed to be in Italy again.

Mary and Jimmy were installed in the beautiful "Villa Taverna," which is the American ambassador's residence in Rome, and we were immediately thrown into a round of seeing our old friends and learning just how they had all fared since 1939. Rome seemed subdued and rather shabby, and there were many signs in the countryside of the ravages of war. Mary and Jimmy were not always with us, because they spent a great deal of time traveling around Italy. Every time a bridge or railroad was rebuilt with U.S. money, they were there to dedicate the opening. When an American ship arrived with a cargo of grain from the U.S., they were on the dock as it came alongside. "If the American ambassador goes and is highly visible, there can be no mistaking which country is sending aid to Italy," said Jimmy. "We might as well get the credit for what we are doing." Jimmy was in Italy for five years as American ambassador and did an outstanding job. The Dunns not only made friends for themselves but, more important, they did a superb job of public relations for the United States. Buddie and I were very proud of them.

One day when we were having coffee after lunch, Jimmy suddenly said, "While you are here, why don't you go up to take a look at Germany?" He told us that the Embassy would arrange the whole thing for us—visas, permission to have scrip, arranging trips. Jimmy suggested Bavaria, because we had known it so well. Also it had been Hitler's favorite countryside and we could go and have a look at his mountain eyrie. We were interested in seeing firsthand the devastation of war. It was something we hoped we would never see again, and this seemed a great opportunity.

So we decided to go. We spent the first night in Verona as traffic in Italy was extremely slow. Seventy per cent of all the bridges were bombed, and although they were being rebuilt, the train passed very slowly over them. All the stations were bombed too, and it was very depressing as it was both foggy and cold.

When we started off very early the next morning things were different. It was bright and sunny. The Brenner Pass and Inn Valley were as beautiful as ever—the larches turning gold, and milky blue glacial streams racing along beside the railroad track. The country, however, looked very sad with the French occupation much in evidence, and when at dusk we found ourselves in Germany, we passed miles of wrecked trains and deserted villages. The station at Munich was only dimly lit and consisted of wooden huts looking hurriedly put together. The total silence of the people was depressing—no greetings, no talking or laughter.

We had no money, so Buddie, who spoke German, was directed to a window where we exchanged dollars for coupons. We drove through the dimly lit and deserted streets to the Vier Jahreszeiten Hotel, which had always been *the* hotel of Munich. We were given a huge newly decorated room with a large bathroom, one of sixty rooms, we were told, that were done over and were in use instead of the two hundred there used to be. We could only eat in the hotel as we had nothing but scrip that could be used only where the American occupation was allowed; so we went down to dinner. The dining room was like something out of a propaganda play—waiters in white tie and tails dashing about carrying silver wine buckets and covered dishes. The orchestra was playing Walther's "Prize Song" from the *Meistersinger*. The guests were American Army sergeants and their wives. Several of the sergeants with blouses undone were screaming out, "For chrissake what's a matter with the service," over the madly playing orchestra. There were three very dignified black men, a couple of peroxided German tarts in cheap fur coats with German businessmen, a finely chiseled young man in Bavarian costume dining with a cynical-looking older man. It was fascinating, particularly as we were all watching each other closely to see what sort of money was being used.

The next day we toured the city on foot. The Deutsches Museum and Residenztheater—gone. The Pinakothek badly damaged. The English Garden—gone. Rubble piled everywhere. The people in the drab streets looked grim and serious, but healthy. We were not allowed to go into any shops except antique shops, and the antique shops were most tantalizing, filled with Meissen and bronzes and Renaissance jewelry; but Buddie was adamant that we buy nothing. So that was that.

Sam Woods, who had been U.S. Consul General in Switzerland during the war and now had the same office in Munich, and who was a customer of Butler, Herrick and Marshall, had called on Bud and had invited us down to his place on the Starnberger See for the weekend. I didn't really want to go, but Bud said he was a very good customer and had married a very nice German-American from St. Louis. "Be careful, though," Bud warned. "He is a very simple down-to-earth person, not at all sophisticated." These remarks did not prepare me for Sam and Minnie Annheuser Busch Woods and their castle "Bernreid." Minnie had been in Germany all during the war and Sam met her when she came up to Switzerland to tell him that she wanted to send some money to her son in America—a sum in seven figures. Sam assisted her, and it was love at first sight.

Their house was fantastic, a vast pile of cream-colored

stucco with round towers at the end capped by shining
gold and multicolored-mosaic onion-shaped roofs. Mrs.
Woods met us at the door surrounded by footmen in red
and yellow-striped waistcoats, a majordomo in a morning
coat and a housekeeper in black silk with keys jangling at
her waist. Mrs. Woods herself was quite wondrous—what
they used to call a "fine figure of a woman," with a vast
hat tilted on one side of her pompadour and a rose stuck
into her ample cleavage. She greeted us warmly and smothered Mr. Woods with kisses. The house was really fascinating—a private chapel, a beer cellar, immense salons, a
charming small dining room in one of the towers done all
in blue and silver stucco and a delightful round pink
frescoed tea pavilion in the Amalienburg style, which was
particularly attractive. The atmosphere was absolutely
feudal. When we woke up early and looked out of our
window, we counted fifty silent people gliding through
the gardens picking off the dead dahlias and asters in the
immense floral parterre that ran the whole length of the
house. In the afternoon, we drove out in an open carriage—
Mrs. Woods and I in the back seat, the men facing us. The
carriage was drawn by two horses and the coachman was
magnificently dressed, wearing a silk top hat with a cock-
ade in it. We each had a bag of lemon drops and pepper-
mints, which we threw out at the children on the road as
we rolled along under the chestnut trees. The children
curtsied and the villagers cried, *"Grüss Gott."* Buddie and
I smiled and bowed and behaved like provincial royalty,
giving the royal beckoning wave of the hand. Mrs. Woods
employed 120 people, and built and gave a house on the
property to all who had been with her twenty-five years.
They were very pretty little Bavarian houses—their windows positively choked with flowering window boxes as
she gave a prize to the house with the best flowers. After a
day and night there, we went on to Berchtesgaden and had

lunch at a U. S. Army hotel which had been done over in 1939 for Hitler's gauleiters, generals and their wives. There were only three of us in the dining room, but a man was playing the piano, and we had a three-course meal of typical army rations, dished out to us by German waiters as though it were cordon bleu, from silver-plated dishes engraved with the swastika. After lunch we went up to Hitler's house, the Berghof. First on the hillside one comes to his private hotel of three hundred rooms, the Platenhof. We walked all through it. Floors uprooted, things twisted every which way, but the stairs in perfect condition. Once again the whimsy of bombing. Then we went on to the Berghof and walked into the room with the huge window and mammoth fireplace that we had seen so often in photographs—usually with Hitler standing in front of one or the other. In the kitchen, the stove (electric) and the steam table were still standing. Bud went upstairs, but I didn't go as the stairs were gone and he had to go by ladder.

We went 120 feet underground to the series of tunnels that connect all of the principal buildings on the mountain. There was no light and a great deal of debris so we did not linger. There were barracks for five hundred troops right next to the Berghof. Also a huge Gestapo house. We saw Goebbels' house, which is lower down, but Goering's house was right next to Hitler's. Goering had the most fantastic double-tiered greenhouse, which was built around the hillside. It was all neurotic and unhealthy, and seen as we saw it that day, in a thick fog, very Götterdämmerung.

The contrast between the people in Munich and the Woodses was almost too much for us. We were glad we went and saw it all, but we were very glad to leave. We had seen the devastation of war and we had seen the survivors. It was an experience I shall never forget. I was glad, too, that I was going home to a real working job that I had started in April 1946.

18

In April 1946, Albert Kornfeld became Editor of *House and Garden*. Albert had been in the merchandizing department of Macy's and in public relations there. He was bright, brash, full of life, and bubbling with ideas. I imagine now, on looking back, that Condé Nast chose Albert for the job in the hope that he would promote advertising in the editorial pages. That, however, was not Albert's idea at all. He intended to make *House and Garden* into a magazine of elegance—the *Vogue* of architecture and house furnishing: rather like the *Architectural Digest* of today. He came and asked me if I would like to be an editor. I had never thought of such a thing and I wasn't at all sure how Buddie would like it. As will be clear by now, I was not a "liberated" woman—at least, not in the sense of that phrase today. I had taken a page from my mother's book, and though I may have appeared sometimes to be dominated by men, it was not really so; in fact it was a role that I assumed and had much fun playing.

My value to Albert Kornfeld was that I could get people to let me photograph their houses, their gardens, their children, their stables, their linen closets, dress closets and kitchen cupboards. At first, when I told Buddie about Albert's offer, he was not quite sure about having a working wife, but he said "yes"—if it did not interfere with our life together. It never did. Buddie was a real sportsman and in great demand for stag parties. When he went to Canada or to the Rogue River in Oregon for salmon and trout fishing, or to Arkansas and the Carolinas and Florida for quail, railbirds, duck and wild turkey shooting, then off I went for *House and Garden*. It was a perfect arrangement, as neither felt that they were neglecting the other.

Buddie was particularly pleased, as he loved being outside all day with a congenial group of men, followed by an evening of sitting around the fire and swapping yarns. Buddie was an extraordinary combination: He was a "man's man," and yet, at the same time, he adored the company of women.

I might mention here that I always thought that the nickname "Bud" or "Buddie" was most inappropriate for him. He was anything but a "buddy" or a "good old boy." He was, in fact, quite standoffish. It took a long time to be considered his friend, but once one entered that category, Buddie was totally loyal. His friends meant a great deal to him. He loved the company of men, but as I have also said, he adored women and was extremely attractive to them as he always had a sympathetic ear for their woes. No woman could resist telling him of her frustrations and problems (which we all seem to have).

The only time in our married life when I really made a scene was just because of this engaging trait of Buddie's. It was an evening when we had two other couples to our apartment for dinner before going to the theater. During dinner (I had ears like a fox in those days), I overheard one of the ladies pouring out the troubles of her married life to Buddie. I knew that he had always been fond of her, which was, perhaps, why my hearing was so particularly keen. Anyway, I heard her say as dinner was ending, "I want to ask your advice about this, but we can't talk anymore," and Buddie replied in a low voice, "What about lunch tomorrow?" She nodded yes. And he said, "I will

call you in the morning," I got up from the table and
rushed everyone out and down in the elevator, saying we
were going to be late for the theater. What the play was, I
don't remember, but as we were driving home together
along the East River Drive in the little Rolls Mrs. Marshall
had given us, I said, "Buddie, I would love to see your new
office before we go to London." (Buddie's firm had just
moved from one address on Broad Street to another and
larger office, and we were off to London in three days.)

"Great," said Buddie, "but have you time before we
leave?" "What about tomorrow," said I sweetly. Buddie
hesitated and quite out of character he said, "I can't tomorrow. I have a luncheon at the Downtown Association
with 'some men.'" "No you haven't," I said coldly. "You
are not telling the truth. You are lunching with Elsie. I
heard you make the date." As I talked, I grew more and
more furious, reminding him of what I had been through
with Dryden, which I emphasized, saying I never intended
to put up with such things again and finally to give more
meaning to my words, I rolled down the window of the
car and, taking off my three jeweled guard rings, threw
my wedding ring out of the window. "There," I cried, "I
am through with you. It is all over between us." Bud said
nothing, but at four in the morning, I heard a door opening. As I called out, "Who's that?" Buddie answered, and
said that he was going out with a flashlight to look for the
ring. Naturally he couldn't find it, but we went to Car-
tier's in London and bought a new one. We had champagne for dinner and drank to each other, declaring that
we both had been very silly and that it would never happen again. Of course I was wrong to have asked Buddie.
He still remained attractive to women; I wouldn't have
wanted him otherwise; just as he liked me to be attractive
to men. No one wants to be married to someone no one

else wants. It is a simple fact of life. The moral of this little episode is: "Be cautious."

I, at that time, was starting my career as a lady editor. A lady editor at Condé Nast's in those days wore a hat all day—only lady editors had this privilege—and could have her pet dog tied under her desk. My very first day I did not realize how privileged I was. I just sat at my desk, opening and shutting drawers and writing notes to myself, as I had no idea of what I was to do for $100 a week ($84 take-home pay). I certainly wanted to justify this sum that Albert had so recklessly offered me. Fortunately, on that very first day I found that Albert had chosen two other women friends of his to be on the staff. They were Suzanne Gleaves and Rosamund Frost—both of them in the copywriting department. Suzie was the senior as she had had more experience, but they were both intelligent, attractive, as sharp as tacks, and with good sense and sense of humor as well. We three became great friends and stood together over the years; starting our friendship on that first day when Albert took over as Editor, and Richardson Wright, the Editor-in-Chief, had not been notified. It was a rather unhappy start for all concerned.

We were fortunate in having really great photographers; some of them were fashion photographers who only photographed for *House and Garden* occasionally, as it bored them. They preferred live models rather than empty rooms. However, André Kertesz was a photographer who rejoiced in whatever his camera could catch. We often worked together, and sometimes I grew impatient when he would insist on waiting all day to photograph a garden to catch the afternoon shadows, or the angle of a book left carelessly on a chair—his signature. With his unerring eye for just the right object and his total dedication to perfection, he taught me a great deal.

On trips I often worked with Tom Leonard, an excellent photographer of interiors and a help in dealing with people in other cities as he was a very good representative for *House and Garden*. A trip that he and I took to Atlanta stands out in my memory as one of the most successful I ever made. We drove down, stopping on the way to photograph some National Trust Houses which were not very interesting—preserved, but with no personality—like some old women one knows. Atlanta was totally different—the New York of the South as it was called—but it was more than that. It is—or was—quite the prettiest city I have ever been in. The Garden Club of America was started in Athens, Georgia, which is close to Atlanta, and its influence is very marked in Atlanta proper. The houses were usually back from the street, with well-kept lawns covered with a mixture of pine trees and dogwood trees. In the spring, it is a dream—a veritable bower of blossoming dogwoods and fruit trees.

I had letters to several people starting with Mrs. Henry B. Tompkins (Isabel), who opened many doors to me—and what doors! In the 1920s, Neel Reed was a popular young architect in Atlanta. His taste ran to the European, so one saw French *manoirs* and English Georgian—one of the houses, "Swan House," the home of Mrs. Edward Inman, was an exceptionally beautiful Georgian baroque, almost Italian in style. The interiors were equally dazzling, not over-decorated, but appropriately done in the style of the house. Mr. Reed was also a skilled landscape gardener, creating perspectives and illusions that defied the limitations of a city lot. He unfortunately died when quite young, but he certainly had a tremendous influence on the taste of Atlanta.

The Francis Abreu house by Regency architect Philip Schutz was another beautiful house in a modified Georgian style. It was very splendid inside, with superb carving de-

signed by the architect and a dining room with mandarin
yellow walls painted with graceful figures in the Chinese
manner by Allyn Cox. It was all fantastically opulent, and
Tom and I worked almost around the clock.

Ralph McGill was, at that time, the Editor of the
Atlanta *Constitution,* and in March 1949 he wrote the lead
article for me. It was entitled "Give Me Georgia" and the
subtitle was "Classic Porticoes and Tobacco Road Are
Both Native to Georgia, a State Where Strangers Are
Welcome, Even Republicans!"

Albert Kornfeld could sometimes be quite naughty. On
this trip to Georgia I might have created a real disaster, because I took it for granted that Condé Nast was paying for
our trip. It was only when the public relations office of
Rich's store kept calling me and asking when I was coming
down to see their merchandise—particularly their new outlet for Baccarat—that I began to get a feeling that there
was a reason for these calls. Tom and I went down to the
store, and fortunately, before we met the owner of it, we
were told by the public relations people that Rich's were
picking up the tab for our visit to Atlanta. We could have
appeared extremely ungracious and unaware.

I was furious with Albert, of course, as our time was
limited and I was only able to do a small feature on the
store and its owner at the very last minute. From there we
went on to the Calloway Guest House, ostensibly to photograph the one-hundred-year-old garden done by itiner-
ant Italian workmen. But when we arrived there just in
time for a late dinner, and I went to the bathroom to wash
my hands and saw bath towels in all colors piled in luxurious stacks on shelves all around, I sensed that this was not
just a "garden" feature. At dinner I asked the housekeeper
exactly what the Calloways did. I was told that they man-
ufactured towels and that I was expected at the mills the
next day! When I got back to New York, I marched into

Albert's office complete with hat and dog, and spoke out in no uncertain terms. Albert took it all as a joke and roared with laughter. I think that the real secret, though, was that Albert had really "had it" with advertising. He really hated it, and wished to shed every vestige of his Macy's past. Alas, it was his undoing. In the end (after I had left) the advertising department of Condé Nast won out, and Albert was fired. It really broke his heart.

Before I left *House and Garden* late in 1952, I had learned a certain amount about combining advertising with the editorial part of the "book." It would have been stupid not to, as advertising is the lifeblood of a publication. I did "ladylike" features, such as getting Sacheverell Sitwell to do a short piece on Mme. de Sévigné and then showing photographs of four chic and well-known ladies at their writing desks (a once-in-a-lifetime pose, I think) while on the opposite page were photographs of all types of writing paper from the different manufacturers.

Another feature that I often used, and it always worked, was to write a piece about buffet suppers or formal dinners, or Sunday brunch in the country, with menus and recipes, and then arrange and photograph a table that was completely laid with the glass, china, and silver of our advertisers. I loved doing these tables as I could use my imagination as to whose table it was—a newly married couple; a jet-set couple; a woman alone; a man alone; a Christmas party; a children's Easter egg party—it was all grist to my mill.

Some of it was not quite honest. To make a room furnished in cheap factory-made furniture attractive, we would rent a thousand-dollar-a-month worth of plants or use a rare antique as a table ornament and never mention it in the price list. When *House and Garden* decorated a whole house, I was often called in to put in the "living touches"—books, flowers, toys, a luxurious bed, after-dinner coffee by the fire. I would run around in a smock helping to unpack and sometimes even helping to lay a carpet. It was all a game to me. The Merchandise Mart in Chicago was quite a magnet for us. Editors, senior and junior, went out en masse. It was hard work going to every shop on the twelve floors, but it was a bit of a junket, too, particularly for the junior editors and secretaries, who were known to bring a whole suitcase full of dirty clothes in order to have them cleaned at the hotel. Pots and pans were glamorously presented, and we pushed hard to have casseroles painted in the *House and Garden* color of the year. Education of children, studios, Christmas trees, bathrooms, wedding receptions—I worked on everything but funerals. The uncommercial side was easier in a way, but sometimes the social people were almost as demanding as the advertisers. "I must have six pages or I won't allow my house to be photographed at all," one haughty matron told me.

Aside from Atlanta and a few houses in New England (Manchester and Arlington, Vermont; Salem and Gloucester, Massachusetts; Providence, Rhode Island)—one of my best features was on "Winterthur," at that time still the home of Henry F. du Pont at Wilmington. He was about to make it into a museum, and would not allow anyone to photograph it. However, through my sister-in-law and Buddie, who were great friends of Harry du Pont's, I had gotten to know him, and he finally agreed that I could photograph it in both black and white and color. He also gave permission to Millicent Fenwick, a good friend of mine and his, who was then working for *Vogue* and who is now Congresswoman from New Jersey. Millicent and I were there at different times as it would have been pandemonium to have had so many photographers there together. I stayed at the Hotel Dupont in Wilmington. Ruth and Harry du Pont were in Southampton and the house was already halfway into becoming a museum of early

Americana (that was to be Harry's gift to the state). Their new house on the grounds was not yet habitable. I was not alone at the Hotel Dupont as I had with me four photographers and two of their assistants. Some of the photographers only worked in the daytime, others preferred to work at night. There was one man who was tops for color and who lay flat on the floor for half an hour between each shot; if anyone so much as entered the room while he was photographing or resting, he insisted on taking the shot over.

Winterthur is an immense house. I had people stashed away in different rooms, and ran around like a mad thing, dashing up and down the many staircases, getting lost, constantly losing my notes, my pencils, and my purse. It took five days to photograph, and I never got to bed until 3 A.M., but I had four full-page color pictures in the issue and at least four pages of black and whites; so I felt very proud and pleased. Joseph Downs, curator of the museum and an outstanding authority on the American decorative arts, wrote the text—"Two Hundred Years of American Decorative Arts." So all in all, it was a success and Harry du Pont was pleased, too.

Harry was quite an extraordinary man. His taste and color sense were impeccable. He had four different sets of curtains and slipcovers for each room for the four seasons of the year in order that the room colors would not clash with the flowers. We photographed the room where these curtains were hung, and it looked like a medieval hall, but alas, the photograph was never published—a minor defeat for my feature. The gardens at Winterthur were famous for their azaleas and beautiful trees. When the Du Ponts were alive, there was a private golf course and indoor and outdoor tennis courts, a great herd of Hereford cattle and a butcher's shop entirely for the benefit of the people living on the place. The museum was arranged and supervised by Harry du Pont during his lifetime, and is open to the public and well worth a visit. The rooms are all totally authentic and vary from the extremely simple to the very grand. There is also a cobblestone court in the interior of the museum with facades of early nineteenth-century houses and an inn with a circular travelers' table sitting invitingly just outside the inn door. Harry worked with Jacqueline Kennedy at the White House and I contributed (after I became Mrs. Vincent Astor) some painted wallpaper (American, 1804) which Harry had found. It was on the walls of the family dining room at the White House. It was of the Hudson River in Revolutionary times, done in soft colors, and I thought it quite beautiful, as did Mrs. Lyndon Johnson. One of the President's wives after Mrs. Johnson had it stripped off, but it is now back in place.

Harry du Pont taught me an important thing, which is that a person who really knows his subject is never irritated when someone who knows less about it than he does asks him a question. I blush to think now of some of the really dumb questions I asked him, but I always received a completely simple and knowledgeable answer back. He took endless pains to explain or simply to place the period of a piece of furniture or the name of a flower or tree. I was very lucky to have had the sense to ask questions and to have had the good fortune to have known the Du Ponts. They were wonderfully understanding friends and were intelligent and lively people, full of curiosity about everything.

I also photographed Monticello and Williamsburg, thereby increasing my knowledge and enjoyment. Then, after another bout with electrical appliances, portable houses, and cheap garden furniture, I went out to Lake Forest to do a feature there. Thanks to Mrs. Howard Linn (Lucy), I photographed her house, her way of entertaining, etc., and she introduced me to Lake Forest. She was very imaginative and original and well worth a feature all to herself. It is said that once after a full day's fox hunting in Middleburg, Virginia, she took a night plane to England in her riding habit and was driven directly to join a famous hunt in England. I also photographed the William McCormick Blair house and the Stanley Keith house. The Stanley Keith house was designed by David Adler, who was the brother of Frances Elkins. Frances Elkins had decorated the Keith house and I especially remember two slender four-poster ivory beds in the guest room. The beds were held together with carved silver bolts, and the bedside lamps were huge hunks of rock crystal with a light shining through them. The library walls were covered with squares of waxed vellum, and all the books were bound in the same vellum but with colored titles. Another time, I went to Bloomington and Libertyville and Evanston, Illinois; and also St. Louis. All of these trips were scattered over the years that I was at *House and Garden*.

In the spring of 1947, my second year at *House and Garden*, I went out to Coronado and rented a little house two doors down from my family for a two-week holiday. I was to be alone there for a week and then Buddie was coming out. Airplane service had begun then, so that California was much more accessible for us. I installed myself in the rather unattractive little house and settled down for the usual happy visit with my parents. Father had had heart trouble for quite a while—a deterioration of the heart —but he looked well, and as he never spoke of ill health, I never worried. There were certain signs, though, that he was not up to doing what he used to do.

In the first place, Mother, the year before, at the age of sixty-six, had learned to drive a car and did all the errands of the house. Father would never have allowed this if he had really felt himself. He also no longer went to the never ending Coronado cocktail parties. The first big dinner that Mother had already accepted for me, two nights after I arrived, he said that it would be too long an evening and that he was staying home. Both he and Mother seemed not to be particularly concerned, saying only that Dr. Churchill had said that he must not tire himself. Well, the dinner party was at the Naval Air Station, and Mother and I went in our best bib and tucker.

There was the inevitably long cocktail hour, and when we finally sat down to the table, there was a glass of tomato juice standing up in a little nest of ice at each place. I took a sip and in doing so realized that it was not pure tomato juice but a mixed drink. "What is this?" I asked the person next to me. "Clamato," he answered. "Half clam, half tomato." I looked down the table quickly to where my mother was sitting and saw to my horror that she had finished her glass. Mother was violently allergic to all fish, but most particularly to shellfish. Twice she had almost died as she became instantly dehydrated.

I jumped up from my seat and ran down to Mother. As she was seated next to the host, I explained that I must take her to the hospital at once, and would he please call the hospital and alert them to have a stomach pump ready. The small Navy hospital was fortunately quite near, but even then Mother was already wretchedly ill by the time we got there. She had a horrid session with a doctor and nurse in attendance, and it was after eleven when we finally got home. I saw Father's light on, but I put Mother to bed before going in to say good night to him. He was sitting up in bed and I told him what had happened and said he was not to worry as Mother had been given a mild sedative and would be all right. He smiled, and patted my hand and thanked me, and I went home alone to my dreary little house.

I have been nervous at night ever since I was chloroformed and robbed at the Kusers' years before; so I prowled around, first to examine every window and door, and then spent an uneasy night hearing mysterious noises. For some reason I was especially nervous. The next day, when Mother was out playing bridge and Father and I were alone, sitting under the pink eucalyptus tree, he told me that the reason he had been awake the night before was because he had had a sharp heart attack and was just recovering when we arrived. "Dr. Churchill says that my heart is deteriorating rapidly," he said, "and I may not be around much longer."

He was smiling as he said it, "I don't mind it a bit," he said. "I have had a good life and I have faced death many times. It is only your mother I worry about. Who will look after her?" "I will," I said. "Don't worry, Father darling. I will always look after Mother." Father laughed. "Thank you, Little Woman. I know that you will." After that, I cannot remember exactly, but Father spoke of wanting to be put in a plain pine box and buried in Arlington, where he already had a plot reserved. I insisted that as he and Mother had lived twelve years in Coronado and had so many dear friends there we should have a service at the Episcopal church and let all his friends have a chance to pay their respects.

He was reluctant at first, but I finally won him over and we were talking about singing the Navy Hymn, "Eternal Father, Strong to Save," when we heard the front door closing and Mother calling out to us. "Not a word to your mother," whispered Father as he then called out cheerily to Mother. I was always glad that we had had this talk, sad as it was, because four days later, fortunately the day after Buddie arrived, the telephone rang at 2 A.M. with Mother frantic, saying that Father was having a heart attack. Buddie and I threw on our clothes and ran over. The Navy doctor arrived the same moment as we did. He gave Father

a shot and said he would get an ambulance to take him to
the hospital.

Buddie stayed with Mother while I sat in the dark with
Father holding his hand—waiting, it seemed, an eternity
for the ambulance. Finally it came and we three followed
in our car. Father was immediately put in an oxygen tent—
doctors and nurses hovering around him. We sat outside,
only peeking in occasionally. At six o'clock the doctor in
charge came to us and said that he thought that the worst
was over and that we should go home and rest. We argued
that we wished to stay, but he said that there was nothing
we could do and that he would ring us if things changed.
This he did at seven-fifteen. We rushed over, but Father
was already dead. I asked the nurse if he had spoken. She
said that he had opened his eyes and looked around him.
She asked if he wanted some orange juice. Then he said,
"Brooke," and died. I knew what he meant—"Remember,
Brooke, to look after Mother."

19

Father died on a Thursday morning—the day when his article should have gone into the San Diego *Union*. After we
got back to the house, I walked into his room just to kneel
by his bed and say a prayer. As I knelt, I saw on the bedside table a large yellow pad covered with Father's familiar
handwriting. After my little prayer, with my eyes still
filled with tears, I touched the pillow where Father's head
had lain just a few hours before and I picked up the pad.

When I read what was on it, I realized that it was the complete article. I took it in to Mother, who could hardly bear to look at Father's writing, but she agreed that I should call up the *Union* and ask them to send for it. Mother and Buddie were sitting in the patio, and when I walked through Mother's room to telephone I glanced at her desk. Under the date March 5, she had written in a bold hand "John died today." Poor Mother—that brief note showed me more than anything else her total sense of loss.

Father's article was published on Sunday. His funeral took place in a crowded church on the following Monday. The little house was besieged by friends afterward. The next day, we three left for Washington by train as Mother wished to accompany Father's body. The commanding officer at the Marine Station in San Diego had spoken to the Commandant of the Marine Corps in Washington and all arrangements had been made for the funeral at Arlington. Some friends from San Diego had lent us an apartment in Washington, and we stayed there, with friends pouring in to see Mother, until March 17, St. Patrick's Day, when we set forth for Arlington.

It was snowing lightly; we followed the cortege down the winding road from the upper gate of the cemetery grounds just below General Lee's home. Ahead of us were the riderless horse with stirrups reversed, 1,500 Marines marching at a slow pace, and 250 blue jackets. To make it even more poignant, the minute guns marked off the passing of time with their somber boom. Father's grave is on a hillside. By the time we arrived, the Marines standing with stacked muskets, and the sailors saluting, were ranged from the gravesite on the hillside all the way down to the road, where we got out of the car. As Mother stepped out, with the Commandant of the Marine Corps escorting her, the Marine Band struck up Chopin's funeral march, and the

Marines and sailors swayed solemnly to the music. Buddie and I followed Mother up to the grave, where, under a tent, a minister, an Honor Guard of Marines and many friends were waiting for us.

After the prayers had been said and the coffin was being gently lowered into the grave, a bugler standing by played taps, a volley was fired, and two marine officers who had been great friends of Father's lifted the flag from the coffin, folded it, and handed it to Mother. She clutched it to her, but she behaved wonderfully, speaking to everyone and throwing back her veil to show that she was a true soldier's wife. We walked down the hill through the snow and drove slowly away. Father had left this earth forever, but he has never left *me*. His spirit—what Mother called "a merry saint"—is forever in my heart, and to this day, is a guidepost and a comfort. Father would certainly have laughed at the very idea, but he was in my mind an "old soul"—someone who is full of wisdom and knows more than an ordinary person can accumulate in one lifetime.

In that same spring of 1947, Tony, while still at Brown University, had announced that he was engaged to a girl whom he had met at Brown (she was actually at Pembroke, which was affiliated with Brown). She was a freshman, and only eighteen, and Buddie and I felt that they were too young and emotionally immature to marry. I recalled my own early marriage and hoped that Tony would not repeat my mistake. However, the more we tried to talk him out of it, the more determined he became. He was married in June of that year. Around the same time Dryden sued Tony, trying to get back the money that had been settled on him. Dryden maintained that since Tony had taken Buddie's name, he was no longer entitled to Kuser money. We went to court down in Foley Square before a judge who obviously took a cynical view of the whole matter as just another family wrangle about money.

I hated having to do it, as I rather agreed with the judge—people who fight over money never seem to me to deserve to have any! Fortunately, Tony for some reason had kept all of the letters in which Dryden was forever asking for money. The climax was the letter Dryden wrote to Tony, just before he was sent to the Pacific, asking him to insure his life for $250,000 in Dryden's name. The judge handed down his decision from the bench in our favor. Dryden paid me the compliment of hissing in my ear, as I passed him in the corridor of the courthouse: "You always were a bitch, but you are still damned attractive!"

After Tony had won the suit, and as he was getting married and would have his own home, I no longer wanted the allowance I had had from the trust, so my salary from Condé Nast was more welcome than ever. I had had a raise by then, and it gave me a feeling of security and confidence to feel that I had money that was my very own. I paid for all my clothes and all the extras, such as flowers for the apartment, and a bathhouse for the swimming pool in Tyringham. As the years went on and my salary increased again, I bought more and more, especially as I got a decorator's discount. I bought every kitchen gadget imaginable and enough casseroles for a hotel. I was like a bird who flies home each day with a twig in its beak to embellish the nest.

Tyringham was my home—our home—and I loved it dearly. I had lived there longer than I had lived in any other house. I was no longer a *Patchwork Child*, but a sedate and happy woman, married to the man I loved, who was always close—to help me and guide me. Tony's wedding was a sadness, as we could see from the very beginning that they could not cope with married life. After one year more at Brown, and right after his graduation, Tony went to work for the government in Washington; and he

Lady Ribblesdale with Alice. A true Edwardian.

Vincent during World War II.

In the apartment in New York City just before the ball at the St. Regis. Cecil Beaton.

All dressed up in my Balmain, posing next to the portrait of the Astor family. Cecil Beaton.

Ferncliff at Rhine-beck, a copy of the Grand Trianon by Stanford White.

My bedroom at Ferncliff.

The hall at Ferncliff after I redecorated it.

Swimming pool, Ferncliff. The first indoor-swimming-pool/tennis-court building built in this country by Stanford White, 1903.

The Wicket in Phoenix. The lawn is for croquet.

The only happy picture of Vincent and his sister, Alice, taken on his birthday.

Dragging Vincent to a ball given by Cornelius Vanderbilt Whitney.

Fourth of July 1976 at Battery Park in New York with Mayor Beame and Brendan Gill. The crowd is shouting, "Brooke, Brooke!" Camera 1.

Riding Tussie at the opening of the Southeast Asia Plains, Bronx Zoo. New York Zoological Society.

The new Ming Courtyard in Soochow to be duplicated at the Metropolitan Museum. Seth Jane.

and his wife bought a very nice little house in George-town.

Mother stayed on in Coronado, living in the same house there. Then she decided to rent it, and bought a smaller house; then finally she sold both houses and came East to live in Norwich, Connecticut, in order to be near her sister, Aunt Roberta, who had a beautiful old white wooden 1820 house in Norwichtown. Aunt Roberta was the widow of Ebenezer Learned, a cousin of the famous New York judge Learned Hand. She was interested in local politics, in needlework, and in genealogy, and she was quite content with widowhood.

Mother hated every minute of life in Norwich. She had a pretty apartment in an old house, but after the gay and cosmopolitan life she had always led, she felt suffocated by the provincialism that had become second nature to dear, easygoing Aunt Roberta. I suggested that she might go back to Coronado. But having once pulled up her roots, she had no inclination to return to the place where she had been so happy. Unfortunately, I had not enough money of my own to rent an apartment for her in New York; and I did not like to ask Buddie to do it, for I felt that he was worried about money although he refused to talk about it. She came often to Tyringham, as she got on very well with our friends there; and when Buddie and I went abroad, which we usually did once a year, she stayed either in the apartment or in the house in Tyr-ingham.

We went to Portugal one year and had a splendid time. We stayed at the Hotel Aviz in Lisbon. It has since been torn down, but it was a very deluxe little hotel, originally a private house. It was only five stories high, and was covered entirely on one side by a mammoth purple bou-gainvillea which climbed right up to the roof. My bath-room had a sunken tub, and the bougainvillea came right over the balcony through the long window to hang on a trellis over the tub. I felt very exotic as I lay in my bath with an occasional purple blossom floating down over me.

There is another memory of Portugal—not at all exotic —but rather amusing. In the dining room at a small table close to the wall, I spied a rather dried-up elderly gentleman sipping vichy water and eating boiled carrots. Between sips of the vichy and a nibble on a carrot, he was perusing a long sheet of paper which rolled out around his feet like a scroll. I called Buddie's attention to him, and his reading matter. "He is reading a financial sheet," explained Bud. The captain, who saw whom we were looking at, bent over our table. "That is Monsieur Gulbenkian," he whispered. "He owns the hotel."

Mr. Gulbenkian, as it turned out, not only owned the hotel, but 5 per cent of the Iraq Petroleum Company. He was an Armenian by birth, and his hobby was collecting art objects from all over the world. Though rich beyond imagination he chose to live in two rooms at the Aviz, thereby avoiding taxes. His son lived in England and was quite different. There is a story—perhaps apocryphal—I have often heard about him. Mr. Gulbenkian, Jr., was very fond of fox hunting and belonged to one of the best hunts in England. One day he appeared at the meet with a large purple orchid in his buttonhole. This sight astonished and aggravated the gentry gathered together before the start of the hunt. Sensing the feelings of his compatriots, the master of hounds rode up to Mr. Gulbenkian and said, "I say, my dear fellow, we have never seen an orchid in a buttonhole at a hunt before." Mr. Gulbenkian gave a hearty laugh. "But then you have never had an Armenian in your hunt before," he responded. I hope the story is true, because it shows real style. His father may have made all the money, but he didn't look as though there was much wit in him.

Aside from seeing the mythical recluse, Gulbenkian, we saw many fascinating museums and palaces. I particularly remember the French silver, which is considered the finest collection in the world, and the carriage museum with the most extraordinary carriages. One papal nuncio, for instance, being a Prince of the Church, traveled in *grand luxe* when he made his trips to Rome. He not only had day and night coaches, but also a beautiful dining coach, round inside, with red-velvet-covered sides and red velvet banquettes gathered around a spacious round table. There was also a kitchen carriage, resplendent with glistening pots and pans and a sturdy portable stove. Another thing I remember was that all the illegitimate children of royal or princely houses had the family crest on the coach door, but tilted to the left.

The little pink and white and green baroque Palace of Queluz, set like a wedding cake in its formal garden of clipped hedges and white pebble paths, is a real gem. The rooms inside are full of fantasy and charm. One room was covered with pale green trellises decorated with roses and fruits. I picked up many ideas for *House and Garden* there. The castle at Cintra on its hilltop is where the last king of Portugal, Charles I, and his son barricaded themselves in 1908. They were dragged out and assassinated, and yet it looks almost impregnable. In spite of its gloomy past, it is quite a cheerful place, and contains a very amusing room filled with furniture made entirely from antlers.

We met the Duke and Duchess of Palmela in Lisbon and visited their magnificent house there, which occupied a whole block in the heart of the city. Many of the floors and doors were made from the finest Brazilian mahogany imported in the eighteenth century. We did not visit their country place, but I was told that when the Duke looks out of the window there, for thirty miles in every direction he only sees his own land. We did go to the Duchess' sister's seaside villa at Cascais. The Duchess' sister was the Marquesa Spirito Santo, and was the mother of fourteen. They were very charming and welcoming people, and after all these years I remember them vividly.

The next year we went back to Bavaria, in particular to visit the small baroque churches and the fairy-tale castles of Hohenschwangau and Neuschwanstien, which were the brainchildren of the mad King Ludwig II. Before that, we took a "cure" at Bad Gastein, drinking the radioactive waters and taking the radioactive baths. We were supposed to take it easy in between these treatments, but Bud and I could not resist the wonderful walks and walked for hours every day until one day, on coming back to our room, I lay right down on the floor in my raincoat and with my hat on my head and said that I was too tired ever to get up.

Buddie handed me a glass of slivovitz, which helped me to rise to my feet and throw myself on the bed. It was Buddie, though, who really had a bad turn on that trip. We were motoring back to Munich and stopped at the Königssee for lunch. After a huge mug of beer, Buddie got quite carried away and ate an enormous fat black sausage. It was a dreadful-looking thing and I cautioned him about it; but he said that it was absolutely delicious. That night, though, at the Vier Jahreszeiten, he woke me up in the middle of the night and said that he had a frightful chill, and was nauseated. We had no medicine of any sort with us (it seems unbelievable to me now), so I piled comforters on top of him and put my arms around him and held him close to try to warm him. But it was no use.

Finally I went to the telephone and called our consul general, who was Charlie Thayer. (He had married Cynthia Dunn, the Jimmy Dunns' younger daughter.) Dear Charlie came rushing over, bringing a doctor with him, who declared that it was an attack of indigestion and gave Bud some medicine to take. We stayed on for a few days, as Buddie still felt very shaky. It was no hardship, as I had known Cynthia since she was a child, and Charlie was an extremely bright man and a brilliant raconteur. He had plenty to recount as he, Fitzroy MacLean, and Randolph Churchill had been parachuted into Yugoslavia during World War II on a fact-finding mission. They sought out Tito, who was living in hiding surrounded by guerrillas. This trio of men saw in Tito a different brand of Communism from that of Russia, and reported this to Winston Churchill, who relied on their advice in his future dealings with the Yugoslav government.

As I write now, I am writing about my older self, not the young Brooke of the first chapters, so now when I am confronted with a blank sheet of paper and take my pencil in hand, all the people I have known begin to crowd in around me and I suddenly see in my mind's eye a ballroom, a café, a mountaintop. In these places, I have danced or sat and talked to a friend, and little vignettes and voices come back to me. My past becomes the present. I don't think that I have put into this memoir all the fun I have had in life. I have left out all the "side dishes" and have stuck to the main course—even bypassing all the laughs I have had. It seems that I have written too much that is, if not exactly sad, certainly not gay; yet what has really held me together has been my sense of humor. People often tell me that I should go into politics, but I could never take myself that seriously. A sense of humor about oneself can easily kill one's sense of self-importance (and kill a love affair, too, by the way—a laugh at the wrong moment is disastrous to someone else's ego).

Buddie also had a sense of humor, but it was gentler than mine. We had fun together because we were interested in so many of the same things, but Buddie was not given to wild laughter or to the totally absurd. Our trips to

Europe were our greatest fun, because there we were together and absolutely carefree. As the years went by, Buddie became quieter and worried more. I often asked him
what he was thinking of and what, if anything, was worrying him. He once woke me in the night to tell me that
he was going to give me power of attorney, but when I
asked him why, he couldn't say. Our trips as the years
rolled by became the most relaxed times in our lives. That
trip to Munich was our last trip.

20

From 1947 until 1952 my only real worry was my mother.
I had always thought that if Mother died first, Father
would have just quietly withdrawn himself from life and
died of a broken heart. With Mother surviving Father, I
had no fears. I thought of her as a tremendous extrovert
with an unquenchable zest for life that would enable her
to survive anything. I had no doubt that she would manage
her life very well. I was completely wrong. I began to realize that Father had been the Oak and Mother the Vine.
Without his constant adoration and protective care, she
was totally lost.

Mother was in her middle sixties and still attractive and
amusing when she wanted to be. Sumner Welles, after his
wife Mathilde died and before he fell in love with Har-
riette, asked Mother to go to Europe with him as his guest.
He and Mother were old friends and had known each
other even before Sumner was High Commissioner to the

Dominican Republic at the same time as Father was High Commissioner to Haiti. They had often exchanged visits then and had seen one another in Europe. In fact, once in Paris, when Mother was there alone, they had seen quite a lot of one another and Sumner had given Mother a first edition of James Joyce's *Ulysses,* which she prized greatly. I gathered that they spoke on many esoteric and controversial subjects—the sort of conversation that Mother loved —and Buddie and I urged her to take the trip. Vis-à-vis Norwich, it seemed a gift from heaven!

But Mother would not accept. She was overcome with qualms that in her younger years she would have laughed at or ignored. "It would not be proper," she said. "I couldn't possibly take a trip alone with a man. Your Father wouldn't like it." She was right. Father would not have liked it; but we thought that at her age no one would raise an eyebrow and she would have a good time. How times have changed in the last twenty years! Today, with the geriatric liberation, the old folks are having a heyday— traveling together all over the world, spending vacations in the most out-of-the-way places, and always being invited together to their friends' houses. Today, Mother could probably have gone in the same cabin on the ship. It was all very hard on Mother, who much preferred the company of men to that of women.

There was Lewis Einstein, an American diplomat whom my family had known in Peking. His wife, who was older than he, was a Levantine and a fascinating woman. As Madame Ralli, she had had a daughter who became the Marchioness of Tweedale. Mother used to tell me how Madame Ralli Einstein, when feeling slightly indisposed, used to receive callers on her "At Home" day in her bedroom. She lay back on lace cushions with a silken cover over her, dressed in a bed jacket of ribbons and satin and lace and fur, and would carry on a lively conversation with the guests grouped about her bedside. Mother, as a young woman, was fascinated by this Proustian character; and so when she died, and Lewis came over to America on a visit, they renewed their friendship—talking mostly about the old days in Peking. "Do you remember that picnic that Lambert gave at the Princes' Tomb?" "Do you remember when Lady Jordan's train got caught under a chair and was ripped off, exposing her corset and *pantalons?*" On and on they went. Lewis came over several times from his apartment in the Place des États Unis in Paris. He was a friend of Nancy Mitford and had a very attractive group of people who were devoted to him.

Buddie and I watched this friendship with approving eyes, but Mother began to grow tired of Lewis. It turned out that he was a teetotaler, or practically one, because only sometimes, on a rare occasion, would he sip a glass of sherry. "I could never marry a man who doesn't take a cocktail before dinner," Mother firmly declared. "It would be too boring." A strange thing happened. One night Buddie and I were dining with Pauline and Walter Hoving at their apartment in New York. They often asked a fortune-teller called Dolly to come in after dinner. She told fortunes with cards, and she was there that particular night. I had never had my fortune told because, if it is true, I don't want to know it and if it isn't, why bother? But Pauline that night for some reason was very insistent, so I went into Pauline's sitting room, where Dolly was ensconced.

I sat down facing her at the card table; and, as she slowly dealt out the cards, she told me several things which I can't remember, then, suddenly in a loud voice, she said, "I see a widow here, grieving—and I see a marriage to a very rich man." I went out of the room exultant and, laughing heartily, I told Buddie on the way home that Dolly had predicted that Mother was going to marry Lewis Einstein. "Great!" replied Bud. "She will certainly be a lot happier." But the months passed and nothing happened. The widow Dolly saw was not Mother.

Buddie and I had come back from Europe at the end of August and we went directly to Tyringham. We spent every weekend there, getting up at five-thirty on Monday morning in order to get back to New York in time for the office. We usually stopped and had breakfast at a diner in Millbrook on the way. Sometimes I stayed over and went in by train if I was busy writing a feature at home or going on an assignment in the Berkshires.

The pigpen had been completely done over (as you can imagine, it *had* to be), and was turned into a bindery. Buddie's father had collected a library of leather-bound books—no first editions, or anything very rare, but a very complete "gentleman's library" of the late nineteenth and early twentieth century—Dickens, Thackeray, Scott, Walpole, the English poets, Macaulay, Boswell's *Johnson*, etc. Buddie started out by learning to take care of the bindings. We coated the books with a special grease, left them off the shelves for forty-eight hours, then rubbed them down with lamb's wool. Through doing this, Bud became interested in the bindings themselves and started lessons in bookbinding with Mr. and Mrs. Gerlach in New York. It was a great resource and a great pleasure for Bud. He bought a press and tools, and when we went to Europe, he bought skins and attractive end papers—both of which are hard to find in this country. The first book he bound was Dickens' *Christmas Carol*, which we always read every Christmas Eve, leaving out the gloomy parts. It was a marvelous relaxation for Buddie, who was always on the go, to have time alone working in the bindery, totally absorbed; and it was very rewarding for him to see a book that he loved decked out in a beautiful new costume.

Tyringham was magical in the autumn. The maples along the road to the village turned their very special gold and scarlet and across the valley, a row of color marched over the summit of the hills. We loved lying out in long chairs on the lawn drinking in the beauty of those last golden days; and then, when the sun set behind the cobble, we would come in, light the fire, draw the curtains, and have a drink. We were not alone all the time. We had many friends in Stockbridge and Lenox and Great Barrington as well as those who lived near us in the valley.

In the middle of October we usually closed up the house. That is, the couple who kept house for us came into the apartment in town. Then we changed everything about. Buddie and I still kept our rooms, although dressed in slipcovers, but the drawing room and library were closed up, with shutters drawn. We used the back stairs and turned the dining room into a sitting room. The furniture was all moved out. A plain carpet was put down and the porch furniture was brought in—the big bamboo sofa and chairs to match—and it all looked very different and neat and comfortable and easy to keep clean. We ate in the staff dining room, just off the kitchen, unless we had guests. When we had guests, we had a buffet in the dining room.

I learned to be quite a good cook. All one has to do to be a good cook is to love food, to be able to read a cookbook, understand a stove, and have plenty of time. The only good cooking is slow cooking. When the shooting season started, I had plenty of time. Buddie went off Friday and Saturday to a little gun club that he had joined; and while he was away I was busy cooking a pheasant or making pheasant soup, making desserts or casseroles because we often had people in for supper, and casseroles can be kept waiting. The gardener's wife came and cleaned up after the weekend, but I usually left the house cleaner than I found it. We always spent Thanksgiving in Tyringham because somehow the country gives one the feeling of what Thanksgiving originally was and the city does not. One Thanksgiving we really had a different time from most. We went up on Wednesday, and I got out a very small turkey and all the ingredients for our dinner. Buddie was to go shooting, but when we woke up in the morning, the ground was covered with thick snow. Buddie tried to get the car out without any luck, and I was just as glad, because it was snowing hard and I was afraid that he would never get back. We went out and shoveled snow and played with the dogs, but when I came in to make a light lunch, the electricity was off, and so was the telephone. We ate some bread and butter and cheese, got out all the candles we could find, and then tried to walk to the village for more, but the snow was too deep. Meanwhile the house was getting cold, as the heat had gone off.

Our gardener, Lucian, came up from his cottage, but there was nothing to be done except to lug in a huge load of wood from the back porch and build up the fire in the dining room and my bedroom. As it grew dark and we grew hungry, we wondered what to do. I remembered hearing somewhere that potatoes cooked in embers were delicious, so we banked the fire, threw in six potatoes, poured ourselves two generous Bourbons and sat on the bamboo sofa in front of the fire, the room lit by its flickering light. It seemed so unlike our real life—so romantic and such fun—that we refilled our glasses and talked as though we wanted to compress the whole of our lives in that one moment.

Time must have fled by, because I suddenly remembered the potatoes. We fished around with the fire tongs and finally found that they had shrunk to about the size of a small crab apple and were all charred and black. But we ate them, blackened or not, and Buddie said, "Why don't we have good things like this in New York?" and we decided that we wanted to live always in the country, and

never never see New York again, and to hell with electricity! We drank to the joys of fire and candlelight and
thanked God for each other; then went to bed, where the
gentle noise of the fire in the bedroom and the firelight
gradually becoming a rosy glow lulled us into a dreamless
sleep. It seems a trivial episode to stand out so clearly in
my memory, but it is not always the grander moments
that count the most. It is often these little unexpected moments that bind the pattern of one's life together. Although Bud and I had so many happy times, I remember
this one because of its sheer absurdity—with both of us behaving quite out of character—and also because of another
Thanksgiving.

It was the Thanksgiving after our return from Europe
—Thanksgiving 1952. Mother was coming over from Norwich, and Buddie had planned three days of pheasant
shooting. Mother met us in New York, and we drove up
together. Mother was writing a book of vignettes of her
life. She was an excellent reporter, always able to put
down on paper a mood, an event, a character, in a few
well-chosen sentences. The trouble was that she never
finished anything. She was like Grandfather, who, all his
life, was busily engaged in writing a history of famous
crimes. Grandfather's style was a bit stilted, more like a
law brief than lay reading, but Mother really had talent.
On the three-hour drive to Tyringham, her recollections
made us roar with laughter.

One was about her friend Lady ffrench in Peking.
Lady ffrench, though happily married, was pursued by a
young member of the Italian Legation who was madly in
love with her. How far this affair went, Mother did not
tell us; but one day, when Lady ffrench had made a ren-
dezvous with her suitor, she was not feeling well and sent a
chit around to the young man saying she could not meet
him as she had taken to her bed. This delay drove him to

madness. Knowing when Lord ffrench was at the office, he brought a ladder and climbed through the window into his loved one's bedroom. Lady ffrench was not expecting his visit and did not look her best. She covered her face with a lace handkerchief and begged him to leave as she was too ill to speak. Spying a bottle of pills on her bedside table, he took up the bottle, said, "I wish to share everything with you," and poured most of the pills down his throat. Then kissing Lady ffrench's hand (which by this time was the only bit of her showing, as she had slipped down into the sheets), he went back down the ladder. The sequel was that he had to send his regrets to a dinner at the Italian Legation that night, as unfortunately the pills were a strong laxative. All of Peking knew the story in twenty-four hours; and it was the end of the love affair.

Another story was about a cabinet officer who came down to Haiti during Prohibition. Father and Mother naturally gave a large dinner party for him but as it was Prohibition and their house was government property, the dinner had to be "dry." Knowing this, a cocktail party had been arranged beforehand and the cabinet officer, accompanied by his aides, arrived for dinner rather the worse for wear. Dinner was served almost at once since no one wanted ginger ale or tomato juice. The high official was seated on Mother's right, and next to him was the wife of one of the leading American businessmen in Port-au-Prince. Minister X took one look at her (she was no beauty and had a long red nose) and demanded to know where the wine was. "This house is dry," responded the lady. "It is considered to be American soil." The Minister took another look at her and gave a long whistle. "My God, woman," he cried. "Don't tell me you got *that* nose on water." With this remark, he threw a napkin over his face and let out a war whoop. The lady got up from the table and Mother, seeing her agitation, followed her. They went up to Mother's room, where the lady threw herself down on the chaise longue and burst into loud sobs. "If he couldn't respect me as a woman," she moaned, "he might at least have respected me as the wife of the head of the chamber of commerce."

"I will read you some of my vignettes tomorrow night," declared Mother, who saw that we were obviously enjoying her stories. "Do, do," we said. So in this merry mood, we arrived at "Milnhouse" and happily unloaded the car.

The next morning, Thanksgiving Day 1952, Buddie got into bed with me and we lay there with Maxl, Buddie's German shorthaired pointer, across our feet, and watched the sunrise. When Buddie got up to get dressed, he looked out of the window and saw a bird on one of the bare branches. "It's a bluebird," he exclaimed. "How marvelous to see it on Thanksgiving Day!" "It means happiness," I said. "Yes," answered Bud, giving me a kiss. I rushed downstairs in my dressing gown to get breakfast ready. After a hasty bite, Bud went off to the pheasant shoot and I took a tray up to Mother. So began the day—a beautiful day, warm for the season, but cool enough to have a fire in the evening. Lucian came up and laid the fire; his wife made the beds. I called up a few friends to come in for tea and a drink, and went about the business of cooking. The turkey only needed heating up and the mince pies were made, so only the vegetables had to be done and some sandwiches made for tea. Mother wrote most of the day, and I walked in the woods, picking up pinecones and twigs.

Bud returned at dusk with two brace of pheasant, which we hung on the back porch. Our guests arrived soon after—only four or five good friends. The fire was blazing away, the teakettle was boiling and the drinks were laid out. We had a great time, and one of Bud's shooting companions was reliving the day's shoot with him. Tea-time merged into drink time, and the guests stayed on.

The room grew hot, filled as it was with people, and I was astonished when I saw Bud throw an immense log on the blazing fire. "For heaven's sakes, Bud," I said. "It's absolutely boiling in here, don't do that." "I feel cold," he answered. I looked at him sharply. He looked pale. "Why don't you have a whisky," I said. "That will warm you up." "No," answered Bud. "Remember, I was told by the doctor not to drink for two weeks—and the two weeks aren't up until Tuesday." I remembered then that Bud had not been feeling well, and had gone to the doctor, who, after examining him thoroughly, said he found nothing wrong with him except that he might have an incipient ulcer. Bud drank some hot tea, and continued talking with our guests, who left in a group, all of us hugging and kissing one another and saying, "Happy, happy Thanksgiving."

After they had gone and Mother and Buddie were emptying ashtrays and tidying up generally, I set the table, brought in the small turkey and we three sat down. Mother and I were drinking wine and Buddie poured just a mouthful in his glass. "I wish to thank God for all my blessings," he said, "particularly, for my dearest wife, and I want us to drink a toast together to our next President—Eisenhower." So we drank to Eisenhower and the next four years. After dinner Bud and I cleared the table, and he set up his breakfast tray for the next morning, as the shoot was going to start early and he was going to make his own breakfast. He was going to clean his guns, but Mother called out to us and said that she was all ready to read; so we went back to our places by the fire.

What Mother read was amusing, but I could see that Bud was looking a bit bored and restless. As a matter of fact, so was I; and I was pleased when Buddie got up and

said, "Excuse me, Mrs. Russell, but I think that I will go
up to bed as I have to get up very early and as I am too
tired to clean my guns tonight, I must do it before I leave
tomorrow." Then he went to the back door to let Maxl
out. I started to talk to Mother when I heard a noise and
thought I heard Bud call. I ran out laughing through the
kitchen, thinking he might have something special to tell
me; but when I got to the back porch, there was Bud on
the floor—his eyes closed, his hands moving.

"Bud!" I cried as I knelt beside him. "Bud, darling,
what is it?" I put his head on my lap and loosened his collar and called out to Mother to call Lucian to get a doctor
at once. As I sat there waiting with Bud's head in my lap, I
thought he must have had a stroke. I remembered that we
had promised each other that if one of us had a stroke and
was totally incapacitated, the other would not keep him or
her alive as a vegetable. "Is this a stroke?" I thought. "Do I
have to make that decision?" I whispered to Buddie not to
worry, but he must try to give me a sign. It was very quiet
on that back porch. Maxl had disappeared, and the only
sound was the sough of the wind in the pine trees.

At long last, Lucian and the doctor arrived. He was a
young doctor from Lee, and as he knelt beside me, his first
words were "How long has this man been dead?" On
hearing this, I let out a shriek that I am sure must have
been heard through the entire valley. The doctor went
into the house to call the undertaker and I sat there with
Bud, still not believing it. Lucian brought a coat to put
over my shoulders and I just sat there. After a while, the
undertakers came, and at almost the same moment, friends
arrived—the ones who had been there at tea—one of whom
had called and heard the news from Mother—Lisa and
Jack Kennedy, Lee and "J" Gould, Monty and Sym
Livermore. J went immediately to clean Bud's guns (they
were a pair of Purdey guns given to Bud by his mother) as

he, J, had been shooting with Bud. It was a dear thing for him to do as it would have meant so much to Bud to have his guns well taken care of, and later I gave them to J.

When I saw my friends, I began to cry and could not stop. What does one do when one's whole life seems to come to an end? Why are tears necessary? In my heart I felt absolutely finished while the foolish tears ran down my cheeks. Of course I had to call up the family. Bud's sister was in Europe. I could not reach his daughter. I got Tony, who said that he would be there first thing in the morning. My friends were marvelous. They stayed, telephoning, consoling, sharing my grief, because Buddie was loved by all who knew him. At last they left, saying they would come in the morning. Mother went to bed and I wandered all over the house, including the rooms that were shut, saying to myself, "Buddie, where are you? Why have you left me?"

When I went to the kitchen, I saw his breakfast tray. I could hardly bear it. Buddie had placed it there just a few hours before. Finally, I went to Bud's room and, as I had done with Father, I said a prayer. Then I went back to my room, where that morning we had been so happy, where Buddie had stood at the window and seen the bluebird. Why should he have seen that symbol of happiness? Did the bird come to take him to another life? It was almost dawn when I finally went into a fitful sleep.

Early the next morning, our couple from town arrived. I had called them the night before to bring me a sealed letter that was in my desk. It was Buddie's instructions, and on the outside was written, "Brooke, to be opened after my death." It contained the most minute instructions for his funeral service—the prayers, the hymns, and the pallbearers. It was of enormous comfort to me to know that what I did was all planned by Buddie. Tony arrived, and when the undertaker called for a suit, Tony took it in to him. It was my favorite brown tweed suit, which looked so well with Buddie's red hair. I also insisted, as I had with Father, that Buddie should have his shoes on. I felt it so undignified to be all dressed and then to have bare feet; but that's what undertakers do if you don't insist.

Buddie came home that afternoon and was taken to his bedroom. Tic and Alma Morgan, who were often our walking companions, had gone out into the woods to gather pine boughs and berries of all sorts. These they brought to Bud, and we arranged them around the room. Friends poured in, and I stood in the midst of them, surrounded by love and not ashamed of my tears. Evie sent word that she was coming as soon as possible, and so we set the date for the funeral at St. James on Wednesday, the third of December. I wanted to be in New York to see Dr. (later Bishop) Kinsolving, the Rector of St. James at that time; so on Monday we went into New York. For the last time, Buddie went down the stairs and out of his front door with Tony walking beside him, his hand on the coffin in never ending affection. Buddie came directly to our apartment in New York and was in the drawing room. It had been quite a fight to manage that as neither the undertakers nor our building were particularly keen about it; but I wanted Buddie to be in his own home near me until he was taken to his last resting place. Flowers, letters, telegrams, cables poured in. In all, I got over 1,500 letters. Such a tribute to Buddie and such an enormous amount of work for me as I answered every one of them. It took me about four months.

The service at St. James was beautiful, just what Bud wanted; even though it was a snowy day, it was so crowded that people were standing in the entrance hall. The coffin was covered with a carpet of evergreens and pinecones and berries. I wanted it to look like a forest floor and it did. Dr. Kinsolving, when he spoke of Bud, said,

"This was a man who was at peace with himself and God. This was a man who was ready to die."

I was swathed in black with a black veil, and we, Evie and Buddie's children, did not walk out after the casket, but went first to the vestry room, then out of a side door on Seventy-first Street. At Woodlawn, I stood by the grave after everyone had gone but Evie and me. Finally, she gently urged me to leave. I reluctantly went, and before getting into the car, I turned for a last look. A little squirrel, oblivious of the falling snow, was sitting in the middle of Bud's "forest floor blanket," busily eating one of the berries, which he was holding in his paws. Buddie would have loved that, and I felt that it was a little message from him.

For the next few weeks, I was practically never alone. Bud had been president of the Brook Club for eight years, and I think that word had gone out through the club that when dusk fell I would be sad; so every afternoon some Brook Club members would drop in on me, and we would talk not only of Buddie, but of the Brook Club, the stock market, politics, our friends. Then all my other friends came. The John Mason Browns, the C. D. Jacksons, Marc Connelly, Mary Spalding (widow of Albert), Albert Kornfeld, and all the people from Condé Nast. Oh, I can't write all their names, but I can only say that without these friends, I could not have survived. Evie's children were marvelous to me, and of course, there was Evie herself and my stepdaughter, Peggy.

I remember one day sitting on the sofa in my library and talking to Norris Darrell, a good friend, and our lawyer. It was just before Christmas and I was feeling very weepy. I could not pass a necktie counter without having tears in my eyes, and the sight of all the people hurrying home with Christmas packages under their arms made me depressed beyond words. As Norris and I talked, he sud-

denly said, "I think that you will remarry within the
year." I almost jumped out of my chair. "How can you
say that?" I whimpered. "Whatever makes you say such a
thing?" "Because," said Norris, "it is the people who cry
the most who marry the soonest. They can't bear to live
alone." I figuratively tossed my head, but I didn't continue
the conversation because I *knew* that I would never never
marry. Norris came to see me quite often because one of
Buddie's worries had been my financial future. Bud's
father had made one of those old-fashioned wills which
said that on Buddie's death, his estate should be divided between Buddie's children—in other words, skipping a generation, thus avoiding double taxation. There was nothing
Bud could do about that, but he had made another contract—a personal one—which committed his estate to pay
out a certain sum annually to someone until that person
died. Buddie had spoken to me often about trying to break
this contract, but had never gotten around to it. He had
finally decided that he *would* do something, and had made
an appointment with Norris Darrell for the Tuesday after
Thanksgiving! Man proposes, and God disposes was certainly the case.

In his letter to be opened after his death, he had also
enclosed a letter to me urging me to take action, as he felt
it unfair that I should have such a small part of his estate.
However, I was in no mood to fight for anything, and
Norris said that, in any case, it would be very difficult and
very expensive. I really wasn't worrying about money. I
knew that I could not afford two homes forever; but,
looking back, I am surprised at how unconcerned I was
about my future. I suppose that I felt I had no future. I
was so busy answering the letters of condolence, weeping
over each one as I wrote. It was truly an outpouring of
love for Buddie; and in reading the letters after a quarter
of a century, I feel that these letters could not be written

today. Friendship such as these letters show, could only be written in a small world—a more closely knit society. Today, one sends a brief note with flowers, or picks up the telephone and sends a telegram. We are all so rushed and involved that there seems to be no time left over for the amenities of life. Buddie and I were, both of us, extremely busy—we did not live a closed-in life. We were just as active as people today are—so I suppose that it was just an end of an era—expressing oneself by the written word has gone out of fashion. I only quote one, which although not describing Bud's qualities, explains a lot about me, and as this book is about me, I thought that I would include it:

> It is impossible to say anything that would convey the sympathy I feel in your loss. But I hope you will understand that how you are is a great tribute to Buddy. Only a woman who has been very happy with her husband would have the particular quality you have—anyone less happy would never have acquired that douceur which still allows you to be piquantly witty and gay. Your sadness is one that comes only after a lifetime of happiness and whatever you do in the future has a wonderful base.

I learned from Buddie's death that one should always go to the house of a friend who has lost a wife or husband. They need not see you if they don't want to, but they are usually so dazed that they need the warmth and affection of friends who show at once that they share in their grief. I used to feel that a family wanted seclusion and wished to be alone. Now I know better. I *take* flowers, I don't send them, unless I am ill, or if it is someone I only know slightly, but have liked. Letters are a great thing, too, because answering them is an occupation, and one must be occupied. I shall never forget the friends who came to see me.

I went back to *House and Garden* off and on, but my
heart was not in it. The nest had been destroyed, and the
bird had lost its eye for twigs. After Christmas the Field
children, Marshall, Barbara, and Bettine, presented me
with a round-trip first-class ticket to Europe. Jimmy Dunn
was Ambassador to France, and Mary had written me asking me to come over and stay with them in Paris. I simply
could not make up my mind about anything, but the Field
children insisted. "You must really have a change,
Brooke," they said, and so urged me. By the kindness and
thoughtfulness of these young people, and Mary's dear letter, I went to Paris. The residence of the ambassador at
that time was the late nineteenth- or twentieth-century
house that Ambassador Myron Herrick had bought and
was the last house on the Avenue d'Iéna. It was not a pretty
house, but wonderfully comfortable, and it gave one the
feeling that when it was built, it must have been filled with
Boldini and Tissot ladies, and that many beautiful women
in full décolletage must have slowly descended the curving
staircase in order to make a grand entrée and a great impression on an immaculately attired white tie group of
chivalrous gentlemen waiting below.

I was given a charming corner room on the third floor
with a wonderful view of the Eiffel Tower even from my
bed. Their two adorable little grandchildren, whom they
had adopted, were there with their governess, and I had
supper with them every night that the Dunns were out or
were entertaining. The little girls, Anne and Lexi, I had
known from their babyhood, but on that visit, I grew to
know them better. Anne, as she grew up, came to
America. Lexi stayed in Rome, then married a Frenchman;
and as the Dunns were living in Rome then, Anne became
like a daughter to me. I had always had a very special
place in my heart for her. She was the embodiment of
Ariel.

Being with the Dunns and being with the children was

a joy, as I felt totally at home; but it was only two months after Bud's death, and every morning I put his picture on my breakfast tray. It was impossible to reconcile myself to my loss. I went to call on Tanta, my mother's eldest sister, who was living in Paris. She was living in an apartment that she had bought for my cousin, Mary Clare, who with her husband, Jacques Bardac, was returning soon from Peking. Tanta herself had been a prisoner of the Japanese for eighteen months. Mary Clare and Jacques had the protection of the Pétain Government (Jacques was the head of the Banque Franco-Chinois) and had stayed unmolested in Peking, while Tanta was shipped off with other prisoners on a crowded cattle car to a Japanese prison camp near Shanghai. She said that when they left Peking, they were told that they were being taken to a country club; so, although they were only allowed to take what they could carry, some gullible characters were loaded down with golf clubs and tennis rackets. One woman wisely carried a pot de chambre, while Tanta wore as much clothing as possible and carried some light blankets and a small valise filled with underclothes and medicine. Even that was quite a load for a woman over seventy.

She was an absolute fiend for cleanliness, and that she weathered the eighteen months was a triumph for the will to survive, particularly as her job was to pick maggots with a crochet needle out of the meat they ate. The camp was organized by nuns and priests, who assigned jobs to everyone. The food they ate was thrown over the fence to them as though they were pigs, and they had to scramble to get it before the birds did. Tanta was brought back to America by the Red Cross, who shaved her head because of lice, fed her orange juice and vitamins, and rehabilitated her in general along with the other prisoners. She was now quite her old self, and had bought a nice apartment for Mary Clare, but at the end of nowhere.

I knew Mary Clare would hate the location, but Tanta

was delighted with it. It overlooked a *parc sauvage*, she said, but when I looked out of the window, all I saw was a raggedy-looking vacant lot. "Now, let me look at you," she demanded, putting her hands on my shoulders and turning my face toward the window so that I would have the full light on me. "Good heavens," she exclaimed. "You have certainly let yourself go. Do you realize that you are at the stage in life where, if a woman takes care of herself, she can look the same for twenty years; but if she starts letting herself go, as you have, she is finished." I did not relish these remarks from Tanta at all. "Buddie only died two months ago," I said, thinking how heartless she was. "I know that," she snapped, "but you are certainly no credit to his taste, looking as you do."

I could hardly wait to get away from her, but I have always remembered what she said. I thought she was dreadful at the time, but in later years, I have realized there was something in what she said. If someone has loved you very much, you owe it to him not to fall to pieces after he dies. You must continue to feel that he would be proud of you—not necessarily in looks, as Tanta said, but in your way of life and what you do.

I stayed about ten days or two weeks with the Dunns; then I began to get restless. I wanted my own things around me. Lela de Talleyrand came to see me one day, and when I told her that I thought of going home, she said that she thought it much better for me to stay in Europe longer. As she was going to her place in Rome, why not go down with her? She intended to motor down, stopping off for the night at Monte Carlo. So, after fond farewells to the Dunns, I started off with Lela.

It had been a very cold winter and the roads were icy. Lela was a very fast and very expert driver, and as we whizzed along, she suggested that we sing as we used to when we were young. I didn't feel much like it, but Lela started off with "I Hate to See the Evening Sun Go

Down." Then, on to "I'd Climb the Highest Mountain." I
joined her when she started on "The Darktown Strutters'
Ball." So here we were, two women approaching fifty,
singing the songs of our youth as the French countryside
rushed by; and to my astonishment, I began to start off on
my own when Lela slowed down. I always was devoted to
Lela, but she was especially wonderful at that moment in
my life. It all seemed a very natural thing to do, and I forgot to think of the last time I had been on this same road
with Buddie.

We spent the night in Monte Carlo. Lela went gambling after dinner and I went to bed. The next morning,
we started off, and were soon winding along the Italian
coast with the familiar golden broom-covered hills on our
left. We stopped for lunch at a primitive little restaurant
where we had excellent pasta al dente and a glorious view
of the sea—then on to Rome. We arrived there rather late,
but supper was waiting for us with a smiling staff in attendance. Lela and Elie's flat was at 3 Piazza Aracoeli in a
palazzo belonging to the Pecci-Blunts. The palazzo gets a
view of both the Vittorio Emanuele Monument and, far
far better, the magnificent Campidoglio with its Michelangelo architecture and equestrian statues. The flat itself was full of great drawings and fine furniture, as Elie
de Talleyrand was also descended from the Marquis de
Biron, who had been a great collector, and Elie had
inherited many of his things. Elie was still in Paris, so I had
his room right next to Lela; but after a few days, I got restless again. For some reason, I was always afraid that I
was about to have a heart attack and so I thought if it was
true, it was better to be at home. So back I came to that
apartment that seemed to echo with emptiness, and tried to
pick up the pieces of my life. I had a remarkable doctor at
that time who was of the greatest help to me. He gave me
vitamin B shots and other strengthening pills (I had become anemic), but most of all, he gave me good advice. I

depended on him, and he did not fail me. I went back to *House and Garden* without much zest, but with enough energy and good sense to try to do a decent job. It was, of course, an enormous help to be occupied. In the evenings I went out to dinner with just a few friends very informally, or would have a man and a couple to dinner at home. The Brook Club was still very faithful, as were other people, so that if I wanted there was always someone to come in for a drink or tea. In this fashion, the winter passed.

In the spring, two things happened. The first was that the C. D. Jacksons (he was Publisher of *Life* and special assistant to Henry Luce) were going off on a trip and then going back to Lenox for the summer. They offered their penthouse on East Fifty-ninth Street as a gift to Mother. It was the most thoughtful and welcome gift. Mother was overjoyed and so was I. She came down from Norwich and installed herself in this delightful apartment, which not only was bright and gay, but had a very attractive garden terrace with comfortable chairs and tables—a very nice place to have cocktails or a small buffet. Best of all, it was just around the corner from me. It was really made to order. The second thing was that Jim and Ellen Bruce came to tea with me one day. They were particular friends of Buddie's as well as mine, and we had gone several times to their shooting place on Pinckney Island just off the coast of South Carolina. Jim Bruce had become president of the Brook Club, and I have a feeling he was one of the organizers of the Brook Club visits. This time they had another mission. "We are giving a dinner party," they said, "and we want you to come." I had not been to any parties, and I was not sure that I felt like facing a crowd. "Just a few of our best friends," they said. "You really should start to go out." It was almost six months since Buddie's death and although I still wore nothing but black, I decided to go. It was a decision that changed my life.

PART III

Vincent

21

When I went to dine with the Bruces, I wore my very best dress. I remember it well. It was black tulle with a large skirt over many petticoats—the "new look" by Dior—and off the shoulders with a ruffled tulle fichu that tied in front. I remembered Tanta's words, and I wanted to look my best for Buddie's friends. I must have dawdled over my dressing because when I walked into the Bruces' large drawing room on Park Avenue, the other guests were already assembled. I knew them all well except for the Jack McCloys and the Vincent Astors. I had known Vincent for years, because when he was married to Helen (his first wife), he had come to Bernardsville, as Helen's younger sister, Alice, was Buddie's wife. We knew a lot of the same people, and I also saw them in New York, but Vincent had his own little clique who went off for six months at a time with him on his yacht, *Nourmahal*, all over the world; but most often to the Galápagos on scientific trips to bring back to the New York Zoological Society the special penguins and giant tortoises that are only found in those islands. I had known Helen, and she had sent a telegram of congratulations to us when Buddie and I sailed to Europe on our wedding trip. Minnie, Vincent's second wife, I hardly knew at all, but she was always very sweet and most responsive when we saw one another. The McCloys I had not known before, but Jack McCloy and I started talking at cocktails. He had a great deal to say of interest as he was much involved in world affairs, and I was really enjoying myself immensely when dinner was announced.

"Let's continue after dinner," we said to each other, and I was delighted that my evening "out" was starting off so well. There were sixteen of us, and we sat at two tables of eight. I sat between Jim Bruce and Eustis Paine. Vincent sat opposite me, and every time I looked across the table, I found him looking at me in an intense way. I could not understand why he was concentrating on me. What had I ever done to him? I wondered what was wrong with him. However, I did not really give it much thought as I was having a very happy time with Jim and Eustis, who were singing Buddie's praises and telling me the latest news of the Brook Club. It was a charming conventional evening, with a feeling of good will pervading, and no passions aroused.

The ladies went into the drawing room, leaving the men to smoke and chat in the dining room; and I had just started talking to Ellen Bruce when I heard a gruff voice behind me saying, "I must talk to you," and there was Vincent. He led me to a far corner of the room and when we were seated, said, "I must humbly apologize to you. I did not write you when Buddie died. I was out in Arizona, but I should have written you." "That's all right," I answered. "I got over fifteen hundred letters." "If we were alone I would kneel at your feet," said Vincent. "Tell me about yourself and Buddie."

I thought him very melodramatic, but I answered him in as matter-of-fact a way as possible. We sat there, he asking questions, me responding, until Minnie joined us and said that it was time to go home and could they drop me? I accepted, and off we went. In the car, Minnie asked me if I could come to them at Rhinebeck for the Memorial Day weekend. I was rather astounded as I was not really a friend; but they both urged me to come and when I got out at Fifty-seventh Street and Sutton Place, they both called after me as I dashed across the street. "We will ring you in the morning."

And so they did—both of them, but separately. Vincent rang to say that he was terrified to see me run across the street "like a small black rabbit," not looking to see if there were cars coming—and could he come around and have tea that day? I said no because I really did have another engagement; but he persisted, and we arranged for him to come the next day. A moment later, Minnie rang, saying, wouldn't I please come up to Rhinebeck for the Memorial Day weekend? Tony's birthday is May 30, and I had planned to spend at least part of that weekend with him. Still Minnie pressed on, saying, "Please think it over." So, as I practically never say no, I said that I would "think it over."

Well, there I was, giving in all along the line. The Astors were not close friends, and at the back of my mind I wondered why they were both so keen to have me. I knew that they had their own group, and that we only had a few friends in common. I was afraid that I would not enjoy myself and might easily bore them. As it turned out, Tony had other plans for his birthday, but I held onto that excuse, saying that I could not come out on Friday, but could come Saturday in time for lunch. Minnie seemed very pleased and said that a car would be at my door at ten on Saturday. All was decided.

Vincent came to tea, and we talked about the Zoo and all his Bernardsville friends. He wanted to give money to the Seamen's Church Institute, as Buddie's friends had all done; but I refused by saying that it was too late. Somehow, I did not feel that it would look right, particularly as I felt that he would probably have given a large sum to please me and not really in Buddie's memory. Actually, Buddie's friends had given so much that for one whole day a year the expenses of the Seamen's Church Institute are paid for in Bud's memory. (It is probably not enough now, but it was then.) Anyway, I refused.

I did not know what this beanstalk friendship was all

about. In my subconscious, I probably thought it was a whim of two rich people to have someone new in their lives. It was, after all, a short visit, and I was certainly no longer shy. Strangely enough, though it is only just now in my old age that I feel really sure of myself. I did not really have an inferiority complex after I was forty, but there have always been some people I cannot get along with—people who are competitive about everything, totally social people, and people who, to my mind, "run on a track." By that I mean people who see the same friends all the time, play cards every night, and games all weekend. They are so insulated that they can scarcely breathe under their coats of smugness. I am not an intellectual snob and I could soon be shown up in a group of intellectuals as being unknowledgeable and badly educated; but Mother taught me to "stretch my mind" and I like to learn something during a conversation. In this extraordinary century that we live in, there should never be a dearth of things to talk about.

When I arrived at "Ferncliff" in Rhinebeck, they were playing croquet in the indoor tennis court. Vincent and Minnie stopped playing and showed me to my room, then went back to continue the game. I came out after brushing my hair and washing my hands to find my old friends Kate and Bill Osborn in the big hall, which was also the main room of the house. Bill and Kate lived at Tivoli, a little further up the Hudson. Kate's first husband, Johnson Redmond, who died after being thrown from his horse while fox hunting in Virginia, had been one of Vincent's best friends. He and Kate had also been great friends of Buddie's and mine. I was pleased to see Kate, and Bill, too, who was an intelligent and attractive man. "I hear that they stopped their game and showed you to your room," said Kate, laughing. "You must be very important, Brooke. Vincent never stops a croquet game and never sends a car

into New York on a Saturday." I laughed. Kate was a
good friend and a great tease.

We were joined by the Olin Dows, also Hudson River
neighbors, and eventually, the croquet party appeared:
Vincent, Minnie, Fulco di Verdura, a lady whose name I
forget and Billy McCann. We had cocktails in the hall,
and I looked around at it. It was really quite hideous—
eighty feet long, with white columns at either end, with a
hall going toward the bedrooms at one end; at the other
end, marble steps led down to an Olympic-size glass-
enclosed swimming pool. It was actually, as I learned later,
the first indoor swimming pool-tennis court ever built in
this country and was designed by Stanford White.

The hall looked out onto a covered courtyard in the
front, where Vincent parked his cars. On the other side,
the huge arched windows looked onto the tennis court balcony. In other words, one might as well have been in the
subway for all the country one saw. The main light of the
room came from a round ornate skylight. The furniture
was uninteresting. I noticed the fireplace was filled with
ashes and no wood, and that the only flowers were Easter
lilies and hemlock boughs stuffed together in a huge vase
on a large table in the middle of the room! As a *House and
Garden* editor, I never would have photographed it. As a
person, I felt I never could live in such a depressing place.
It was the only room aside from the dining room. There
was an unused squash court, filled with trunks and odds
and ends, which I saw later.

During lunch Vincent announced that he was going to
take me for a drive after lunch. They all laughed at that,
and Kate bent across to whisper in my ear that nothing,
absolutely nothing, could change the routine of Vincent's
afternoon nap. The Osborns left soon after lunch as they
had things to do on their own place, and the others went
off to play canasta in the tea house. Minnie had asked me
to come along, but I said that I thought I would take a

walk in the woods and then meet them at teatime. Vincent went to his room, so when I was alone, I looked around the dismal room again; not a bookcase in sight, the unlaid fire and the dreary bouquet of hemlock and Easter lilies gave the whole place an air of neglect and unhappiness. I was glad that I was only spending one night.

At that moment, Vincent appeared from the hall that led to the bedrooms. "All set?" he asked. "Ready for a drive?" "Yes," I answered. "I'm all set." He backed the Mercedes out at a rapid pace from its parking place right next to the front door, and off we went; but we didn't go very far. We stopped abruptly under a tree, halfway between the main house and the tea house, which was only about the distance of a couple of blocks. Vincent turned off the engine, then turned to me. "Minnie wants to leave me," he said, "and up to now, I have refused to give her a divorce, but now that I have met you, I will give her a divorce if you will marry me."

I couldn't believe my ears. "But you hardly know me," I said. "We really don't know each other at all." I know a lot about you," Vincent answered, "and I have never known anyone to have more friends and be more loved and admired than you; and I can swear on the Bible that if you marry me, I will do everything I possibly can to take care of you and make you happy—and earn your love." Well, such suddenness would have thrilled me and elated me at twenty; but in my late forties I was frightened by it. It was something that a woman such as I am—impulsive and responsive—found tremendously appealing and very moving, but at the same time, I could hear Father saying, "Hold your horses, Brooke." I didn't know what to say, and I told Vincent so. I said that I couldn't possibly come to such a serious decision so suddenly, especially as I really had not recovered from Buddie's death. Vincent then said that Minnie was going away in a week to Europe and that he was going to Japan with Dr. Bruce Webster in July.

He said that I must think it over, and perhaps I could give him an answer before he left for Japan. He stressed all our mutual friends, many of whom he had not seen in years and whom, he said, he would like to see again. He gave me a big hug and a kiss and said, "Now we can take a drive."

We drove all up and down the Hudson River Valley while Vincent told me the most fantastic tales of the people whose houses we passed. They all had some eccentric streak in them, and there seemed not a normal one in the lot. "It's the shadow of the mountain that has fallen on them," declared Vincent, waving a hand toward the Catskills across the river. "They are all touched by it." I laughed at the time but later, when I got to know them, I could well believe it. The shadow of the mountain was a strong influence. We arrived back in time for tea, but the others were all still playing canasta. Vincent and I had tea alone. Then I went to my room for a rest.

I really couldn't rest at all because I felt that I was suddenly mixed up in a play and did not know the script. It was all totally unreal. It was far more dramatic than anything that had ever happened to me, and it seemed quite absurd that it should happen to me in middle age. I felt very strange when I joined the others before dinner, but they were all chatting away, and a few neighbors had arrived to add to the party. I wondered if Minnie knew what Vincent had said to me. If she did, it did not seem to matter. She was the same as usual—very sweet and gentle. I left after lunch the next day, and when I walked into the apartment, the telephone was ringing. It was Vincent at the other end of the phone wanting to know how I was and if I had had a good trip down.

Vincent called me constantly from then on and wanted to come and see me almost daily; but I was busy working at *House and Garden* and getting ready to move back to Tyringham for the summer. I had told Al Kornfeld that I was not sure whether I could continue. He told me not to make up my mind quickly but to take more time off and rest a bit. As it happened, I had quite a backlog of features. In fact, even several years after this, features that I had done kept appearing in the magazine. I did not feel guilty when I went up to Tyringham. I had really done quite well at *House and Garden*. My salary was now high up in five figures, which in 1952 was not bad at all. I had worked hard and with real zest because I loved it. It had made me into what is now called a liberated woman. Life held no terrors of insecurity for me anymore. I felt quite capable of earning my own living for the rest of my life if need be.

It was not the money that mattered so much to me, as the knowledge that I, Brooke, was not a parasite, but a person who could strike out on her own. Buddie, I knew, had been worried about my financial future because of his Father's will and his other obligation. He had wanted me to be able to keep Tyringham, which I could not possibly do on my reduced income. I was going back to Tyringham with all its memories to spend my last summer there. After that, I was going to put it up for sale. I had not really faced that fact, but I knew that it was unrealistic to think that I could run two houses. My lawyer still thought it possible to carry out Buddie's wishes as contained in his letter; however, even he was not very optimistic. A contract is a contract, is a contract—and to try and break it would be costly and perhaps futile.

With all these things in mind, and bracing myself for a return to Tyringham, I did not take Vincent very seriously. He was not a part of my everyday life—just an exotic episode—at least that was my thought at the time. I moved up to Tyringham and tried to pretend that Buddie was just off salmon fishing; however, I soon found out that I was not as good at pretending as I had been when I was a little girl in Peking. It was no use. Buddie was gone forever and I was lonely. As Arthur Krock had said to me years before, "Brooke, you are a confirmed bride," and so I suppose, I still was. I wanted someone to come home to, to talk to, to discuss things with, someone who had a strong shoulder I could cry on; someone I could surprise and make laugh—in fact, I wanted a life companion. It was as simple as that.

I agree now with Norris Darrell that people who have had very happy marriages are apt to remarry quickly after the death of their husband or wife. It is, in fact, a tribute to a happy marriage. Bad marriages make for happy widows and widowers. It was in this mood that Vincent began to roar into my life, and he literally roared as he drove like the wind over the hills and made the entire valley reverberate with the sound of his high-powered foreign car. Vincent said that he found my house the prettiest he had ever seen, my food the best, my friends the nicest, and I myself quite the sweetest and dearest "girl" he had ever known. In spite of myself I began to react a bit. It was rather nice to have all these things said to me. "Be careful," said some of my friends. "This is the typical action of a very rich man. They go after something until they get it, then once they have it, they lose interest." Others declared that Vincent had a vile temper, that he was quite impossible at times, and that I had better take a good long look at him. Well, I couldn't take such a long look, because he went off to Japan the first week of July after finally agreeing that it was all right for me to "think it over." "But I don't intend to take no for an answer," he said as he left. "Will you remember that? I shall write you as though all was settled." As he said this, I looked up at him (he was six feet, four inches), but in my heart I was not sure of my decision. I was beginning to feel Vincent's need for me, but I could not be unfaithful to Buddie.

Vincent was gone two months, and during that time, he wrote me at least five letters a day. Having been in the FBI and Naval Intelligence, he addressed each letter to a

different post office, so I was dashing from Great Barrington to Stockbridge to Monterey to Lee to Lenox and
Tyringham—in fact all over the Berkshires. It took up a
great deal of my time, but Vincent's letters were quite the
most beguiling letters I had ever had written to me, and I
had lived long enough to have received a fairly large number. I don't think that I would have married Vincent if it
had not been for these letters. I have the letters and am
going to quote from some of them here—not because I
want to "show off" and have people think, "Brooke must
have been quite a girl." Of course, everyone likes to be
told that they are loved, but I really want to show what
Vincent was like. He was a very private person, a sort of
prickly-pear person who was in fact very softhearted underneath and with a delightful pixie sense of humor. He
invented a dreadful old crone with the eyes of a hawk and
the tongue of a snake who he said was my "chaperone"
but also secretly in love with Vincent. A great many of
the letters contained detailed accounts of her Machia-
vellian tactics in regard to her dislike of me and love of
Vincent. I, of course, wrote defending myself and sending
out crashing broadsides regarding her slyness and duplicity.
I cut pictures out of books. One I particularly remember
was from Cecil Beaton's parody *My Royal Past* which
showed a frightful picture of an old crone walking across a
lawn, who I claimed was our chaperone, and Vincent responded by saying, "Why is that old hag trespassing on
my lawn?"

Vincent loved all of this and so did I. Our sense of
humor was a very strong bond between us. Anyway, as
Vincent said in his letters and as I said in mine, we really
got to know one another through our correspondence. His
sweetness and understanding about Buddie, his real need
for me, and the love that flowed through his letters all
combined to make me feel that if he wanted to make me
happy, I in my turn could spoon out my reserves from

twenty happy years and use them to bring happiness and peace to Vincent.

Vincent kept all my letters. But alas, two old house-maids who had been in his employ for many years, in a moment of misplaced zeal, took it upon themselves after his death to empty his desk of all his papers—not only my letters, but confidential reports from intelligence agencies he had worked with during the war.

When a woman marries a very rich man it is usual to say that she married for money. I know that these letters meant far more to me than money. A woman, they say, "will not die from want of love, but she will wilt." I feel wonderfully lucky that I was loved and cherished just when I needed to be. What woman in her late forties could resist such a hand when it reached out to her?

Here, now, is Vincent—speaking in his own very special way.

Vincent wrote me on the plane going to California. The weather was so rough on the plane that his hand-writing was almost undecipherable. He wrote:

A man must be hit by a nuclear bomb from Cupid to try to write on this damned plane—but write I must.

But Darling you must know by now that my one great ambition is to make you happy; and without the need for any specifications as I tried—perhaps stupidly—to express in my letter yesterday. If you have any lingering doubts of that, please for the sake of your old man, throw them away.

Dearest Brooke, if you wish to make me as great a gift as any woman ever made a man, you will sit down at once and write me that you love me and know that I love you from the bottom of my heart and that you expect me to forever and forever. Your love is the one thing that I most need and must depend on in all this world.

I shall now break my own self-imposed restriction

for mailing this to the over-worked Tyringham Post
Office.

Bless you Darling and please be happy.

From your loving and devoted
V.

Dearest Darling,

This letter is going to start out about me, and not
about you, which is, of course, the greatest mistake any
letter can make.

This place is quite extraordinary and I would not
have missed the trip for anything (although I shall be
glad to be returning to Tokyo in the A.M. after 2
nights). I should think that I am the first American
ever to be here. Furthermore, after my series of cultural
blunders, undoubtedly I am the last that they ever
desire to have with them and this is in spite of the vast
assistance of "Pak" and "Massai." Massai is absolutely
enchanting and gave me a huge pat on the back by
giving me permission to call her by that name which
is her first.

Some of the customs are a bit trying and the first
principle one must remember is that "nakedness is
nothing, but to notice it is unforgivable." While
shaving this morning in the public wash room I was
slightly startled (although forewarned) to have a nice
looking young lady enter, make me a very slight bow,
and then proceed with her ablutions.

Another seemingly odd custom and quite a nice one
too, is that servants are considered to be on equal terms
with their employers. For example, in this place I have
assigned to me as a maid, a really very pretty girl in an
extra grand kimono. At breakfast she shared half of my
peach and helped me to dress, from practical nudity
up, but had I made one "pass" at her, the whole hotel
would have been up in arms and I in lots of trouble.
Another rather odd intriguing custom is that one must
(repeat must) bring one's maid one or more mementoes
of places visited on an expedition. We did go on a

motor trip today (your St. Christopher clip certainly
worked overtime for a bit) so I left to Pak and Massai
the responsibility of getting the appropriate presents
with the following results—one postcard from our
village (12 yen) and one "pearl and diamond" ring
(750 yen = 2.07) from a town through which we
passed. The postcard I must give her tonight as an
evidence that she is not forgotten, but the ring not until
the last thing in the morning as we step into the car.
Furthermore, I must slip it on her finger myself, as
evidence that she earned it honorably. In this remote
valley a tip in cash would be the *injure grave*. Do you
think, Darling, that I can ever get the St. Regis employees to react like that? A bad bet, maybe. Speaking
of the St. Regis, I warn you, dearest "House and
Garden Brooke" that I shall expect lots of help on
doings over there.

This next letter is particularly sensitive, I think. How
could I resist its special appeal:

Your letter, a terribly sad one in parts, arrived
shortly after my breakfast tray. I do feel, Darling,
that you must stop torturing yourself concerning your
memories of Buddie and entirely irrespective of me.
God did dissolve your marriage whereas a court in
Idaho did the same for mine, artificially and not
through an act of God. Of course I understand how
you felt about Buddie's belongings still hanging in the
closet after his death. When Minnie failed to come to
Rhinebeck for a weekend in April, I felt miserable when
surrounded by her country clothes that she was not
there to wear, and her various bathroom gadgets. Those
are the ghosts of purely physical things that you eventually enabled me to forget; to put them right out of
my mind, as indeed I have.

Well, that is that. If you have it in your heart, please
write me a happy letter to Honolulu.

I do hope that you will not think that parts of this letter are too critical. If you should, just know that your old man loves you from the bottom of his heart.

V.

I still could not make up my mind. Mother was no help at all. "I think Buddie has sent Vincent to you," she said. "The sooner you marry him the better." This rather occult idea of Mother's made me wish more than ever that Father was around to put things in a better perspective.

At the beginning of September I went up to Bar Harbor to stay with Joe and Liz Pulitzer. Joe met me at the airport and immediately said, "What is this I hear? I hear that you are going to marry Vincent Astor." "I don't know," I answered. "I am really being torn apart by it all." That night after supper, when we three were sitting by the fire, I read them some of Vincent's letters. They found them just as beautiful and just as interesting as I did. I was very glad that I had read the letters to them, because the next day a cable arrived from Vincent saying that he was going to be in Hawaii on September 11 and would I cable him there saying that I would marry him fairly soon. I showed the cable to Liz and Joe and they both said, "Cable him 'yes.' You are not a woman to live alone. Here is a man obviously in love with you who wants to please you and make you happy and has the added advantage of being very rich. You are very foolish if you turn him down." I knew that they were good and true friends, and I valued their wisdom and understanding. I went into Bar Harbor and sent my cable. The die was cast.

I returned to New York about the same time that Vincent arrived, and it was not long before it began to appear in the papers that we were "an item." This upset me, but pleased Vincent. "You want to wait until after the date of Buddie's death," he said, "but it is much better to be married quickly and not be talked about." I had to agree. There really seemed no point in making him miserable when he obviously needed me. So, eleven months after Buddie's death, Tony, Vincent, and I flew up to Bar Harbor on October 7 and we were married before the fireplace in the Pulitzers' living room on October 8 with only the minister, a lawyer, the Pulitzers and Tony. We had caviar and champagne, and Tony presented me with the champagne cork, which I have to this day. The St. Louis *Post-Dispatch* "scooped" the news, and the New York papers headlined, "Vincent Astor, Incurably Romantic at 61—Elopes."

22

Our honeymoon trip was probably one of the shortest on record, lasting just about an hour and a half. We were in Vincent's *Mallard*, an amphibious plane built by Grumman, which landed on the river in Rhinebeck directly in front of the house. A launch was waiting for us, and half an hour after our arrival we were having tea in the hall.

I felt very strange—a new name, a new house, a new life. The house looked even worse than before, because the pictures had all been gifts to Minnie from Vincent, so the walls were bare, and the little tea house was almost totally empty. But Vincent was funny and dear and began making plans about Milnhouse, my house in Tyringham. His advice as an astute real estate man was to sell it with all the furniture, as he said that I could get a much better price for it furnished than unfurnished. But I did not want to be parted from furniture that I had had most of my life. I

even included a couple of mantelpieces that I wanted always near me (I am sitting by one of them as I write). We
went over once to have a look at the house but I couldn't
bear it and left it to Jepson, Vincent's steward, to do all
the packing up. When Vincent saw all my silver, china,
linen, etc. unpacked at Ferncliff, he said that he had married an heiress. When the dining room table looked particularly nice, he would say, "Pookie, are these yours or
mine?" I also came endowed with a Buick, a station
wagon, and best of all in Vincent's eye, a jeep, equipped
with a snowplow. The cars came over instantly, the other
lares and penates, later, including, of course, all my books,
which were to sit in boxes in the cellar until I could have a
library built.

The first forty-eight hours of our life together were
dedicated to exploring Ferncliff and its 3,500 acres. In
spite of his wretched childhood Vincent loved every inch
of Ferncliff. It was his "security blanket." The main house,
where he was brought up, had been torn down when he
married Minnie, and an octagonal and very pretty tea
house built in its place. Minnie had not wanted to live
where Vincent had lived with Helen, but actually it would
have been a much easier house to run than the tennis court
building which, although lovely on the outside, was extremely difficult to staff. (The staff's rooms were all in the
basement and who wants to come two and a half hours
from New York to sleep underground?) The basement itself was so large that a man was always stationed at the
back door in order to trundle groceries, etc., on a dolly to
the kitchen. It had been built in 1902 on the instructions of
Lady Ribblesdale (then Mrs. John Jacob Astor). Apart
from the indoor tennis court and Olympic-size indoor
swimming pool, it had a squash court, a dining room, six
bedrooms and baths and, of course, the huge main hall.
Aside from being a play house, it had also been meant for a
bachelor guest house.

Lady Ribblesdale, born Ava Willing of an old Philadelphia family, had been one of the great beauties of her day. She kept her marvelous figure by constant exercise and was an intrepid sportswoman. In fact at the age of fifty she was the only woman member of the bobsled team that won the gold medal that year at St. Moritz. It was said at the time of her marriage: "Jack Astor, and she was Willing" (considered to be very witty by the media of that day). She and her husband, Jack Astor, got a divorce when Vincent was fifteen. Divorces were quite uncommon in those days and Vincent, always shy, was very upset by the notoriety and by the curiosity of people his own age. He had lived all his young life in a household full of tension and unhappiness. He disliked his beautiful but habitually discontented mother and he loved his kindly father.

At the time of the divorce, he and his much younger sister, Alice, were given into the custody of their mother. She really could not have cared less about them, but it was the usual thing in those days for the mother to be given custody of children. A divorce was considered so horrid that it was thought that it could not possibly be the fault of a "lady."

Vincent went to boarding school at first, before the divorce, to a small boys' school in England; then St. George's in Newport. The summers were spent abroad with his mother, who was usually entertaining so much that she had no time for him. Fortunately for him, the alternative was to send him off with a remarkable man named H. V. Kaltenborn, who was the very well-known radio commentator and newspaper correspondent. They traveled all over Germany and Switzerland and Vincent learned a great deal from him. In fact, it was Kaltenborn who so interested Vincent in "news" that he, Vincent, eventually founded *Newsweek*.

However, the short school holidays were the happiest for Vincent because he spent them with his father at

Ferncliff, where his father was born. During the winter holidays he went iceboating up the Hudson with his father and played tennis and went swimming in the play house, and in the spring they went sailing and fishing in the Hudson, which was still possible in those days. Franklin Roosevelt, ten or twelve years older than Vincent, was his boyhood idol and was also an expert iceboat skipper. Mr. Robert Huntington, his father's friend, whose daughter, Helen, became Vincent's first wife when he was just twenty-one, was also an influence on him.

Sometimes in the spring, he went off yachting on his father's *Ava* or he would go to the Newport house for a weekend, but not for long. His father loved Vincent, but he was very busy courting younger women. Colonel Astor still lived in the vast house on the corner of Sixty-fifth Street and Fifth Avenue—now Temple Emanu-El—where Vincent was born. He was almost born at Rhinebeck and always deplored his mother's hurried visit to New York. "I should have been born in Rhinebeck," he said, "just like Father." I quite agreed with Lady Ribblesdale that to be in New York in those days was to be closer to a doctor and was safer in case of complications. The noise of the city, however, so shattered her nerves that straw had to be spread all along Fifth Avenue and Sixty-fifth Street in order to dull the sound of the passing carriages while she was convalescing from Vincent's birth. (The Astor house occupied the entire plot where the Temple Emanu-El now stands.)

Vincent was a small morose little boy kept out of the way by ever watchful governesses and tutors and growing more and more aware of being unwanted. I once asked him what his earliest memory was; and he told me that it was when he was four and his Nanny said, "Now I must make you look your best, Vincent dear. Your Mother is having tea in the drawing room and wants to see you." So she set to work and put on his best sailor suit and brushed his beautiful curly hair into a great crest on his head. Then she led him down into the drawing room, pushed him ahead of her at the door, but fortunately stayed quite close behind him—because when his mother saw him timidly standing there as she sat surrounded by friends at the tea table, she cried out, "Nanny, take him away, he looks perfectly *horrid*." Remembering my own happy childhood, this story really broke my heart. How could one not carry the mark of such a remark through life? Vincent did. It made him wary, cautious, suspicious, apprehensive. He was always waiting for the next blow. It took me time to learn this, and sometimes I suffered in consequence. But in the end, when his inner character became known to me, I marveled that he had sought me out and trusted me.

Actually, I was fond of Lady Ribblesdale and had often been to her apartment in New York when Buddie was alive. She was a true Edwardian, rolling her *r*'s and being very witty and cutting. It was lucky that I had liked her before marrying Vincent as in the end it was I who had to deal with her after Alice's death.

In that first week together at Ferncliff Vincent wanted me to see everything—the chicken house, where under electric lights hens were busily laying eggs twenty-four hours a day. The eggs were taken to the St. Regis, where the menu bore the proud boast "No egg served at the St. Regis is more than twenty-four hours old." The smell of the chicken house was enough to turn one's nostrils inside out, but Vincent was quite oblivious as we climbed through all four stories followed by the two chicken men, who had taken on the perfume of their trade. I was told that at one time there had been turkeys there, too, who for the last four weeks of their lives had lived on sherry and walnuts before giving themselves up to the Thanksgiving table. Vincent explained to me that turkeys were so stupid that they hunched together at one corner of their cage and climbed onto each other's backs until they suffocated. This in spite of the good life of sherry and walnuts and walking only on a luxurious floor of suspended chicken wire—a sort of trampoline. However, the poor things were so dumb that they died before their time. Vincent was impatient with stupidity in any form, so turkeys were definitely out. Next, we went to the very beautiful stone barns built by architect Harry Lindbergh on the edge of a big pond. This was the winter home of the 375 purebred Angus—a part of the herd which Vincent, in partnership with Allan Ryan, raised to sell for beef and for breeding. Angus are a beautiful breed of cattle—chunky and square with coal black shiny hides (every inch "pure beef," as the cattlemen said). Later, Vincent put a cattle call horn on my car, so when the cattle were grazing in the fields, I used to enjoy blowing my horn to see them stop grazing and come running to the fence. Whether it was a mating call or a cry for help, I never knew. But the dandelions and buttercups and corn that I brought seemed to please them.

Later the cattle sales on Allan Ryan's property became something I looked forward to. Immense crowds came from all over the world. Hot dogs and hot coffee were served, and the animals were led in one by one to a small exhibition pen while the buyers sat on bleachers encircling it. The bidding was always lively and the auctioneer extremely energetic. The animals looked magnificent and I remember Allan sending to Scotland for a specialist in Angus grooming. He flew over to braid their tails, comb their eyebrows and make their hides extra glossy with some special Scottish ointment. Prices were high, and I remember one young bull going for $300,000.

In that first week, when we had seen the chicken house and the cattle, Vincent took me for a ride on his miniature railway. There were two engines and a train of flatcars capable of carrying seventeen people. Vincent sat straddling the engine and I directly behind him and off we went over the two miles of track, which included quite a long trestle.

Vincent blew the whistle at turns, and I held on to him for dear life; on the first ride I was rather pleased that I arrived all in one piece back at the "roundhouse." Then we toured the estate, inspecting the six wells to find out exactly what their water level was, and drove up the rough road to the top of Mount Rutsen. This was a very wild place full of brambles and fallen trees, but it was the favorite haunt in the summer of the Rhinebeck Boy Scouts, who were given permission by Vincent to camp out there by a small pond. There were five attractive cottages on the place, but my favorite was the Pond Cottage—a little stone house built in 1640 by the Dutch with two-foot-thick walls on a wonderful site on the miniature peninsula which jutted out on to the large pond. One saw the pond from every deep-set window in the cottage, and wild irises grew along the bank in the early summer.

These tours took us most of each day, and I loved them; but things were not so attractive at the house itself. It seemed that there was a legend among the Hudson River aristocracy that there were no bugs on the river. Consequently there were no screens in the house, and I was horrified to see long ribbons of flypaper suspended from the kitchen ceiling. They were absolutely covered with struggling flies. One of the reasons for this tremendous invasion of flies was that Vincent had placed a salt lick for the cattle just near the kitchen windows. (That working part of the house was on the hillside, so it had windows.) The salt lick was placed there because Vincent could see it. This was all very well, but our bedroom and the adjacent porch were just over the salt lick. One afternoon when I was lying on a long chair reading, I looked down and found that I was completely covered from head to foot with quivering black flies. Vincent came into the room at that moment, fresh from his nap, and ready for a drive. "Vincent," I said, "look at me." "What's the matter with you, Pookie?" he said. "You look all right to me."

"Don't you see a resemblance between me and a piece of toast covered with caviar?" I asked. Vincent said something like "You always look better than caviar to me," but I eventually got him to admit that there *were* a certain amount of flies about, although he could not imagine why. I reminded him that the cattle were not exactly free of flies. Finally I persuaded him to have the whole house screened. This may seem a tiny triumph, but it had Vincent's cronies on the river in an uproar. It was a break in the tradition! Vincent's first wife, Helen Hull, was particularly outraged, and it was years before she screened her house, holding out only in her own bedroom, which was never contaminated by screening.

In a short time we settled down to a routine of spending the week at the St. Regis and Fridays to Monday mornings in Rhinebeck. We stayed at the St. Regis because Vincent thought that I would like to do over the apartment at 120 East End Avenue. He was certainly right about that. So while the work was being done we lived at the St. Regis. The apartment at 120 East End Avenue was huge, occupying a whole floor, but we got decorators, painters, etc., to work on it, and we hoped to be able to camp out there, at least, when we returned from Arizona.

In the meantime, I was beginning to learn a bit about Vincent's interests. Up to this time, I had only been made aware of his love for Rhinebeck, but in New York, I began to learn of his real and continuing interest in *Newsweek*, in the United States Line, and the St. Regis. At the instigation of Raymond Moley (who had been editor of *Today*), he had bought the title *Newsweek* in 1937 from a moribund publication and started to publish it in the form which it has retained up to this day. When I married Vincent the editorial office was on Forty-second Street and he went there every day. His real estate office was also there; at that time he was working on getting completely out of real estate except for the St. Regis. The Astors had always been big real estate holders in New York City, starting with the founder of the family, John Jacob Astor, who lived from 1763 to 1848. He is reputed to have lost interest in real estate as his biggest money-maker and gone into the fur trade after he saw four men in gray top hats in church one Sunday. "New York is through as a place to make a fortune," he said. "It is becoming decadent. I must turn to the West." Turn to the West he did, competing in fur trading with the Hudson Bay Co. and continuing his interests across the Pacific to trade with China. When Colonel John J. Astor, Vincent's father, went down in the *Titanic* on April 14, 1912, Vincent, aged twenty, left Harvard in order to start learning the family business, which at that time was confined almost entirely to real estate.

The first thing Vincent did was to sell all the slum holdings. He was horrified to learn that money could be made from someone else's misery. Vincent au fond was deeply concerned with what was going on in the world around him, and was a man who could have dedicated his life to the welfare of the less fortunate. He was, however, a product, and perhaps a victim, of his times and of his inheritance. In those days, a rich young man was not necessarily supposed to interest himself in the workaday world; and there were always people around to suggest that he go off and enjoy himself while they ran the business.

This happened to Vincent—older businessmen whom he admired and respected gave him a pat on the back and urged him to build bigger and better yachts and go off to the far corners of the world. At the age of twenty-one, he married Helen Huntington, the daughter of his father's old friend Robert Huntington, who was, in a way, a father figure to Vincent. Helen was the same age as Vincent, a stately beauty whom he had known from childhood. They were married only a short time when World War I broke out. Vincent immediately enlisted in the Navy and was assigned to submarine warfare, which was in its infancy at that time. This duty took him overseas to Brest, France, which was the home port of his unit. From there, the submarines made their forays into enemy waters. Helen and her great friend Ethel Harriman came over to work for the Red Cross and financed a canteen. (Ethel was the daughter of Mrs. Borden Harriman, who will be remembered as the first woman Minister appointed in the United States. She was sent *en poste* to Norway, where she acquitted herself with great distinction.) I gather that Ethel and Helen were a great combination and ran one of the most popular canteens in France. How different that "War to end all wars" was! Out of range of the guns, life could make a good show of continuing on "as usual."

Vincent rose to be a full lieutenant in the Navy. At the end of the war, he was in command of the captured German submarine U117 and was ordered to return her to the United States. He set out from shore, but no sooner were they at sea when it was discovered that there had been some sabotage and the sub was filled with strong gas fumes. Many of the men became ill, the speed had to be greatly reduced, and they limped into New York twenty-nine days after leaving France. Vincent had the bronchial tubes in his left side badly damaged and had a rattle in his chest for the rest of his life.

I do not know what eventually happened to Vincent and Helen's marriage. Perhaps, as in my own first marriage, they were both too young; instead of growing together, they grew apart. They had no children and lived in the vast gloomy house on Fifth Avenue and Newport and Rhinebeck, which must have been sad with no family. Helen interested herself in music, and Vincent was away for months on his yacht. When he was in New York, he was becoming more and more absorbed in his enterprises and not at all socially inclined. When World War II came around, he was back in the Navy within twenty-four hours and rose rapidly to the rank of captain, which was one of the things that he was most proud of in his life. It was soon after the war started that he and Helen got a divorce, and he married Minnie Cushing, the sister of the late Mrs. William Paley (Babe) and of Mrs. John Hay Whitney (Betsy). Vincent was Commodore of Convoy during the war and was also in the Naval Intelligence. The St. Regis became a "safe house" and William Stevenson, "A Man Called Intrepid," used it constantly. He and Vincent were great friends and at the end of the War, he gave Vincent a gold cigarette case with an inscription inside it which was one of Vincent's most treasured possessions.

Looking back, I feel that those war years took their toll of Vincent mentally and physically. He was not a regular Navy man, accustomed all his life to being at sea. So to be in command, to spend long hours on the bridge, and to be responsible for the welfare of his men and at the same time to be active in intelligence work—all this added up to a very strenuous and fatiguing job. However, when I once asked him (rather smugly, I suppose), "What were the happiest years of your life?" he answered, "You won't like it, Pookie; but I was happier during the war years than at any other time in my life." He paid a price for it in health, but whatever happiness we have in life has to be paid for in one way or another. Vincent's direct contact with all types and classes of men and his camaraderie with them added a new dimension to his life.

All of this I learned during those early months when we were getting settled down and I was fitting myself into the pattern of his life. Now I was to go to another house— in Arizona—which Vincent had chosen for the winter months because of his weak chest and cough. As was his usual custom, we flew out there in his plane, spending the night in Tulsa, Oklahoma, on the way. The Grumman *Mallard*, an amphibian, was very slow compared to the planes of today and Vincent did not want the pilots to fly more than six hours at a time. I must say that flying with

Vincent almost made a basket case of me on each and every flight. Having been a pilot himself—a member of the "Early Bird Society"—he detected unusual sounds in an engine which sounded perfectly normal to my ears. During landing and takeoff, he was particularly sensitive to every vibration. Our first flight across the continent was quite terrifying, but later I grew accustomed to his dire predictions. I wore my St. Christopher's medal and recited to myself the old proverb "Cowards die a thousand deaths, the valiant die but once."

23

The house in Arizona where I was to spend a part of the winter for the next eight years was a small white adobe house on the golf course of the Arizona Biltmore Hotel in Phoenix. Vincent told me that I would love it, and I did from the moment I set foot in it. The house, swimming pool, bathhouse, tool shed, and garage were on one acre, and the other acre was an enormous croquet lawn. A high hedge protected us from the road behind us, and in the front we looked out over the golf course to Camelback Mountain, which was shaped exactly like a sitting camel; and in the late afternoons, it and the other surrounding mountains took on the most marvelous shades of rose and purple. Vincent and I used to sit out beside the pool at "bird time"—the hour before sunset—and watch the absurd roadrunners coming up to our bird feeder and the Gambel's quails and the mourning doves and many other birds such as cardinals, thrushes and blue jays. Vincent had a

huge bird feeder made in the shape of a house, which had a
sign on it saying, "Astor House Annex—Birds Welcome."
Our little house itself was nestled down among flower beds
of snapdragons, ranunculus, African daisies, bougainvillea
(over the walls), and I put in climbing roses—"Break of
Day" and "Paul's Scarlet"—which eventually grew all
around the windows of our bedroom, and at the front door
was a huge bottlebrush tree.

That first winter, though (before we had the bird
house), I was not really content. I suppose that I expected
too much. After the blow of Buddie's death and then my
whirlwind courtship from Vincent, I imagined that I
would settle down with Vincent to a quiet tranquil existence—leading *his* life, but getting great satisfaction from
it. I had not counted on certain ties, and certain claims on
his time, that I found upsetting and humiliating. There
were in Phoenix at that time some people who had captured Vincent's friendship when he had been unhappy
there. He had sought solace with them, and they had taken
advantage of his weakness.

When I first appeared on the scene, they took it for
granted that things would be just the same. They flocked
to the house and behaved as though it was their own, and
the female contingent was particularly active. I went to my
room and wept—how foolish I had been to believe in those
love letters! Perhaps my friends were right: No sooner did
a rich man get something than he was bored with it.
I thought of Buddie and all my friends in the East and my
house in Tyringham. What was I doing out here all by
myself with no one to support me? Once again I remembered Father asking, "How did he behave under fire?" I
was under fire, and I was already wounded. Could I go
on? I looked at myself in the mirror and thought, "You are
a middle-aged woman, Brooke. If you are stupid enough at
your age to have made a bad bargain, you must still see it

through. It is your own fault that you were carried away by your emotions as if you were a teen-ager."

So when I heard them calling me for the croquet game I would slap on my dark glasses and sally forth. At least I had the sense not to make a scene; Vincent would neither have forgiven nor forgotten. Toward the end of our time there, Merton Powell, an old friend of Vincent's and mine, came out to stay with us, and so I had a sympathetic ally who was also devoted to Vincent. Whether or not it was due to Merton's presence or not, I know that before we left Phoenix things got better. These friends to whom Vincent had felt a loyalty began to seem less attractive to him; and as we met more and more people who were to become very good friends of ours, the others began to fade from the scene. In fact, they faded to such a degree that they eventually moved away; and we then made some of the nicest and warmest friends that anyone could possibly have; and I look back on my life at "The Wicket" (as I christened the house) as a very happy time.

Vincent thought that the air of Phoenix was good for him, but it really wasn't. The dust storms were terrible, and often we would spend a whole night walking the floor as Vincent went from one paroxysm of coughing to another; at the same time smoking a cigarette. It drove me quite frantic, but he quoted to me his favorite doctor, who had told him that he could smoke all he wanted and that smoking had never hurt anyone.

When that first winter was over, I went back to Ferncliff for the spring, but not before I had made plans to move our bedroom in Phoenix to the front of the house, where the view was, and to enlarge the cabana by the pool where one could shelter from the sun. I also ordered long chairs with parasols attached because the sun in Arizona is particularly strong.

Rhinebeck in the spring was lovely. The gently rolling hills on the east side of the house were covered with hundreds of thousands of daffodils and the willows by the pond dropped pale yellow-green tendrils in the water. The dogwood gleamed through the pine trees in the woods and even the Hudson was sometimes a bright blue. As the weather grew warmer, Rhinebeck could be very hot. There would be an intense stillness in a late June day, the sky would become overcast, and claps of thunder would send the dogs running to hide under the beds or sofas. "Father Knickerbocker bowling," it was said, as the rain came down in torrents and the thunder clapped.

Then the storm would be over. The cattle would come out from under the trees, the dogs would leave their hiding place, and it would be hotter than ever. This had been the reason for Newport and the yacht; but they were gone—the house sold, and the yacht given to the Navy at the beginning of the war. The solution for Vincent was Europe. He was not really so keen on going that first year, but he said there was so much that he wanted to do with me, particularly to stay with his friend Fulke Warwick (the Earl of Warwick), whom he described to me as a brilliant, cultivated man. "He will take you around and show you all the things that your old man knows nothing about," he said.

We crossed on the *America* of the United States Line and had the "Duck Suite," a really beautiful suite: in fact, the *America* was one of the most attractive and well-planned ships that I have ever traveled on. Naturally, with Vincent's connections with the United States Line, we got superlative service, which added to our enjoyment of the trip. We had a perfect trip in every way.

When we landed, we went immediately to London to Fulke Warwick's house in Swan Walk, Chelsea, a lovely little street one block long which ended at the Thames embankment. Years later I was to have several friends who lived there, but at that time I was new to that part of London. Before the war, the fashionable thing was to live in

Mayfair, which included Berkeley Square and Grosvenor Square and all the streets opening off these squares; but after the war, and the bombing (Mrs. Marshall's house, 6 Grosvenor Square, and the house next to it were totally destroyed) people branched out and lived wherever they could find an attractive house. We stayed there at Swan Walk while Vincent visited his tailor and shoemaker and I went to the Victoria and Albert, the National Gallery and the British Museum. When the weekend came, we went to Warwick Castle, where we had most romantic rooms looking out onto a broad river with a rushing current and a waterfall that filled our rooms with thunder. Warwick Castle—now, alas, the home of Mme. Tussaud's waxworks —was a treasure trove of art—Canalettos stacked up on the floor, fourteenth-century tapestries on the wall—magnificence everywhere, including the famous Warwick Vase, then lodged in a garden pavilion and not looking the vast size which it really is.

Stavros Niarchos, who was a friend of Fulke's, had given him the "bare bones" of a small yacht of his called *Eros*. Vincent was to pay all the expenses and just the three of us were to go on the cruise. Kate and Bill Osborn were staying at Warwick at the same time we were, and I clung to them. I dreaded the trip. I had sensed that after one look at me Fulke disliked me and thought Vincent could have done much better for himself. As Cole Porter wrote, "It was just one of those things" between Fulke and me—but in reverse to Cole's meaning. However we were doomed to be together for two weeks on the misnamed *Eros;* and I was determined to try and make the cruise as happy as possible for Vincent, particularly as I had not been pleased with that little clique in Phoenix and I did not want Vincent to feel that I disliked his whole group of friends. Vincent, of course, saw nothing of all this, and after the weekend, we set off for Paris and were going to head on down to Portofino to meet Fulke there.

We had a glorious time in Paris, staying at the Ritz and doing all the frivolous things that the very rich are supposed to do. Vincent went to all the "collections" with me, and together we settled on Balmain, where I had to restrain him from buying out the collection. Then we drove out into the country for lunch; back to the Ritz for a nap; then either shopping again, or Vincent would go to the Jockey Club and I would see a few friends. My cousin, Mary Clare Bardac and her husband, Jacques, had returned from China, so they often joined us. Either they dined with us, or we went to them in the out-of-the-way, but attractive, apartment where Tanta, just a little over a year before, had told me that I looked a mess and owed it to Buddie to make myself more attractive. Now, of course, she was delighted with me and felt that I had really done the right thing for the Howards. (In case you have forgotten it, my mother was a Howard.)

It was at the Ritz that I did the most frightful thing. Vincent was smoking and coughing like mad and, as a dutiful and loving wife, I approached him with a tablespoon and a bottle of cough medicine. A very dear and touching scene, but, alas, in my hurry to help him, I had snatched up a bottle of tincture of benzoin instead of cough medicine. Imagine my horror when I saw Vincent turn bright red and begin spitting out the dreadful stuff. I called the desk and, thank heavens, a doctor came at once who gave Vincent an emetic and large doses of warm milk. From that day to this, I don't even give someone an aspirin without surveying the bottle carefully on all sides. Vincent forgave me, but I never have forgiven myself.

The trip to Portofino reminded me a little of my trip with the Kusers. We had brought over a large station wagon on the *America* and so we piled into it for the trip. The English chauffeur, Vincent, and I squeezed into the front seat while in the seat behind us, the personal maid and Vincent's valet sat in stately and silent comfort. Behind them, our luggage was piled up to the roof of the car. The maid sulked the whole way down to Italy. The valet tried to talk to her, but she would have none of it. We shed them both, fortunately, after they had unpacked for us in our cabin.

The *Eros*, as I remember it, was neither large nor luxurious—a rather tublike ship with little deck room and pokey cabins. After a quick look around, Vincent was very disappointed. But that was nothing compared to how he felt when he looked up at the large and gleaming yacht *Creole* anchored alongside of us. Vincent's *Nourmahal* had had eleven large passenger cabins, each with bath, a very large dining room, a library and a main living room with a real fireplace. Although she was a motor yacht, she had a crew of sixty and he had sailed the Atlantic many times in her; and as I have already noted, he had also been to Galápagos, Easter Island, Indonesia, etc. And now we were about to go cruising on something that looked to him like a tugboat.

Matters were not improved when Fulke told him that *Creole* also belonged to Niarchos, that we were expected on board for drinks that night and, worse still, that we were to spend the entire two weeks cruising together in tandem. Vincent was furious at these arrangements. He would not have minded if a friend of his had a better boat, in fact he would have enjoyed visiting the yacht from stem to stern; but to be overshadowed by someone he had never heard of (he had led a sheltered life) was just too much. We went on board the *Creole* for a drink, but had dinner in the piazza, which was fine for me as I saw Mario, our boatman in the castèllo days, and Nino, the padrone of the Ristorante Nazionale and all the lacemaking ladies at their bobbins. Vincent loved meeting all these old acquaintances of mine and was quite overcome that I could still rattle off a bit of Italian. When we returned to the yacht, I went to my cabin and Vincent stayed up to talk to Fulke. What course the conversation took, I am not quite sure, but I do know that we left the next morning, unaccompanied by the *Creole*.

We cruised to Sicily—not to Palermo, but to Taormina and Catania. Fulke was not in the mood to sight-see, but Vincent, who was an avid vulcanist took me all over Mount Etna—in fact we had a picnic lunch on the rather uncomfortable black rocks. The weather was perfect, but we had to leave the yacht twice to go to Rome as Vincent had a toothache. This wretched tooth became worse and worse, and finally Vincent had to have it pulled out at Capri, a place which I cannot recommend for painless dentistry. We approached the dentist's office at night, following a guide who, with a flashlight, led us along a winding rocky path. A huge, snarling dog greeted us at the gate to the dentist's villa, but was subdued by a young lady who ran out of the house with a leash. Inside the house was another dog of the same breed—a mixture, I would say, of a Dalmatian and a Great Dane. This dog was most amiable and followed Vincent right into the dentist's office. "He hates to see me hurt people," said the dentist laughingly as the dog put his paws on Vincent's chest. Vincent was about to reply when the nurse stopped him by giving him a tumbler full of brandy to drink. "This is our anesthetic," she said. Vincent gulped it down and that was that. My only comfort was that the dental equipment looked familiar and they told me that it was American, sold by the Army when they were ordered home. Needless to say, our trip back over the unlit path was rather hazardous.

Vincent, who had a navigator's license and was himself a skilled skipper, was extremely apprehensive about other people's skills at sea. He was particularly nervous when the yacht was about to dock, and would rush up to me and say, "Pookie, go below at once. Get into the bathtub with some blankets around you. We are about to dock." His fears were not really justified, but I knew from that first trip that unless he was in total command, we would never go yachting again.

In fact, that whole trip made me feel that Vincent really was happier at home than anywhere else. So after I had picked up my dresses in Paris and we were safely back on the *United States*, I ventured to say why didn't we skip Europe another year. Vincent looked astounded. "I thought every American woman's dream was to spend the summer in Europe." he said. "Not mine," I told him. "I love Europe, but I know it very well and so do you and I don't feel that you enjoy it as much as you did when you were younger." "What can we do?" said Vincent. "We can't stay in Rhinebecky all summer, it's too hot." "What about Maine?" I asked; and so we began planning to go to Maine.

Soon after we landed, we went up there to look for a house and I found "Cove End," a white shingled house on a cove with a fine view of the sea and apple trees and lilac bushes in the dooryard. We rented it for the following summer. Vincent took my word for it, as he had stayed in the car. I was deeply content, for I have always loved Maine, and Vincent also breathed a sigh of relief. He immediately started on plans for a forty-eight-foot cruiser to be built in Holland, and he bought (from a catalog) the smallest fiberglass sailboat available. "We don't want anything that would be capable of racing," he said, "because we would win every race."

24

I suppose that it was Vincent's love of life at sea, with its emphasis on routine, that made him wish to conduct his life on land in the same way. Two months in Maine in the summer; Rhinebeck in the spring and autumn; 120 East End Avenue, New York, in the winter with the weekends in Rhinebeck; and from the middle of February to the middle of April in Arizona. *That* was the way we lived.

He did not enjoy a social life, and the only large party we ever gave was during the first winter of our marriage. It was a dinner-dance for 275 people at the St. Regis roof. The idea of a dinner-dance appalled Vincent, but I felt that we should make one gesture at least to the outside world. Vincent insisted there be no dance music while dining. Instead, we had sixteen violins moving romantically around the room during dinner; and the dance music afterward. The whole dining room of the St. Regis was lit entirely by candles. There were pink tablecloths and huge bunches of pink roses on every table. I wore the most beautiful dress I have ever owned, which we had chosen in Paris and which was made by Balmain. It combined turquoise satin knots over the shoulders, a waist of dark green satin, and an emerald green satin skirt so large that it took two maids to press it. To complete the color scheme, I wore my new aquamarine necklace and earrings and my emerald engagement ring.

It was truly a gala and great fun. Vincent exclaimed

that it was extraordinary that we knew so many people and hoped that we would never feel inspired to give such a party again. Nevertheless he stood with me on a small Persian carpet—the St. Regis' idea of Vincent's importance. He never even noticed it—but he stood on it patiently and shook the hand of every guest. He appeared to have a marvelous time, although he went home early while the rest danced on until after three. When I came home he was still awake, astonished and childishly delighted by the success of the party. But that was our only gala party. From that time on, we had only a few dinner parties and entertained mostly at Rhinebeck over weekends, with longer-staying guests in Arizona.

It was about then that I got to know the English Astors. Bill Astor—Lord Astor—whose mother was the famous Nancy Astor (born Nancy Langhorne of Virginia) —came to Phoenix several times. We had seen Nancy Astor in England; but she never came to Arizona. Though American by birth, she, as everyone knows, was the first woman Member of Parliament and later became Lady Mayoress of Plymouth. She and Vincent disliked each other intensely. She was a teetotaler and a Christian Scientist and Vincent loved his martini and was mesmerized by his doctor. He and Nancy fought like cat and dog over these differences. I found her fascinating. She was a destroyer of people in a way—but in a very witty way, so that one could not help but be delighted by her marksmanship. Bill Astor was really overwhelmed by his mother; and as I grew to know them over the years, I became more and more fascinated by Nancy and more and more sorry for Bill. He seemed to have very little of the Langhorne dash. During the last twenty years, I have known and grown very fond of the English Astors, Michael and Jakie on one side, Gavin (Lord Astor of Hever) and John and Hugh on the other. They have made me feel very much a part of the family and I, having so little family of my own, am very grateful. Michael, who has just died, was really the one closest to me—he and his dear giving wife Judy.

In Phoenix we made friends with the Wrigleys (P. K. Wrigley of chewing gum fame), who owned the Arizona Biltmore Hotel and also the golf course around which houses, including ours, were built. They were a very shy and socially timid couple but once one broke through the barrier, they were marvelous friends. Helen was a tiny woman and reached only a bit above Vincent's waist but she was a great croquet player and usually teamed up with him. He was devoted to her and I loved her. She was one of the few really good people I have ever known and she continued to be my friend until her death. I ventured forth to "Taliesin West," where Frank Lloyd Wright lived as a super guru surrounded by dedicated disciples in a collection of buildings resembling an elegant commune. Vincent refused to go, because in the Imperial Hotel in Tokyo (designed by Wright), the ceilings had been so low that his whole head was covered with scratches and bumps. Apart from that, he and Frank Lloyd Wright were far too positive and sure of their own viewpoints to ever give an inch. There could never have been any light conversation between them. It had been attempted once in Minnie's day with disastrous results. I went several times and was impressed by the power Frank Lloyd Wright wielded over his group. His word was law and no task was too menial for those budding architectural students. To wash the Master's clothes, to vacuum his sitting room, was a joy for them. When the Master and his party walked into their communal dining room, the students all rose silently to their feet and stayed standing until the Wright party was seated on the raised dais.

These students all paid for the privilege of spending the winter months with the Master. The wives of the married students did all the cooking and were busy not only

cooking the meals but preserving and canning all the left-
over fruit and vegetables. They gave plays, too, and concerts; I remember one when Frank Lloyd Wright, clad entirely in white, stood up in the front row and said, "If any
one is paying for this performance, they ought to leave at
once and demand their money back." It was particularly
hard on the performers as it was a benefit for charity and
most of the audience had paid a good price.

The Henry Luces bought a house next to ours after I
had been there a year or two. Clare imported exotic characters like the writer Gerald Heard, who was experi-
menting with LSD, and John Courtney Murray, the brilliant Jesuit priest who was at the Jesuit headquarters in
Woodstock, Maryland. Father Murray was an excellent
croquet player and therefore a welcome visitor to The
Wicket. Merton Powell usually came for at least a month
and I took a piano lesson from him every day in order that I
could accompany myself when I sang to Vincent at
Rhinebeck. Our life at Phoenix was the most social part of
the year as at Rhinebeck we saw only the same "old
Hudson River" characters and, of course, Vincent's sister,
Alice; but in Phoenix we really blossomed out and saw
people constantly.

These nice, genial, kind people were just what Vincent
liked. Best of all, we were away from his doctor, who I
felt encouraged his tendency to hypochondria.

I felt then, as I feel today, that Vincent could have
lived much longer if he had given up smoking, but his doctor told him smoking could do no harm and it was only
when his foot turned black from lack of circulation that he
gave it up. He revered her and thought she could do no
wrong. He had wanted me to go to her too, but I decided
that she was not for me. I told Vincent that, great as she
was, I thought that it would look very shabby of me to
leave my own doctor, who had looked after me for twelve
years, just because I had suddenly become Mrs. Astor.

Vincent understood loyalty; and although he had no confidence in the doctor of my choice, he immediately sympathized with my reasoning.

When his doctor died some time after Vincent's death, I went to her funeral out of respect for his memory. She had a glamorous group of patients and the church was packed. Men of substance and position rose up to eulogize her. As I sat squeezed into a pew, I felt a dreadful pain in my heart and I thought to myself, "This is it. The old witch is going to strike the unbeliever dead." But then my father's example took hold of me and I knew that I had never harmed her while she was alive, and that if the human spirit knows truth when it leaves the body, she must at that moment be aware of that fact. However, I was glad to leave the church quickly and did not linger to feign grief.

Vincent's sister Alice and her four children lived in the house next to us at Rhinebeck. I had known Alice slightly for years and always thought her a most unusual person. She had the look of a Persian princess, with a rather secret oval face and coal black hair. She was tall and very slender and dressed in a way all her own: never eccentric, but always becoming and, in the evening, romantic. She was eleven years younger than Vincent and they had never gotten on very well. It started, I think, when Alice got a divorce from Serge Obolensky, her first husband. She had married Serge, who was older than Vincent, when she was in her early twenties. Serge, His Serene Highness Prince Obolensky, was a marvelous-looking man until the day of his death—tall, aristocratic, full of life and courage. When Alice married him, he must have been like a fairy-tale prince. He rode beautifully, danced like a dream and up into his eighties could still do wild Russian dances dressed in a Cossack costume. Vincent was devoted to him and admired him for his great physical courage, which he demonstrated particularly in World War II, when in his early fifties, he became a paratrooper in the U. S. Army and took part in three invasions. After the war, he dropped the title of Prince and preferred to be known as Colonel Obolensky.

He and Alice were married several years and produced two children, Ivan and Sylvia. I was not married to Vincent then, and so am not sure just what happened, but Alice fell in love with Raimund von Hofmannsthal, the son of Hugo von Hofmannsthal, the Austrian poet who wrote the librettos for Richard Strauss, and she left Serge in order to marry Raimund. Vincent was furious and stuck to Serge and that was the beginning of a rift between brother and sister. Subsequently, after having one child by Raimund, she divorced him. While staying in England during the war, she fell in love with Philip Harding, whom she reputedly met while she was manning a gun. (The idea of Alice manning a gun is enough to terrify anyone who knew her, but she was brave.) She married him. After the war, on returning to America, she was divorced from Harding, by whom she also had a child, and married David Pleydell Bouverie, a cousin of Lord Radnor. They were already divorced when Vincent and I were married.

When I came to live in Rhinebeck, Alice was again single and was surrounded with an interesting group of friends: John La Touche, Tennessee Williams, Gore Vidal, Aldous Huxley, Tchelitchew (who did a portrait of her), Iris Tree, and from England some of her nicest friends including Osbert Sitwell and his sister Dame Edith and Frederick Ashton, the choreographer. Later on her friends grew more and more exotic. They even went so far as to make her feel that she might be the reincarnation of an Egyptian princess, thereby causing her to start learning Sanskrit. Alice, like Vincent, was a victim of her childhood and had deep roots of unhappiness. She was endowed with so much—looks, distinction, intelligence, a very special aura and charm and a very soft heart—but alas, she had very little common sense and no sense of humor. In spite of her eccentricities, she was a marvelous housekeeper. Her meals were superb and her houses both in Rhinebeck and in town were cozy and intimate. She created an atmosphere that has meant much to her children and she left a strong imprint on them.

Vincent and she were on bad terms when I came to Rhinebeck, but I tried to bring them together. When Vincent talked about Alice *in absentia* he always spoke fondly of her; but her friends and her "causes" irritated him, and when they were together things did not go so well. She died three years before Vincent, and he was very upset by it. I am happy that on Vincent's birthday, the year that she died, she gave him an old painted Sicilian cart for our donkey Piccolina. I have a picture of Vincent pulling it with Alice sitting in it; and I love it because they are both smiling, which was rare for them when together. But even though Alice and her coterie irritated and bored him, I never saw him do a really unkind or nasty thing to her. The same with Lady Ribblesdale, who made Vincent indignant when she returned to New York at the beginning of World War II. He felt that as she was the widow of an Englishman, she should have stayed there. He had very strong views about patriotism and duty to his country. However, when Lady Ribblesdale came to New York and most of her money was tied up in England, he helped her out very generously.

Lady Ribblesdale was a period piece and even in old age a classic beauty. I loved to go to lunch or tea with her and get her to talk about Alice Keppel, and Lord Curzon and "the Marlborough House set." She had a very direct way of summing people up, sitting at her richly laid tea table, with a small hat tilted to one side over her still beautiful face, a large necklace of pearls around her snow-white throat, and a cigarette in a long gold holder in her lily-white hand. She would look at me with her piercing blue eyes as I plied her with questions. "Tell me what it was about Lord Ribblesdale that you found the most attractive?" I asked, seeing in my mind's eye the Sargent portrait of Ribblesdale as the very acme of elegance in his riding clothes. Lady Ribblesdale blew the cigarette smoke out of her mouth before replying. "He was so suave," she answered. It seemed a strange quality to look for in a husband, but as she faced me across the table, I could see how such a man would fit into her life. On another day we were speaking of a man who had recently come on the New York scene and whom she had met and disliked. "You must forgive him, Lady Ribblesdale," I said. "He is a rough diamond." She answered rolling her *r*'s, à la Marlborough House set. "Not a rough diamond," she said, "a r-r-rhinestone." I used to laugh with her and always came away quite exhilarated with her tales of London at the beginning of the century.

Vincent and Alice had one thing in common—they were both terrified of their mother. Alice always sat on the edge of her chair looking nervously about and jumping up to draw a chair near the tea table for a new arrival or rushing out to call the butler—anything to keep busy and out of range of Lady Ribblesdale's sharp inquiries. Vincent, on his part, always put on a blue suit when he called on his mother and wetted down his curly hair so it would lie flat. He only went to see her when I goaded him on and then he asked if it could just be the three of us. Lady Ribblesdale's secretary would say yes, but when we got there we always found two or three of the sort of tabby-cat men who like to court rich old ladies. Vincent would give them a glare and, after one perfunctory cup of tea, would say that he had to leave. It was really quite sad, because all three of them—Lady Ribblesdale, Alice and Vincent—needed each other. They wanted to be a family, but it was impossible for them.

Soon after we were married, I discovered that Vincent was extremely jealous. He was jealous of my old friends, particularly those associated with Buddie who had been a very important element in my life. He did not want me to see any of them. One has to nourish a friendship. When it is deprived of meetings, or telephone calls in which joys and sorrows are shared and innocent gossip exchanged, friendship withers like a plant in winter. Of course it can be renewed, but I lost many friends forever. Worst of all, Vincent was jealous of Tony. Tony was not happy in his own life at that time; so this was very hard on me. Vincent did, however, adore my twin baby grandsons and we often had them to stay with us. Vincent carried them around in a huge dog basket in the evenings after their supper and played all sorts of games with them. As they grew older, he also led them around on Piccolina, the donkey, and when they spent a summer with us in Maine, he took them sailing almost every day. He said that he thought that we should adopt them as we "had more sense than their parents"; but I never broached this subject to Tony or his wife as I knew quite well what the answer would be.

Vincent really had a phobia about the telephone, and he asked me never to telephone my friends when he was in the house. As he never went out until 10 A.M. and was back at three, this pretty well cut me off from telephoning.

Sometimes I got depressed, thinking of all my friends chatting away together and seeing one another daily, but I have a naturally happy and cheerful nature. I also knew that Vincent loved me deeply. It was *his* life that I had made up my mind to live, *not* my own. I had had so much happiness and love, and he so little. In his heart he was still that same small boy who had been locked in a cedar closet by his mother and forgotten. He was six feet four with a booming voice and a great air of authority and assurance, but underneath he was very vulnerable. I gave up my friends. I saw very little of Tony. I concentrated on Vincent. It was what he longed for and needed desperately and it was what I had to give. I made that gloomy house into a cheerful, attractive *home*. I played croquet and sniff (a domino game) and backgammon. I would play the piano (badly) and sing for hours at a time while Vincent sat near me urging me on with, "Play the 'Dritte Mann' again, Pookie," or, "Let's have 'Wouldn't It be Loverly' just once more." He claimed that I could have made a fortune on the stage or at a nightclub (not true!). He did it sometimes to tease his first wife, Helen Hull, who took her music very seriously and practiced several hours a day, but he would extol my accomplishments to her. "She's nothing like you, Pookie," said Vincent to me. "Just tinkle, tinkle blue note." This, of course, was totally untrue, but I can't say that I minded it. My greatest bond with Vincent was a mutual sense of humor. No matter how depressed he felt about some business matter, or by his morning sessions with his doctor, I could always pull him out of it by making him laugh. I tried in fact to do what I had set out to do after I married him: to make him happy. I hope I did.

One of the benefits of not being social was that we discussed anything and everything that was of interest to one of us, or just what came into our minds. We talked about whether *U. S. News and World Report* was coming up as a rival to *Time* and *Newsweek*; whether all reporters should have by-lines; how much stock should be given to editors and whether only to senior editors. We talked about the running of the St. Regis and whether the freighters of the United States Line could have roll on/roll off containers without having trouble with the Maritime Union. We talked about the farm. "Give up the cattle when I am gone," he said. "It's not a woman's game. You wouldn't stand a chance against those cattlemen." We talked about the U. S. Navy and its future and the Vincent Astor Diagnostic Clinic at New York Hospital and the future of the Vincent Astor Foundation, which during Vincent's lifetime had a rather small income for a foundation. "You are going to have a hell of a lot of fun running it, Pookie," he used to say, and by "fun" I knew that he meant satisfaction. Looking back, it makes me happy that we had those talks. Vincent always said that he was going to live for at least ten more years but that he wanted me to know everything about his interests. Thank heavens I did know something, because the cards were already being dealt in ways we had never anticipated.

25

The first blow was Alice's death from a heart attack in 1956. We were up in Maine when Alice's son Ivan called us and tried to break the news gently. Vincent at once noticed his tone of voice and demanded to know the facts. We, of course, prepared to go to New York immediately. Our plane unfortunately was having its annual checkup (Magnaflux) at Pratt and Whitney, so we had to pull every wire to get on a commercial flight as Maine was not very well endowed with an air service at that time. Lady Ribblesdale was staying at the hotel in Northeast Harbor, so I rushed over to tell her that we were going down to see Alice, who was quite ill. I could not leave her to face the news of Alice's death alone, and wanted to tell her the sad fact on my return.

It was a very depressed and confused little family who greeted us. The two older children were there—Ivan and Sylvia, married; Romana, engaged, and Emily, only fourteen. Ivan and his father, Serge Obolensky, were making all the funeral arrangements, which were to take place at Rhinebeck. We went out to Ferncliff, and the first night two men drove up to the house and asked to see Vincent, saying that it was most important. Vincent saw them at once in the library and when they left a half hour later, I could hear him at the front door in a towering rage. "Get out, and don't ever let me even see you again," he roared. I ran out to the hall to join him as I heard the door slam. "Tell Jeppie to mix me a double martini," he said, "and not to let any of the household use the telephone. I am expecting a call." I sat down beside him after telling Jepson about the martini and could see that he was literally trembling with rage. "For heaven's sake, Vincent, what is it?" I asked. "Whatever is the matter?"

Vincent then told me that these so-called friends of Alice's had come to him to say that they thought that she had committed suicide and that if Vincent would give them a rather large sum they could prevent the coroner's office from performing an autopsy. They hinted that unless the autopsy was stopped, there might be some very disagreeable publicity. He said that he told them to wait while he got his doctor on the telephone. In their presence, he asked her to have the Chief Coroner of New York City, Milton Helpern, perform an autopsy at once and to telephone Vincent when it was completed. "That's my answer," said Vincent to the two men, and when they lingered, he showed them to the door (none too politely, as I had overheard). "I must know the truth about Alice," said Vincent, "and her children should know. They should not go through life in doubt about their mother's death." We waited impatiently until at last the call came through. Alice had died of a heart attack. There was a trace of one drink and one mild sleeping pill; if this combination could kill, there would be a great many more people in the cemeteries. Vincent hated publicity of any sort, but he wished for the truth, no matter how unpleasant.

Alice's death affected Vincent very deeply. He may not have seen much of her in life, but he missed her and, I think, felt sad that they had not been closer. We had Emily, Alice's youngest daughter, come to us in Maine and she and Vincent got on famously. He taught her how to sail, which later became one of the passions of her life. When they got into that tiny sailboat together and set off toward the islands, they seemed blissfully happy. Vincent was proud of Emily's aptitude and began to talk to me about adopting her. I was all for it. Emily was an enchanting child, and as Vincent had no children, she would have filled an important lack in his life. Unfortunately, we lingered too long. By the time the summer was over, Romana, who was married to Rory McEwen and living in England, had already had herself declared Emily's legal guardian. Romana loved Emily very much and felt that she was the one to look after her. Of course she knew nothing of our plans.

It was too bad in a way, as it would have meant so much to Vincent. However, life with Romana was a much gayer and of course a much younger household. We, after all, were growing rather dull. Before Emily left to live in England I did have the fun of finding a boarding school for her. We scoured the country looking at schools, finally settling on Garrison Forest outside of Baltimore, where Miss Marshall on Emily's graduation told me that Emily was one of the most brilliant girls she had ever had there. Emily went on to Barnard, where she won the Woodrow Wilson Scholarship, but gave up her education in favor of marriage. As a footnote, Emily thought of me as an "Auntie Mame" type. In fact she called me "Auntie Mame" and I played that up in our relationship. It was fun.

Alice's death had other repercussions. She had been a marvelous daughter to Lady Ribblesdale even though she received little recognition or thanks for it. She had visited her every day and had worked behind the scenes to keep the household running smoothly. With Alice gone, I felt that I should take on the job, but I could only do it to a small extent as Vincent grew more and more dependent on me. Lady Ribblesdale, like a great many rich old ladies, fell into the hands of secretaries and disagreeable maids; and although she disliked them, she was dependent on them.

There was one scene that I remember that was like a Maupassant short story. It was near the end of Lady Ribblesdale's life and she was confined to her bed. She had, however, called me and asked me to come to tea at five o'clock on a Thursday afternoon. I arrived there on the dot and was ushered into her bedroom, where, propped up by dozens of lacy pillows, with a pale blue bed jacket on and her marvelous pearls around her still beautiful throat, she lay looking absolutely regal. Her lawyer arrived a few minutes after I did. The tea table was brought in and laid with lace cloth and silver tray and she asked me to pour. After we had all had a cup of tea, she rang a bell and summoned her maid Clara. "Clara," she said, "bring my jewels from the safe." Clara disappeared and returned with a huge tray laden with suede and leather jewelry boxes stamped with the names of the best jewelers of Paris, Rome, London and New York. The tray was placed beside her ladyship on the bed and she said to her lawyer (who happened to be a younger member of her law firm), "I want to give Mrs. Astor a present. I want her to choose what she would like."

The lawyer and I drew near, as dusk was falling and the room was lit only by one lamp. Lady Ribblesdale then proceeded to start opening the boxes. The first one was empty, the second one, the third and so on. There must have been at least thirty boxes. Halfway through the lawyer and I begged her to stop opening them, as she became more and more agitated, but she insisted. When all were open, she threw herself back against the pillows and let out a dreadful scream. "Clara, Clara," she shrieked. Clara, who must have been just outside the door, came in with a smile on her face. "Yes, m'lady," she said. Lady Ribblesdale was almost beyond speech and I was terrified that she might have a stroke. "Where are my jewels?" she gasped. "Don't you remember that you sent them all down to the safe-deposit last month?" said Clara righteously. Lady Ribblesdale screamed again and the lawyer and I started to leave. "Must get the jewels another day," she said, but he and I both felt that we could not go through such a scene again.

I could have killed Clara then and there. I know that Lady Ribblesdale was bad-tempered and not easy to live with, but such cruelty to a person near the end of her life was so brutal and vengeful that I felt Clara could have been at home as an overseer at Dachau. Lady Ribblesdale died two years after Alice, but her death was not a shock for Vincent as she was in her middle eighties and she never had really understood or liked him. The jewels, thank heavens, were all intact in the bank and were divided up among the children. Only Lady Ribblesdale's flawless ruby ring was left to Clara "for faithful service." An important piece of jewelry had always been intended for Clara and was the reason she had stayed with Lady Ribblesdale all those years, but the ring was rather special as it had been Colonel Astor's engagement present and was worth hundreds of thousands of dollars.

I was left some lovely antique silver for the table and some rare and beautiful Chinese ornaments that I had often admired with a very dear note attached. In spite of all her faults, I was fond of Lady Ribblesdale and I know that she was fond of me. She had depended on me since Alice's death and I regretted that I had not been able to do more for her.

Vincent at the time of her death was preoccupied with a business deal in real estate. He had not been interested in

real estate for years but against his own better judgment
had been advised to invest a great deal of money in buying
the block of land on the east side of Park Avenue between
Fifty-third and Fifty-fourth streets, where the Citibank
Building now stands. It was not a bad investment at all, but
as time went on, Vincent realized that it would be at least
twenty years before he would receive any substantive income from it and in the meantime, a large part of his capital would be tied up.

This was not all to his liking. His philosophy about his
fortune was that he did not want to make any more
money. He simply wanted to keep what he had. He began
to worry night and day. He was always pulling little slips
of paper out of his dressing gown pocket at breakfast
which were covered with figures showing just how much
he was losing each day and how many years it would take
to get any return on the investment. It was to be called
Astor Plaza, not that Vincent cared a hoot about that.
What he did enjoy was to walk around the excavation and
watch the men manipulating the bulldozers. Anything me-
chanical intrigued him. He was also interested in the architecture, and his office was filled with models. He liked the
idea of having the sidewalk in front of the building made
of a mosaic in bright colors in a design of a map of Manhattan Island.

However, after visiting the excavation he would say to
me, "Your old man must have had a hole in his head when
he invested in *that* hole in the ground." The novelty of the
architectural models and the visits to the building site were
transient pleasures. The rest of the time he was in the
deepest gloom. Whether we were sailing in Maine or playing croquet in Rhinebeck or sitting in the library of 120
East End Avenue, he would suddenly say, "Pookie, we
have to get rid of that damned building, otherwise we will
have to sell almost everything we own. It will be the death

of me, and you, poor Pookie, will be left with a paltry
sum, no foundation and a thousand worries."

I already had a very real worry, which was that this
constant pressure might cause Vincent's death. Stress, the
doctors say, is what brings on heart attacks and strokes.
Vincent was certainly under tremendous stress, which
caused him to smoke more than ever and to cough all night
long. I began to feel that 399 Park Avenue had a curse on
it.

Luckily in the autumn of 1958 Cardinal Spellman
offered me seats to the coronation of the next Pope—soon
to be elected. I thought it would be a very interesting and
fascinating event to attend, particularly under the wing of
Cardinal Spellman, who would have me asked to all the
Masses and receptions, but I did not think Vincent would
go. As it happened, Vincent was all for it. He felt that it
would be a marvelous opportunity for me. I could fly
over, stay with the Dunns and he decided that he would
take the *United States* and meet me in London. In this
way, he would be having fun, too, as he really loved every
inch of that ship. It was a most welcome invitation and I
hoped would pull Vincent out of the doldrums.

26

Who should I find waiting for me in the Dunns' apartment
when I arrived, but Cardinal Spellman sitting in the drawing room, beaming and cheerful and full of plans. He had
seats for us at the Mass of the Holy Spirit at St. Peter's,
which takes place just before the Cardinals are locked up

in the Vatican for their electoral vote. He had superb seats
for the three of us, intended for his own family. These
were almost at the altar for the coronation, and he had
procured invitations after the coronation for the time-
honored reception at the Spanish Embassy in the Piazza di
Spagna. Jimmy and Mary also had invitations to the Embassy as Jimmy had been Ambassador to Spain.

All of this was very exciting and when I told Vincent
about it over the telephone, he was vastly pleased, particularly that the Cardinal was there to greet me; as he wrote:

> I do think that "Mr. Madison Avenue" being in the
> Dunns' house so recently after your arrival and to greet
> you was just about the nicest gesture ever. Of course
> "gesture" is completely the wrong word. He obviously
> is really fond of you, and I hope of me. Please, if you
> have an opportunity, give him my respectful best.
>
> It would be nice if New York and Rome were not
> so very far distant from each other. However in five
> days the U.S. will be at sea, coming this way, and in less
> than another five, I may be walking in to the [Hotel]
> Connaught door to find my Pook.
>
> Meanwhile, bless you darling and all my love. V.

Vincent called me or cabled me every day with detailed news of himself and the dogs. He sounded very
lonely. This was the only time in our married life that we
were separated and fascinating as it was to be in Rome at
that moment, to hear all the speculation and gossip about
the impending elections, I felt guilty every minute and
missed him terribly. I had wished him to be dependent on
me, and to need me, but until I was away from him, I had
no idea what a strong hold that was. To be needed is indeed an iron trap in a velvet covering. With Vincent it
was not the tyranny of the weak over the strong, because
he was stronger than I was. No, perhaps that is not so, perhaps I really *was* stronger. I had not been neglected as a

child. I had never been rejected. I had never been let down. My strength came from this, whereas Vincent had gone through a sad childhood and then the position of a sought-after rich young man. After being neglected for so long, he always felt that people were after him just because of his money. As for me, I do not count being rejected by Dryden. He made me very very unhappy, but I was not yet a person in my own right at that time, so that it left no mark on my spirit.

Our seats at the Mass of the Holy Spirit were far up on the right side almost next to the altar. In front of us sat the Cardinals (on both sides of the altar) with their secretaries sitting at their feet. Directly in front of us sat Cardinal Spellman with Monsignor (now Bishop) Ahern at his feet. Next to him sat József Cardinal Mindszenty, the Hungarian Cardinal who had been imprisoned for being anti-Communist. Before his trial, he had issued a statement that anything he said at the trial was not to be believed, which was wise because under the influence of drugs or pressure, he declared that the allegations against him were true, and he was imprisoned. It was the first time he had been seen out in years. He was a tall blond man with a fine-boned ascetic face which showed deep marks of suffering. I remember him so well because sitting so close to him and watching his expression, I could feel the enormous spirituality of his being. To him, that Mass, with his fellow priests and Cardinals around him must have meant so much because of all that he had been through for his faith.

The Mass was in the late afternoon, as the light faded, which always makes for more mysticism, and in that richly adorned basilica the crepuscule mixed with the cloud of incense and the flames of the candles created an atmosphere of unreality. The hundred or so Cardinals in their red robes ranged on either side of the altar, their secretaries in purple at their feet made a bright spot in the descending dusk. The Mass itself is a particularly beautiful one, and sung as it was, it echoed through the huge edifice. It was a Mass for understanding and guidance and strength, and when it was over, the Cardinals filed slowly out on their way to be sealed in conclave until they had elected a Pope.

We dined with old friends at one of those little-known restaurants that are always being discovered and always have the "*best* food." It was the season for funghi—those huge delicious mushrooms—and I remember making an entire meal of them. The next two days we spent in St. Peter's Square watching the little stovepipe on the roof of the Vatican wing for the white smoke. The square was packed like a sardine tin with people and I thought how clever it was of Bernini to have designed the quadruple elliptical colonnades, which were like arms coming out from St. Peter's to embrace the crowd. At last, the smoke was white, the crowd cheered, kissed one another, and fell on their knees to pray. It seemed almost at once that a Cardinal came out onto the center balcony and announced to us, "*Annuncio vobis grodium magnum habemus papam,*" and then the crowd roared, "*Abbiamo un Papa.*" Pope John Paul I appeared, his white vestment standing out in contrast to the red robes of the Cardinals. He gave us his *Urbe et Orbe* blessing and then stood there a moment while the crowd roared its approval. He was not the Pope who had been expected, but as it turned out, he was an excellent choice for that moment. He was a man of the people, a man of great strength of character who had been Cardinal in Venice and who had a real sense of what the Church could do to inspire both confidence and faith. Subsequently he became known in Rome by the affectionate nickname of "Johnnie Walker" as he went so often among the people.

That afternoon we went to the reception at the Spanish Embassy. It was like something painted by Vibert, who made a speciality of painting cardinals—only a little

grander, because the Spanish Embassy is an extraordinary
palace. It has the atmosphere of a fortress palace with its
high walls, huge gates and great stone entrance stair. As
we climbed the flambeau-lit stairs the Ambassador was
coming down, escorting a Cardinal who was leaving. A
footman in knee breeches walked ahead and another one
behind. We passed them and the Ambassador greeted
Mary and Jimmy and then we were in the long central
hall. Before us was a stone table, about twenty feet long,
and on it were laid the Cardinals' crimson cloaks, each one
topped by the large crimson hat. Footmen, of course, were
everywhere. One of them escorted us into an immense
salon which was filled with beautifully dressed women and
men equally well turned out by the famous Italian tailor
Caracini. I looked around for a Cardinal, but there was not
one in sight. At this moment, a Cardinal, followed by a
small entourage, came through a doorway and everyone he
passed knelt before him even though they had a champagne glass in their hand. After he had passed, I asked a
friend where he had come from. "From the Cardinals'
room" was the response. "As the Spanish Embassy has always been very close to the Vatican, they have a room
which is only used by Cardinals; but if you would like to
go in, I can take you. Whom would you like to meet?" I
asked for Cardinal Spellman, but he had already left. So I
asked to meet the French Cardinal Tisserant, who had a
glorious snow-white beard and was most imposing-look-
ing, a bit like my idea of Moses. My friend led me into a
room which, like all the rooms, was of vast proportion, but
here the walls were covered with crimson brocade and the
woodwork was all of gilded wood and stucco. The Cardinals were seated on gilt and crimson chairs around small
tables which were covered with red brocade and white
lace. They were eating cakes and drinking champagne and
toasting the new Pope. It was a merry scene. They were
all obviously pleased with work well done. I was pre-

sented to Cardinal Tisserant, made an awkward curtsey
and left. It was, however, a moment of history, short as it
was, and I doubt if such a sight will be seen again. The
coronation of a Pope will never have the pomp and ceremony that I saw. It was already a thing of the past.

The day of the coronation we arrived at the North
American College at seven o'clock in the morning in order
to be escorted to our seats. Monsignor Rigney was the
head of the college at that time and was a most delightful
man. Mary and I were in black as that was the prescribed
costume. Mary had a black lace mantilla that she had used
in Spain and I had one that Cardinal Spellman had given
me. I had brought practically no jewelry with me but Sir
D'Arcy Osborne, the British Ambassador to the Vatican,
told me that one simply must have some jewels on. So I
had put the only pair of diamond pins I had on my mantilla, wore pearl and diamond earrings (very small ones),
and a diamond bracelet, which was all that I had. Mary
was more dazzling with several pins and a rope of pearls.

When D'Arcy had told me about the jewels, he had
also said, "I think that women never should wear anything
but black and diamonds or white satin and pearls." Rather
nice if you can get away with it!

It was fortunate that Mary and I at least had a little
glitter, because the Italian nobility who surrounded us
were in tiaras and earrings and parures that really defy description. The sight of all the women in black and jewels
made an extraordinary contrast to the men in orders and
diplomatic uniforms and the ambassadors from Asia and
Africa who were ablaze with color.

Then there was the procession of the prelates from all
over the world in their richly embroidered robes and capes
and variety of hats—a dazzling collection. Above all was
the Pope himself, standing in his golden robe (it weighed
sixty-five pounds) and looking both saintly and human.
The ceremony lasted almost five hours but I never even

felt the slightest twinge of fatigue or boredom. The pageantry, the mystery, the singing of the Vatican choir and the stirring music of the Eastern Orthodox Church—all of it rising like incense up into the 410-foot dome of St. Peter's. The pages of history seemed turned back many centuries. I only give this short description because I suppose it is all very well known; but to be there is always more moving than to see it through the eyes of television. To be able to say, "I was there," still means something.

Almost immediately after the coronation, I left for London. Vincent did not arrive for twenty-four hours so I saw Jimmie Smith (the Honorable James) and Rhoda Birley and one or two other friends. Then Vincent arrived and we went to his tailor and ate potted shrimp for tea and grouse for dinner. Then off to a weekend with Bill Astor at "Cliveden," who had, I think, among others the C. P. Snows (now Lord Snow) staying—he, of course, the scientist and author; she, Pamela Hansford Johnson—also a witty novelist. It may have been later that I met them, but they became great friends. Cliveden had no central heating and Vincent caught a cold and so did I; but we had said that we would stop and have lunch with Arthur Salter (Lord Salter) at All Souls College at Oxford, where he was a Fellow, on our way back to London. The Salters were old friends from Tyringham and I was looking forward immensely to the lunch. We had drinks in Arthur's lodgings at All Souls and then lunch in the All Souls dining room, one of the loveliest in Oxford. It is truly imposing, with a wonderful view of the dome of the Bodleian Library. Lunch was excellent and my seat at table perfect. I sat between Arthur Salter and Maurice Bowra; but I did not enjoy myself as Vincent did not look well, quite aside from looking extremely bored. The conversation was so bright with all the literary lions roaring. I longed to linger on.

But we left even before coffee was served and I sent the

Salters a veritable garden of flowers with profuse apologies. I was upset as they had taken so much trouble; but indeed, Vincent was not well. He had a low fever which the doctor could not diagnose except as fatigue.

We saw a few friends—Judy Montagu, Rhoda Birley, Sheila Milbank Dimitri, were among those who came to our suite at the Connaught for tea and gossip. Vincent amused himself by having old Mr. Bulgari come over from Rome to discuss an emerald necklace and earrings for me. Mr. Bulgari, a sophisticated and worldly old man, stayed for lunch in our sitting room. He promised to assemble some stones and to send his designs. Vincent was very pleased with himself. "Even though your old man is laid up, he has done a fine bit of work for Pookie," he said; but his fever continued and his cough got worse. An x-ray machine was brought in, its great coils wandering over the Connaught lobby and up the mahogany staircase to our suite on the first floor. "It is a good thing he has given up smoking," said the doctor to me, "but he has a shadow on his lung. He should have an extensive checkup when he returns home."

I was frightened by these words, but Vincent miraculously got better. In fact, he felt marvelous and was able to go to the tailor for a fitting, to the shoemaker for his shoes. He seemed jaunty and full of spirit and in this mood we embarked on the *United States*.

It was during the trip that I really saw Vincent in action. It was soon after the *Queen Elizabeth II* had been put in service, and it was said in the papers that she would break the speed record for Atlantic crossing, thereby relegating the *United States* to a back seat. We were having a leisurely lunch in the upper deck dining room of the *United States* when a smiling waiter came up and said, "If you look out of the window, sir, you will see the *Queen Elizabeth* just behind us." Vincent took one look over his shoulder at the *Queen Elizabeth* looming over the horizon, and saying to me, "I am going to the bridge," threw down his napkin, and dashed out of the dining room.

Within five minutes as I was sipping my coffee, the whole ship began to shake, and the passengers, bewildered, jumped up to see what was happening. I went out on deck, and hanging onto the rail, watched as the *Queen Elizabeth* disappeared below the horizon behind us. Eventually, I went down to our suite, where Vincent appeared, beaming from ear to ear. "Miss *United States* kicked up her heels, Pookie," he said. "She wants to keep her record, and we will dock hours before the *Elizabeth*." The United States Line, alas, have gone with the winds of time. Air travel and the unions have done away with leisurely trips across the Atlantic. To be once again wrapped up warmly in a deck chair sipping tea at four o'clock would be my idea of heaven.

As we were passing Ambrose Light, Vincent was seized with the most dreadful pain in his legs. I got the ship's doctor, who gave him a sedative and said that he would order a wheelchair and an ambulance as Vincent should not strain himself by walking. Vincent was not so sedated that he could not hear the doctor. He refused an ambulance and said that he would walk off the ship. "I am not going to be lugged off the ship like a part of the cargo," he declared, "I refuse to be photographed in a wheelchair." So walk off he did and was in a dripping sweat when we got into the car.

For the next couple of months Vincent had ups and downs. When up, he went to his *Newsweek* meetings and United States Line in the morning and in the afternoons after his rest, he would often have someone from the office come up to the apartment to talk over business with him. When he was down, he would run a fever and his doctor then would tell him to take his temperature every half hour and write it down on a chart. I can see him now sitting in his red leather chair with the red leather footstool—

a thermometer in his mouth, a yellow pad and pencil on his lap, looking terribly depressed, busily writing down the time and his temperature. His doctor refused to tell me, or did not know, what was the matter with him, and I grew more and more depressed. One day, when he felt particularly low and said that he wished that he could have stayed with that nice doctor in England, I jumped at the chance and suggested that we call someone in for consultation. I found out from my own doctor who the best man to have was. "A man above hospital politics," he told me, as Vincent would only stay within the bounds of his doctor's hospital. I called the man mentioned by my doctor, but he said that he could not come unless Vincent's doctor called him in. I immediately called her, but she was most reluctant; and only when I kept saying slowly and with emphasis that *Vincent* wanted another opinion, did she give in.

The opinion I finally got was that Vincent had a bad cardiovascular condition; that he should get away to a better climate, avoid stress and, of course, never smoke again. He had already given up smoking, but I knew that the unexpectedness of Alice's death and worry over 399 Park Avenue had affected him deeply.

At this particular moment my mother had a very serious operation and Vincent had fun sending her an absurd gift every day and also telling me that I must go and see my mother, that I was a very bad daughter always staying with "Wincie." Well, mother pulled through and came back safely to her apartment. Vincent began to feel 100 per cent better—no more fever—and was looking forward to Arizona, where he felt sure that the air would benefit him.

We were to leave on February 4 and the morning of the third, he woke up feeling so well that we went to the St. Regis Hotel for lunch and sat at our favorite table in the corner. We said good-by to John and Rudi, the two headwaiters, adding that we would be back at our table the end of April. That night we were to dine with the Malcolm Muirs at their apartment at the River House, but Vincent begged off as we were leaving fairly early the next day. He thought, however, that I should go to dinner as Malcolm (who was editor-in-chief of *Newsweek*) was going to play *Newsweek* records of the editorial part of the magazine which were a new venture and were meant for the blind. Vincent wanted me to hear the record and report. So I had a "before dinner" drink with him beside his red chair, then off I went to the Muirs.

We had a huge Cadillac built especially for Vincent, which could seat about nine people. The ceiling of the car was so high that it could accommodate Vincent's six feet four inches with a top hat! It really looked like an ark and not since the Kusers' Crane-Simplex had I ever ridden in such a car. Now after five and a half years, I had grown accustomed to it; but its greatest drawback was that with all that space, we were always the ones to take everyone home. That night was no exception and although the party broke up early as they all knew we were leaving the next day, I did not get home until almost eleven.

The moment I walked into Vincent's room I saw a dreadful change in him. He was propped up in bed and gasping. "So glad you're here," he said. "Medicine." I put a nitroglycerin tablet under his tongue and then as he was in pain, I broke up a Demerol and crushed it in a teaspoon with water. But I could see that he was very ill. I went into my room and called his doctor. She came in an incredibly short time. She was with him only a few minutes when Vincent seemed to be in unbearable pain and fell back against the pillows. She turned to me and said, "Vincent is gone, Brooke." She put her arms about me and comforted me. I clung to her and when the undertakers came, she took the wedding ring I had given Vincent off his finger and gave it to me. She spent the night and was kindness itself. We were both united in that moment by

our love for Vincent. I am sure that she loved him too and
that whatever she did for him it was from love. But I think
that her love blinded her skill and she had wished to please
Vincent and keep his affection. That night of comfort and
sweetness to me was her final tribute to Vincent; and it
was a godsend for me. Without her, I would have been totally alone and also tormented for the rest of my life by
the feeling that I might possibly have saved him. I may
have felt harshly toward her, and she wounded me often in
the future, but that night she did everything that a compassionate human being could do for another.

27

Vincent's death was like a volcano in my life. Everything
erupted. I was faced with people who were suddenly totally different from the way I had ever seen them before. I
became, overnight, a person to be manipulated, talked to,
and asked to behave in a way that was completely contrary to my character. It surprised me and hurt me deeply.
I did have one laugh, though. I was driving down to the
lawyer's office on Wall Street. I was dressed in the deepest
mourning—still wearing a veil (that was twenty years ago,
when widows literally "took the veil"). Beside me in the
huge Cadillac sat one of the men from Vincent's office
who was supposed to help me with all my problems. "He
will be your minion," Vincent had said. "You can count
on him." As we rolled along the East River Drive, the gentleman said: "Now, after things are settled and the will
probated, you should go on a round-the-world cruise. The

only thing is"—and this is his own elegant expression—"you will have money coming out of your ears, so you will be attractive to men and had better watch out." This was certainly a vision of myself that was new to me. I wondered how he imagined that I could have married two very attractive men who had not been attracted to me because of money.

Among those whom Vincent had trusted, there was one man in particular who wished to take over the running of the Foundation. I had never before seen the claws and teeth of men climbing the status ladder. I had only known men as I met them socially. They might be attractive or dull, clever or stupid, fun or a bore, but they were to be relied upon because supposedly they were versed in the ways of a world of which I knew nothing.

It did not take me long to lose that illusion. I had become an obstacle, a menace to their smugness and security. I turned for advice to two old friends of Vincent's who were not connected in any way with his business. "Of course, Vincent expected you to run the Foundation," said his oldest friend and former lawyer. "That was always his intent, and the will is drawn up so that you have full control of the Foundation. It is a great tribute to you."

Buoyed up by this, I told the aspirant that I was going to be president of the Foundation. I was seated at Vincent's partner's desk at the Foundation office as I said this and I could literally feel my feet growing cold beneath me. He was furious and never forgave me. I am still surprised at myself in retrospect. That day marked the beginning. As the ads point out: "You've come a long way, baby!"

I had always looked upon Vincent's will as a diversion in his life. He used to change his will constantly. It was a game with him—almost a social event—and it always put him in a merry mood. He would say to me in the morning, "Pookie, tell Jeppie to have drinks and sandwiches out about five o'clock. Some men 'tried and true' are coming

to witness my will." He used to joke that the carpet
around the chair at his desk was worn threadbare by the
restless feet of these trusted men. I was always delighted
when they came, because Vincent would say, "Go off and
have your hair done," or, "Go see one of your girl friends.
I am going to be busy." Now his will began to take on another aspect.

I did not know or care about the will. If we had been
married thirty years, and had had children, I probably
would have wanted to know details. But I had been married to Vincent only five and a half years in all. I certainly did not feel that it was any business of mine what
Vincent did with his money and I was not going to ask
him, "What's in it for me?" He had already settled a comfortable sum on me by a "prenuptial agreement." That
phrase had made me laugh at the time. It sounded so pom-
pous—like minor German royalty; but Vincent had
insisted. "You must be able to give to your own charities
and buy things you want, like a present for me," was what
he said. I knew that he was leaving me our home, Ferncliff,
at Rhinebeck, even though I had said that I could never
live there without him. It was far too big for me alone. He
insisted that I needn't live there if I didn't want to. I could
sell it or give it away, but that he was leaving it to me just
the same; and he wanted to be buried there under the
ginkgo tree looking across the croquet lawn to the five
enormous English elms.

Well, Vincent's will was no sooner probated than Jack
Astor (whom I have never met even to this day) filed suit,
claiming that he should have half the estate and that Vincent had been non compos mentis for some time. Norris
Darrell was my lawyer, and although some people urged
me to settle and avoid unpleasantness, Norris urged me to
fight it. He was not a trial lawyer so he turned my case
over to another member of his firm: Judge David Peck.
Dave Peck was the happiest, luckiest choice in the world

for me. He became my knight in shining armor. Without him, I never could have carried on. It is not an easy thing to have to stand up in a courtroom and hear one's private life described as seen through the eyes of disgruntled servants or by people who had no knowledge of how decent people live. But Dave said to me, "Never be afraid when you are speaking the truth. The truth will always be recognized. You have nothing to fear from these people. Their lawyer has never met anyone like you."

The contest took place in the courthouse in Poughkeepsie. I was on the stand quite a few times. But Dave gave me such confidence that I found it very easy to answer questions. When Jack's lawyer said: "Didn't you think it strange that Captain Astor was getting out of the real estate business when the Astor fortune had always been associated with real estate?" I answered "No I didn't think it strange." And when he asked, "Why?" I said that Vincent had told me that he got out because he didn't like the sort of people who were getting into real estate. When he said, "Did you know that Vincent had liquor in his room at the New York Hospital?" I said "Yes, I did. I brought it there. We always had a drink in the evening." To try to prove that Vincent was non compos mentis was quite absurd. He was as bright as a button right up to the end, and I was overjoyed that Dave Peck had given me the courage to prove it.

The next event was the sale of the St. Regis. I insisted on giving large severance pay to all the employees who were non-union when we sold it. They were the head people in the departments, maîtres d'hôtel, captains, housekeepers, head chef, etc. It was an expensive thing to do, and my advisors were against it, but all those people were loyal and devoted to Vincent and I knew that I could not let them down.

Newsweek was another problem. There were several bidders, but the only one who really stood out was Philip

Graham; although Doubleday was a close second. Graham offered fourteen million dollars, which was the highest bid; but it only cost him eight as there was six million cash in *Newsweek*'s account waiting to be spent on another "property" which Vincent had intended to buy. Vincent felt that *Newsweek* needed another outlet, which he thought would put new life into the organization. He wanted to develop editorial talent.

Phil Graham took on all the *Newsweek* editors except Malcolm Muir, who was to be a sort of roving ambassador for the magazine and had a ten-year contract of $100,000 a year. The three young top editors at that time were Osborn Elliott, Benjamin Bradlee and Arnaud de Borchgrave. They kept coming to the office telling me of their troubles with Muir. I felt that it was important to keep them together, and I listened to them sympathetically. Phil Graham took the trouble to write up a program and a philosophy of what he intended to do with *Newsweek*. This came into the Foundation office at the same time as the contract on April 14, 1961, and when I saw at the bottom of the page of the contract the signature Philip Graham and then wrote Brooke Astor, I was tremendously moved. By a stroke of my pen, I was signing away something that Vincent had given so much of himself to. Of course I had to sell it, as it was left to the Foundation and not to me; but just the same, I felt impelled to write Philip Graham a personal note. It seemed to me that the transfer of *Newsweek* was not just an exchange of material value; one man's vision was being passed on to another man who had the same passion for truth and excellence.

I wrote Phil Graham to this effect and ended by saying, "God bless," and wishing him all the joy and satisfaction that Vincent had had. He was staying at the Carlyle at the time and I sent it around by hand. He came to see me the next afternoon and we had a marvelous talk. He described himself as a "Florida cracker" but he was far from that. He was a brilliant and fascinating man, full of originality and charm.

The conflicting advice I had concerning the sale of our property in Arizona, the cattle, and our large apartment made my life complicated and hectic. I slept very badly and was depressed.

The Foundation was the matter that concerned me most directly. As Vincent had a suspicious nature, it touched and amazed me that without a word to me, he should leave the running of the Foundation to my sole judgment. It gave me a feeling of exaltation and dedication. I was determined to make it the very best foundation of its size. But how to do it? The people around me were urging me to expand the organization, to hire researchers who would dig up new ideas, and at the same time go on giving to the "safe" well-established charities. Somehow this was not what I felt Vincent meant when he had told me that I could have a lot of "fun" with it. To sit in an office and read "meaningful in-depth studies" of something I had never heard of before and would probably never see was certainly a not very stimulating or productive thing to do. Without a husband to look after, and with no one who needed me, I could direct all my energy to the Foundation. I wanted the best possible advice I could get. I telephoned John D. Rockefeller III, and asked him if I could come to see him. He asked me to lunch at the University Club, and it was there that he gave me the advice that has been my principal guideline for the last twenty years—"The person who has control of the money should also be personally involved in the giving. It is a lot of work, but it is worth it," John told me. "You should control both the money and the giving," he emphasized. I returned to the Foundation full of gratitude for this, and with my mind full of anticipation at the idea of really starting to work.

Fate intervened at this moment. I had always had the

most marvelous health, and yet I suddenly became ill. I could not walk from one room to another without bursting into tears. I felt weak and was unable to eat. I felt as though I had swallowed a red-hot poker. I went to the New York Hospital for tests and was told that I needed to have my gallbladder out. At that moment I really did not care *what* I had out, as long as I could get well, and start work. So into the hospital I went—Room 1719 in the great white tower. Everything was set for my operation the next morning, when my doctor came in. "Well," I said, "what time is the operation? What did they [meaning the surgeon] tell you? My doctor shook his head. "They didn't tell *me*," he said. "I told *them* you are not going to have an operation."

I was in despair. I wanted so desperately to get over with whatever it was and be once more my healthy self. "Your blood is not normal," said Dr. Murphy. "There are far too many white cells and I am suspicious of the quality." I don't know to this day what was wrong with my blood, but I do know that I was tested for every possible type of infection, mononucleosis, hepatitis, Malta fever. Different teams took my blood twice a day. I moved from room 1719 to 1720, which is the best room in the hospital, and there I languished for weeks.

One night when I was chatting with a young resident, I said, "What on earth is the matter with me? What do they think I have?" "Well, if you want the truth," he answered, "they have come to the conclusion that you have leukemia." I am not particularly knowledgeable about medicine, but I knew what leukemia was. A little boy just down the hall from me had died of it the day before. The next morning I asked to speak to the chief medical doctor of the hospital—not because I did not trust my own doctor; I trusted him entirely—but he was such a good friend that I felt he might wish to protect me.

When the chief medical doctor came, I asked him at

once. "I want to know if I have leukemia," I said, "because if I have, I am not going to stay here. I have things to do to put 'my house in order.'" He answered that they really did not know what was the matter with me. There had been a significant and worrying change in my blood, but if it *was* leukemia it was a slow type and would not really become fatal for another ten years. When he had left, I lay there in bed wondering just what to do. I turned on the television to distract my thoughts, and there was John Glenn going around the earth—a man a great deal younger than I was, with a young family dependent on him, risking his life for the sake of his country and for mankind. It hardly seemed right for me to loll in bed. I might as well do what Father always advocated and "die with my boots on."

I called my doctor, who released me from the hospital on condition that I stay around for another month having blood tests. This I did, but after the month was up, I chartered a large yacht and took a party of friends down the Yugoslav coast and to Capri and Sardinia, ending up at Monte Carlo. Some days I felt so badly that I just sat on a curb while the others went sight-seeing.

The yacht was very comfortable and attractive and even though I felt shaky, I enjoyed the trip. Feeling relaxed and being with people I liked was a great tonic for me, and I came home much refreshed. I now think that all the worries and vexations I had been through were too much for me, and that though I threw them off, the chemistry of my body was thoroughly disturbed. My subconscious is more sensitive than my conscious. I once went blind for three days from a shock which I had completely discounted. After three days at the Eye Institute, my sight had returned. The doctor could find nothing wrong with my eyes and said, "The only time I have ever seen a case like this before was on the battlefield with men in shock. Have you had such an experience recently?" Only then did I remember what had happened to me.

Faced with the fact that my subconscious was not toughened up, I found that my life became much simpler. I want no unpleasantness, no hard feelings. I never want to hurt someone else even unintentionally if I can help it. It is a form of protection. I try to avoid disagreeable and aggressive people. I want to hear good things about people; the weaknesses are too easy to find.

I returned from my trip renewed in health and spirit, and started to look around for things that I was interested in. I wanted the Foundation to be alive, to be innovative. I found that once the interests of the Foundation were known, there was no need for researchers. The path was soon beaten to our door and we had a wide range of interesting choices. It was just up to us to define our guidelines. And this we did.

A strange thing happened just at this moment. Mr. Bulgari, the Italian jeweler, sent over a colored transparency of the emerald necklace and earrings for which we had selected the stones in London in 1958. With the transparency there was an impatient note from Vincent asking how soon it was to be finished as he wanted it for my birthday. Now here it was, two years later. I certainly did not feel in the mood to buy such an expensive present, but I went to see my banker, who said, "Vincent ordered it for you and wanted you to have it. If you like it yourself, I think you should buy it." I *did* like it. Vincent loved jewelry and had very good taste. It is pretty and not ostentatious but very elegant, and so I bought it. Considering that it was really Vincent's last personal gift to me, I am very sentimental about it, and I felt that it was a sign of encouragement from Vincent.

PART IV

Brooke

28

As I have loved every house that I have ever lived in and have always felt comforted to open my eyes in the morning amid familiar and pleasant surroundings, my heart goes out to those who open their eyes and see a hated four walls. How can one start a happy day in a dark room with flaking plaster and grimy walls?

It was with this in mind that an idea for a Foundation gift began to germinate in my head. Why couldn't we do something about housing? I started to read everything I could lay my hands on about housing, and I was particularly impressed by Jane Jacobs' book *Death and Life of Great American Cities*, which had been recently published and in which she advocated that shops and other facilities should be located within the housing development. I remembered back to Bernardsville when I was on the Board of the Maternity Center and in that capacity visited the "new housing" at 123rd Street and the East River Drive. The buildings were only five or six stories high, and therefore manageable. They seemed more homelike than what I saw around me forty years later. "High rise, high crime" is no meaningless cliché. Could we not go back to an improved and modernized version of that type of housing?

Allan Betts, who was Director of the Foundation at that time, was a friend of Mayor Robert Wagner. So we went to see the mayor and I asked him what the Astor Foundation could do for housing in New York. It was naïve even to think of housing in connection with the Foundation at that point, because this was long before we thought of invading the Foundation's capital. Although the income was ten times what it had been when Vincent was alive, housing is one of the most costly of projects, and of course the Trustees and I did not want to tie up all our income in one venture.

Bob Wagner listened patiently to my rather sketchy presentation and then made an appointment for me to see the housing authorities. "They are the people who make the decisions," he said.

I should say at this point that the only guideline Vincent had made for the Foundation in his lifetime was "The amelioration of human misery"—a pretty grand statement, but it could include a very wide range of action. As I did not take it to mean physical misery only, I had laid down two guidelines myself for the Foundation. As the original Astor fortune had been made in New York, and as five generations of Astors had contributed to the life of the city, I felt that the Foundation money should be spent only within the five boroughs. I also decided not to make individual grants—or to give to "bricks and mortar" (a hidden invitation for constant future giving). The Trustees agreed thoroughly with me on these principles. We have, of course, given scholarships to individuals, but through programs supervised by other charitable organizations.

Thanks to Bob Wagner, the appointment with the Housing Authority was made. I shall never forget when I walked into their board room down on lower Broadway. They were gathered around a long table smoking cigars; and though they greeted me politely, I could see from the look in their eyes that they were thinking, "Here comes another Park Avenue lady with an impossible, impractical scheme in her head." I sensed their weariness at having to suffer through half an hour with me in order to please Bob Wagner.

However, I was not daunted. I knew that I had to win them over, and that was a challenge. I sat down and began to explain what I would like to do. That was in 1961, before vandalism had become rampant and the "rip-off," a way of life. In fact I feel that if they had put shops in at that time it would have worked. Now it is too risky. If we had then been able to build shops within the development *run by the tenants,* if there had been a supermarket and a drugstore and a pub so that old people would not have to walk blocks for their shopping or a friendly gathering place, it could have created a neighborhood feeling. People could have gotten to know one another in an easy way and been able to judge one another—adults vis à vis adults, children vis à vis children. We could have had little villages within a development instead of these bleak aseptic buildings. But the men around that table were against it. When I saw that there was no point in pushing any further, I suddenly got an idea. "How about making the courtyard into a park?" I asked. Remembering Santo Domingo, where I had once spent a summer as a young girl, I began to elaborate, suggesting a bandstand in the middle. Talent from the outside, or even the tenants themselves, could give concerts at night or over the weekends. I remembered how in Santo Domingo in the cool of the evening there was the *paseo*—the girls walking around the bandstand in one direction, the boys in the other, so they could meet eye to eye and flirt discreetly under the watchful eyes of the *dueñas* on the benches at the edge of the walks. As we have so many people of Hispanic origin in New York, it seemed to me that this might be a way of continuing their culture and making them feel at home. Thus did I plead my cause.

Most of the Board looked skeptical, but I found a champion in Ira Robbins, a very dedicated and influential member of the Board who was most enthusiastic and spoke up warmly for me. Finally I got permission to see different sites with Ira and then to come back to the Board with a plan. Thanks to Ira, I saw many housing developments and finally we both agreed that the George Washington

Carver Development was the one for our experiment. It had enough space and—even more important—it housed people in the lowest income bracket in the city. The inner courtyard was four blocks long, from East Ninety-eighth to 102nd Street, and we used every inch of it. Ira helped us to pick out the architectural firm of Pomerance & Breines, who brought in Paul Friedberg, the landscape architect. We worked it out with them. The plot was divided into different levels to give it interest, and also to separate the age groups. The upper level had built-in chess tables and niches with benches against a sunny wall for old people and a sand playground for small children. Then there was a vine-covered pergola, in front of which we placed a bronze statue of George Washington Carver as a boy. He was a slave as a child and grew up to become an outstanding agricultural chemist of international repute. The statue was produced by the Housing Board from the archives of the city, and it is a lovely one of a barefoot boy with a bright intelligent face.

Beyond the pergola were steps going down to the main plaza, where a small fountain was placed, and instead of a bandstand (the authorities were against that, for some reason), we built a small brick stage, where we spent a fortune on lighting. We also put in trees around the edge of the park. If I ever had any qualms about the reception that this "outdoor living room" would get, they were dispelled when I was told by the rent collector that the tenants thought it would be marvelous if Pablo Casals could play there on the opening day.

We did not have Pablo Casals, but we *did* have the lady mayoress of San Juan, a truly dynamic lady, Doña Felicia Calderón, and Bob Wagner, and Ira Robbins, and Ed Sullivan, who was our master of ceremonies because he had lived in that neighborhood as a boy and offered his services to us. Unfortunately on opening day it was pouring with rain and we all sat on the stage while impassioned

flamenco dancers, undaunted by the downpour, performed
to spirited music with shouts of *olé, olé* from the crowd
who filled the entire open space and looked down from all
the windows. I made a speech, first in English and then in
Spanish. The Spanish speech was a triumph, and the people crowded around me afterward, touching me and kissing me and talking to me in Spanish. Alas, that faraway
summer in Santo Domingo had left me with a fairly good
accent, but absolutely no vocabulary. My English speech
had been translated for me by a friend who was fluent in
Spanish. All I could stammer out was "*muchas gracias.*" It
was our first effort in outdoor living rooms—and my *first*
and *last* attempt to make a speech in Spanish. I did not
wish ever again to disappoint people.

We have done many of these outdoor living rooms
over the years; and as the times have changed, we have
changed with them. One of our most successful efforts,
and certainly the largest and most expensive, was one we
did in 1965 at the Jacob Riis housing on the Lower East
Side at Sixth Street and Avenue D. It was a large plot of
three acres, and as before we turned to Pomerance &
Breines and Paul Friedberg. A great deal of digging had to
be done, so once again we were able to work on different
levels. The dust and dirt were frightful while the excavat-
ing was going on, so we had huge billboards painted to
show what the park would look like when it was finished
in order to divert the minds of the tenants. The children
were fascinated by the pictures and followed the workmen
around asking if they could help.

I came down often from Maine that summer to see
how the work was progressing. The children clustered
around me shouting, "Mrs. Astor, when you coming to
visit us again?" and one little boy, Poppo by name, wanted
a swimming pool and tagged around after me saying,
"Please, a pool." I wanted one for them too, but it meant
so much maintenance, with a lifeguard, etc. that it was im-

possible. However, we did put in two channels of water with sprays on each side. These channels were only about eighteen inches deep, but running through them when the sprays were on during the hot weather could be a lot of fun.

As at Carver, the older people were on the higher level, and the stone steps that led down to the open-air theater could seat a thousand around it and had well-appointed dressing rooms behind. The stage was separated from the audience on two sides by the water channels. There was a walk up to an overhanging balcony and an open space beyond for skating; beyond that, the first "adventure park" for children ever built in this country. I had met Lady Allen of Hurtwood at a friend's house, where she had spoken on "adventure parks" as the "answer to the boredom of children." "When a child is bored, he becomes naughty," she said. "He throws a stone, he breaks a window, he climbs a fence he shouldn't. Put him down in a playground with nothing in it to distract him, he will soon do something destructive." The "adventure playground" has a little element of danger and was originated in Sweden. It consists of doing things which call for a certain skill, like jumping from one flat-topped totem pole to another one, two feet away, and lower down; climbing up difficult ladders, swinging from rope to rope and landing either on the top of a small hut, or jumping off onto the soft bed of sand below.

Paul Friedberg liked the idea enormously and produced a fascinating playground, adding many of his own features such as climbing poles, and ladders. The opening day was a triumph with Mayor Lindsay and Lady Bird Johnson inaugurating it, bands playing lively tunes, and politicians smiling happily at their constituents. The only thing we forgot was a "comfort station," which was added several years later, as the park was so popular it was used by the entire neighborhood, not just Riis Housing.

I first came to know Lady Bird Johnson as a very much admired "First Lady." As the years have gone by, she has become a good friend whom I have never ceased to admire. I was a member of her Beautification Committee when she was in the White House, and it was because of her that in 1966 we gave our only Foundation gift outside of New York: in Washington, D.C. In Southeast Washington there is a public school called Buchanan School. There we built one of our outdoor living rooms to be used during the day by schoolchildren and in the evenings as a community center. Walter Washington (later mayor of Washington) spoke at the opening, as did Mrs. Johnson, and I said a few words. I am glad to say that the next year, when there were bad riots in that sector of Washington, shops were looted and buildings burned, but Buchanan School was untouched. We had spent all in all about three quarters of a million dollars on it, and it really was lovely. I have always believed that if you give people the best, they will recognize it and respect it.

One little personal touch about Buchanan. Lady Bird had asked my son, Tony, and me to come back to the White House for lunch after the ceremony at the school. I had supposed that she was having a lunch party and had very thoughtfully included us as we had come down from New York. But not at all: it was only the three of us, and we had lunch in a tiny corner room, which had been Lincoln's press room (too bad that the press can no longer be contained in a room of that size) and looked out toward the Washington Monument. It was an historic occasion for us and so very like Lady Bird to have given us that special pleasure. Tony and I often talk about it.

There was one time when I sought Lady Bird's help. It had not been decided where the Temple of Dendur, which the Egyptian Government had given to the American people, was to be placed. The Smithsonian Institution wanted very much to get it and planned to place it somewhere by the shores of the Potomac. The Metropolitan Museum, because of its very extensive Egyptian collection, was also most anxious to have the temple and were willing to raise the money to build a wing to enclose it so that it would always be in the proper temperature to conserve it. Experts on the conservation of buildings from New York City's Institute of Fine Arts had said that if it were placed outside in the humid climate of Washington, the temple would not last twenty-five years. A panel had been appointed to submit an opinion, but the President had the final vote.

I was asked by the Executive Committee of the Metropolitan Museum if I would call Mrs. Johnson and ask her for her help. I called Lady Bird, who said that she knew our Egyptian Collection very well and that she would speak to the President. But naturally she could promise nothing, since he did not discuss decisions of that sort with her. I understood her position perfectly. We were all overjoyed, however, when, a few days later, she called and said that we had it. We lived up to our promise to house it well. It now stands in its beautiful glass wing at the Met with the waters of the "Nile" at its feet.

Not all our parks have been big. We have given tiny vest-pocket parks—like the one behind the Jefferson Market Courthouse Library and one up on West Eighty-ninth Street. Our Foundation has been effective up and down in the city, on the East Side and on the West Side, including the only football field outside the meadow in Central Park. It is in Asphalt Park (built where an old asphalt plant used to be) and is opposite Gracie Mansion. In Central Park itself we have supported summer projects for young people who are taught by experts how to plant, how to grow and how to conserve. This serves the double purpose of training them and helping to conserve the Park itself. We are currently interested in rehabilitating the "gothic" dairy to be used as a small exhibition gallery.

Where the old Rupert Brewery stood, and before the present housing was built, we supported a community group who grew vegetables and flowers on the vacant lot and either ate the vegetables or sold them. We have built greenhouses in housing developments, we have helped young people grow worms in basements in order to enrich the soil of backyard gardens, and we have paid for rakes and trowels and other simple garden instruments. To paraphrase a great man's saying, we gave them the tools and they did the jobs which, when accomplished, were very satisfactory.

As the years go by, we are inclined to give large gifts. Yet sometimes it is the small gifts that give me the greatest joy. It is my proud boast that the Foundation never gives to anything that I do not see. I do not feel that I can report properly to the Trustees unless I speak from personal knowledge. A group can come into the office and describe what they are doing and make it sound really marvelous: just the right answer on how to keep the children off the streets, to see that old people are cared for, or to improve education or rehabilitate old tenements. *But* when you go and see for yourself, you may find that the place they described as a beehive of activity is empty, or that it is badly organized, or in the wrong neighborhood, or just a plain ordinary boondoggle. My present directress, Linda Gillies, now does a great deal of scouting and weeding out for me, but I still go and look myself before we make the final decision: That is the fun of it all. Giving away money should be exhilarating. I keep reminding myself of what Vincent said: "Pookie, you are going to have a hell of a lot of fun with the Foundation when I am gone."

The nearest we came to housing itself was Bedford-Stuyvesant. I had been interested in Bedford-Stuyvesant for quite a while, and knew it well. Many people I knew had spoken to me about it and I thought that some day we might be able to do some sort of development and encour-

age the tenants to maintain the pleasant but rather dilapi-
dated one-family houses. While I was wondering what, if
anything, we could do about this, I read in the paper that a
committee had been formed called the Bedford-Stuyvesant
Restoration Corporation. It consisted of a group of businessmen who were going to put up the money to make it a
going concern.

Among the names on the committee was that of
Douglas Dillon, whom I had known for years and with
whom I sat on the Board of the Metropolitan Museum.
(He is now Chairman of the Museum Board and was President for eight years.) It so happened that Walter Washington, my old friend from Washington, had just come to
New York to work with John Lindsay as Head of
the Housing Authority; and I was giving a lunch for him
the next day. I called up Douglas and asked him to the
lunch to meet Walter Washington and discuss Bedford-
Stuyvesant. He said no, that he couldn't, but why didn't I
ask Bobby Kennedy? Well, I didn't know Senator Kennedy, but Douglas gave me his telephone numbers. I called
him. He couldn't come, but two days later he and his
friend Tom Johnson came around to tea with me and we
talked for hours. The Senator, of course, could get federal
funds. But what was needed was not only money for four
blocks to be made into super blocks, closing down four
cross streets, thereby obtaining playgrounds with trees in
the center and good lighting; but, also, they needed money
for the plans for the entire area. The Bedford-Stuyvesant Restoration Corporation brought in I. M. Pei, the
Chinese-American architect, to make the plans.

The director of the Vincent Astor Foundation and the
Trustees were all most enthusiastic. We gave a million and
a half dollars to get the thing started including paying for
the architect's plan for the whole project and for the
building of the four super blocks. The Corporation chose
Franklin Thomas—now President of the Ford Foundation

—and John Doar to run the entire development, and a magnificent job they did. The super blocks were great but, to my mind, the rows and rows of neatly painted houses, with an R in the window (meaning that with the help of the Bedford-Stuyvesant Restoration Corporation they had restored their home), were really more impressive than the super blocks. I had the pleasure of dining in one of these houses and I defy the famous and exclusive area of Georgetown in Washington to show anything more attractive. The main building of the Corporation, with its shops and offices, is both practical and impressive and the theater, to which we gave more money later, is exquisite. It is an elegant showcase. I am happy to say that I visited Bed-Stuyv just the other day, and it is an ongoing concern.

In doing these parks and bits of housing we have not neglected people. Directly opposite the Jacob Riis housing, and actually before we built the outdoor living room, we built a clubhouse for the Boys' Brotherhood Republic. It is one of the few neighborhood clubs for boys in that part of the Lower East Side. I was very much impressed by Ralph Hittman, the Director, and so we decided to take a gamble and build a really impressive building. I felt that something called a Republic should look imposing. It should stand out, as a seat of government. We were offered land on the Rosenwald Development facing Sixth Street, and there we built a large granite building with the emblem of the Boys' Brotherhood Republic on it and a flagpole overhead. Inside it is cheerful, airy and, if I do say so, beautifully equipped.

As it is run as a republic, the boys pay "taxes"—$1.00 a year for younger boys; $1.20 a year for the older ones. In addition, each boy must contribute one hour of work per week. The younger boys, aged six to eleven, come directly after school and stay until five-forty. The older ones (aged twelve to twenty) come at 6:30 P.M. and stay until 10:30 P.M. Each age group elects its own mayor and officials and they run the Boys' Brotherhood Republic during their appointed hours. The desk at the door is manned by boys who are office holders and part of the government. It is run like a city, with mayor, cabinet, judges and elected officials. If a boy is late, causes trouble or gets into trouble, he has to appear before a court. A jury is chosen. There is a judge, a prosecutor and a defense attorney. The court-room is paneled in real oak and the judge, who can range in age from eleven to twenty, sits majestically in a great leather chair, properly dressed in his robe, with the American flag on one side of him and the Boys' Brotherhood Republic flag on the other side. The jury is in the jury box and the witnesses are sworn in by the clerk of the court. When I see twelve-year-olds from the inner city learning the principles of law in that courtroom, with their faces solemn and in rapt attention, I feel that any money spent on the beauty and dignity of the room is well worth it.

There is a basketball court big enough for professional games—the "Knicks" have played there—with rows of seats for onlookers. There is an auditorium for the club and for the community, and behind the auditorium there is a large and spotless kitchen, where the mothers of the boys pre-pare meals for special events. There are workshops with every sort of up-to-date machinery from woodwork to radio repair. There is also a library, a reading room and spotless locker rooms and toilets. After eight years, there are no graffiti and no signs of wear and tear; yet there is tremendous activity going on all the time. Ralph Hittman is an inspiration. Born in that district, he knows what is needed. It is thanks to him that out of that building many fine young men have gone to make a name for themselves in the outside world. Of course, we have helped out with maintenance from time to time, just as in the parks we have financed programs during the summers.

We have had many programs in Harlem, but our larg-est gift has been to Moran Weston's St. Phillip's Church

Parish House, which was largely financed by us with well over a half million dollars. It is a very intelligently thought-out and much needed building. At one time we gave large amounts to the Neighborhood Houses Fund and left it to them to divide the money among the different neighborhood and settlement houses. It seemed such a waste of time and a duplication of effort for people from different settlements or neighborhoods to come asking for the same thing.

However, we have found that certain neighborhood houses often have projects that especially appeal to us. We become interested in helping a pilot project that we feel might be beneficial to the community at large, because a good pilot project will soon catch on. Lenox Hill Neighborhood House, for instance, under the leadership of Celine Marcus as Director and John Pierrepont as President, has done a job for the elderly that is outstanding. They have brought teen-agers into a program called Scope, in which two teen-agers "adopt" an elderly person who is either totally housebound or too feeble or too afraid to go out alone. The teen-agers take a course of instruction at Lenox Hill. After that, they go to the apartment of the elderly person and proceed to do what they have been taught, which is to be particularly sensitive to what the old person needs and wants. It can mean shopping for them, or taking them to the doctor, or sitting with them on a bench in the sun, or just being with them in their apartment and letting them talk. The young people are paid the minimum wage, and they take great pride in their job. They might not be interested in their own grandparents, but these old people are their "clients" and they look forward to their bi-weekly visits. They are supervised, of course, by the management of Lenox Hill and have to write progress reports.

In England, over 11,000 young people are doing this sort of work. Since it started at Lenox Hill, I have already

heard of several similar programs. Lenox Hill Neighborhood House has an indoor swimming pool and gym
(left over from the days when it was a boys' club); and
once a week fitness programs for the elderly are held
there. The rest of the time, it is used by the young and the
very young. Lenox Hill is fortunate in that next to it is a
new apartment house built just for the elderly, so that the
"clients" who live there find it very convenient to step
next door for their one hot meal of the day. Every
Thanksgiving the Lenox Hill "regular" senior citizens can
invite a guest if they so wish to a turkey dinner followed
by dancing. I go as often as I can to this event and act as
"wine steward," carrying a huge jug of wine from table to
table. I love it because there I answer to the call of "Miss,
oh, miss, some wine here, please." I feel like skipping to
them, because I am as old, if not older, than most. That
word "miss" brings out the springtime spirit in me. Jackie
Onassis came once when I was there, and there was a veritable stampede. It made for a red-letter evening.

We have participated in all these activities; as we also
have down at the Henry Street Settlement, where the hot
meal program and the craft program have attracted a
happy and busy group of senior citizens. We gave them
their new kitchen and dining facilities, and on opening day
we were serenaded by their Good Companion Group,
singing to us like larks and all of them well over the Social
Security age. As I grow older myself, my heart reaches out
to these people as I see how responsive they are to a little
touch of TLC. Love, or at least an affectionate concern,
can make an otherwise dreary life bearable. Also, as these
gatherings have both men and women in their ranks, ro-
mances flourish. Thornton Wilder said in his play *The
Matchmaker*, "Money is like manure. It should be spread
around." Thanks to this wonderful legacy that Vincent
left me, I can spread money around and participate in the
happiness of so many people. Giving the money away

would not mean nearly as much to me if I never saw what comes of it. I really don't even have to be called "miss" to enjoy it.

We have given to girls' clubs on the Lower East Side too, supporting basketball and soccer and track teams for girls, especially Hispanic girls, who often feel so inferior to the "macho" boys. We give to the boys too, and one of our sponsored basketball teams won the Whitney Young trophy, which they proudly brought to me. I have it in my office. Perhaps even before this book is printed, one young Hispanic girl may be running on an Olympic team. We have hopes. As her proud teacher told me, "Mrs. Astor, you may find your name in the New York *Times* one day soon when Tiajuana (the girl's name) wins the Olympics." I think of Tiajuana often, waiting for that proud moment. I can't go through all the projects and programs we have given to—Wiltwyck School, East Harlem Recreation Center, East Harlem Jaycee Foundation, Harlem Prep School, Kips Bay Boy's Club, United Negro College Fund, A Better Chance, YMCA of Greater New York and the YWCA, Youth Development, etc. All of these were given grants from $100,000 up.

I have always wanted to help to develop leadership in our country, and so I asked an English friend of mine, Noel Annan, now chancellor of London University, a man deeply involved in education, how he would act if he were I. "I would seek out the gifted children," he told me, "and at the earliest age I would start giving them the finest education possible."

When I returned to New York I discussed this with my directress, Linda Gillies. She became as enthusiastic as I was, but where to start? Luckily, hidden away in the inner recess of the Board of Education, we were told that there was a lady who had been talking about just such a program for years. Her name was Dr. Virginia Ehrlich, and when she came to our office Linda and I both felt that if anyone could help us, she certainly could. It took many meetings with all the top brass of the Board of Education, and after that with the principals of the schools who would be involved, because the program needed its own classrooms and special teachers. As there was no program for very young gifted children, we took them at the age of four and kept them until they could enter into the Board of Education's program, which began with the fourth grade.

Virginia Ehrlich was an inspiration. Linda and I were thrilled when we visited the classrooms. It was a monumental task, but Dr. Ehrlich was totally dedicated and tireless. It was heartwarming to talk to her. The Trustees were tremendously interested, and were impatient to hear our reports. There were approximately five hundred children in ten schools under direct funding from the Astor Foundation; and when the program moved from private funding to public funding, the numbers increased because of the increased number of classes. In all about fifteen hundred children will take part, which is a considerable step forward.

The program was a great success, but after the four years which we had contracted for, we kept it on one more year. We had never intended to keep it up forever as it was a pilot program and usually we do not give to any program for more than three years in a row. This was an exception. The children were fascinating and quite extraordinary and so were the teachers; but the gratifying thing is that at least four schools will be carrying out Astor Program philosophy in Manhattan, District 1, made possible by a federal grant. District 22 in Brooklyn has obtained a federal grant to replicate the Astor Program. This will affect several schools; and even more exciting is that the St. Paul Foundation in St. Paul, Minnesota, is implementing an Astor Program in St. Paul. So in the end we really achieved what we set out to do, which was to give a head start to the gifted.

We decided to go from children to gifted teachers. St. John's College at Annapolis, Maryland, is a college dedicated to the humanities and runs a summer program at Santa Fe, New Mexico, where they have a four-year course that runs for two months each summer. We started by sending four teachers and we now send twenty-four. Many other foundations are also in on this summer school program. For the Astor Foundation the Board of Education picks out a group of New York teachers, and a dean from St. John's makes the final selection. Married teachers take their families with them. I usually have a tea party in the fall, when Linda and I meet with the teachers and St. John's faculty and any Trustees of the Vincent Astor Foundation who are available come too. I have it at my apartment and look forward to it tremendously. St. John's is run on the tutorial system, which in itself is a great advantage. The teachers study subjects such as the ethics of Aristotle, the language of the Bible, the philosophy of Santayana, Comparative Religion or nineteenth-century English novels as compared with French novels of the same period.

The teachers when they come to tea say to me such things as, "Santa Fe is like Athens. If you have a philosophical problem, you can stop anyone in the street and talk to them about it!" It makes me want to go myself. Perhaps one day I shall. It must be exhilarating and the teachers tell me that when they return to New York their own attitude toward their students is different. They feel that they try harder and get more response.

We have tiny projects, too, such as uniforms and instruments for the Fife and Drum Corps, a young people's band; and one of my particular pets, free care at the Animal Medical Center for pets of indigent old people over sixty-five. An interesting fact is that old people tend to

have old pets: one dog died there at the age of twenty-
four! The veterinarians at the Animal Medical Center treat
their patients as humans, and are so advanced that they can
put pacemakers into the animals who have bad hearts and
perform back fusion operations—mostly on dachshunds. It
is open twenty-four hours a day and we have received
many letters telling us what an investment in happiness it
has been both for the animals and for their owners. One of
our Trustees took a dog there and wrote me a glowing letter about the treatment. The Trustee, not being indigent,
paid a fee. We have just endowed this program in perpetu-
ity as so many doctors have written us telling us of its
therapeutic value on the elderly.

There are so many institutions and charities we have
been interested in, that I cannot mention them all; but
there is one that Vincent himself started. It is therefore
one of the most important to us, and is the only commitment we have for regular annual support. It is the Astor
Home for Disturbed Children at Rhinebeck—now simply
called Astor Home. It was built by Vincent in memory of
his father and was originally meant to be a vacation home
for boys run by the Episcopal Church. But after the war,
the Episcopalians could no longer maintain it. Vincent was
a staunch Episcopalian, but he was also an admirer and
friend of Cardinal Spellman. He offered it to the Cardinal,
who accepted it. It is now run by the Sisters of St. Vincent de Paul and financed by Catholic Charities of New
York City, the state of New York and the Vincent Astor
Foundation. The Sisters have developed it into an outstanding example of what can be done with disturbed children, and there are now both boys and girls there. TLC
combined with Ph.D. degrees have worked miracles. During the twenty-five years I have been associated with it, it
has had over a thousand "graduates," all of them able to
take their place in the world and some of them supporting
their own young families. The work there has been so suc-

cessful that at the spring seminars they usually have up to eight hundred doctors and social workers who come from all over the world to study the system and to hear papers read. Vincent, I feel, would be very proud of it today.

At the twenty-fifth anniversary, Cardinal Cooke and I were standing out in the garden receiving the guests. One small boy after bowing low as he shook my hand, having been coached by the nuns to say, "Thank you, Mrs. Astor," but then, as he stepped up before the Cardinal in all his robes, became overwhelmed and stood stock still. His Eminence, smiling, bent down and, shaking his hand, asked him his name. The little fellow responded, then speaking up, said, "Are you Mr. Astor?" The nuns must have indeed been eloquent in singing my praises!

None of these things could have been accomplished without a very dedicated and co-operative staff and a group of lively and truly interested Trustees. I am president; Linda Gillies is my much younger and very able directress; Mary Earle is Program Director. We have two other ladies—one a secretary, the other an accountant. Price Waterhouse visits us regularly and we are proud of the way our books are run and our "house" kept in order.

A word here about Linda. Before Linda, I had two men directors. One was both director and vice-president until his retirement. The other left to practice law in his brother's firm; but even before that I began to feel that working with a man was not always easy. They did not see eye to eye with me. One day I was lunching with Waldemar Nielsen, who wrote *The Big Foundations*. (At that time we qualified for inclusion, but now, because of invasion of capital and the slump in the market, we are no longer eligible.) Waldemar said to me, "Brooke, I think that you would be much happier working with a woman. A woman would be interested in the things you are interested in, and you would enjoy your work at the Foundation a hundred per cent more."

I took his word for it, and it has meant a world of difference to me. Linda and I usually see things through the same window, and my life has been much happier because of her. The Trustees all admire and respect her, and they particularly like the delicious teas that appear at our office when we hold our meetings—a feminine touch that was not there before. Those teas are just another tribute to Linda's sense of organization and a nice fringe benefit for the Trustees. Speaking of fringe benefits, we give each Trustee $10,000 a year to be given in their name through the Foundation to a recognized charity in the city of New York. No gift can be less than $2,500 as we do not have the staff to cope with so much bookkeeping.

When I went to Washington to talk to the late Congressman Patman regarding the future of foundations, he told me that we and one other foundation were the only ones that gave trustees such a fund. I found to my amazement that some trustees were paid large fees and had expense accounts. He was supposed to be very much against foundations, and as he told me of the abuses of these so-called "charitable funds," I was horrified. I was also very proud and pleased when he and his two young assistants said that if all foundations were run like the Vincent Astor Foundation, they would never attack them. I walked away from his office with a great sense of pride and a feeling that I had been given guidance as a Trustee way beyond my own limited capacity. Someone had helped me do the right thing—my guardian angel must have been watching over me.

29

Now I come to what I call our "Supporting the Crown Jewels" program. "The Crown Jewels of New York City" on our list are the Metropolitan Museum of Art, the New York Public Library, the New York Zoological Society, Rockefeller University and that smaller marvel, the Pierpont Morgan Library.

We gave a million dollars to the Metropolitan for air-conditioning the Western European Paintings Department; a million to the Michael Rockefeller Wing for Primitive Art; and a much larger gift to the Endowment Fund. We have also shared with the Fairchild Foundation the expense of keeping the Museum open to the public on Tuesday nights. This appealed to me particularly because so many people are not free to come during the normal daytime hours. We are at the moment building an authentic copy of a Chinese courtyard (circa 1600) in the Museum. Opening off it, we intend to build an early Ming room, for which we have already acquired the furniture. The courtyard will probably be finished and opened to the public in the early eighties and is the first permanent exhibition to be devised jointly between the People's Republic of China and a Western country. Thirty Chinese arrived in New York on December 31, 1979, to work on the courtyard and will be here for eighty days, until the completion. However, the courtyard will not be opened until September 1980, as the American Wing is opening in June and the Metropolitan did not wish to have two large openings at once.

The New York Public Library was started by the original John Jacob Astor, who left his extensive personal library and a cash gift of $500,000 (a princely amount at that time) to fund a "new" New York Public Library. I say "new" because John Jacob Astor's library was already built down at Astor Place, and when James Lenox died and left his extensive library (then housed on the corner where the Frick Collection is now) to the New York Public Library, there was talk of amalgamating the two. But it was not until Samuel Tilden died, leaving not books but money to build a New York Public Library *reading room*, that the three gifts were amalgamated.

The city contributed the land, which was then a reservoir, and employed the firm of Carrère and Hastings as architects. But what with one thing and another, the building as it stands today was not completed until 1911. Five generations of Astors have supported the Library and their names are carved around the main hall including the Astor Foundation and my own name, because of a personal gift from me. Last year, the Foundation decided to give five million dollars to the Library if it could raise ten. Four million have already been raised under the leadership of Richard Salomon, the Chairman of the Board. The Library gave me a wonderful dinner party there, and the main hall was then christened "Astor Hall." They wished to name it after me personally, but as it is Astor money, not mine, it seemed inappropriate to me.

I took Vincent's place on the Board of Trustees, and sometimes over the years I have grown so discouraged because of the lack of funds that I have almost resigned. But when I go into that magnificent reading room and see it packed with every sort of person, all bent over their books under those green lamps, I say to myself, "How can you ever let these people down? This is one of the great research libraries of the world. It must never be abandoned." In order to take pressure off that reading room, we gave three floors of the Arnold Constable building just across from the Library on Fifth Avenue. It is called the Mid-Manhattan Library and is used mostly by students for its textbooks—and for its massive armory of Xerox machines.

I have always loved animals and through the years my friendship with Fairfield Osborn kept that interest alive. Fair Osborn was President of the New York Zoological Society and ruled it in a very special way. He loved every inch of it and his personality and charm were such that those who worked for him absolutely adored him. He made everything an adventure. I remember one day when he came in his car to take me to see the Zoo's aquarium, which is situated in Coney Island. As we started off, he turned to me and said, "This is going to be an historic day for you. You are going to do something you have never done before." I tried to guess what it was, but he wouldn't tell me. He was rather a wild driver, and suddenly we shot down into a tunnel. "This is it," he shouted. "You are in the tunnel going to Brooklyn. Isn't that wonderful? I'll bet you have never been in it before!" I hadn't, but as we tore through it, I began to feel quite elated. What an excitement! That was the magic of Fair. The Brooklyn tunnel was the entrance to Wonderland and I became Alice.

Fair's enthusiasm was as contagious as the mumps; and so the Foundation gave the World of Darkness, a coal black building with no windows and a white pebble roof which contains not only nocturnal birds and beasts, but animals who live underground like moles and aardvarks. It took quite a time for these creatures, who came from all over the world, to get accustomed to the time changes. They were put into individual cells and the lights were gradually adjusted until now they are all awake during *our* day—so that we can see them—and sleep during our night. Quite a *tour de force* to accomplish.

When John Lindsay was mayor, the city began to look

covetously on the forty acres of land just across the Bronx
River which the Zoo owned, but had never built on. As I
am a Trustee of the Zoo, I asked what could be done about
it. It seemed sad to lose land that belonged to us when land
is so scarce. Bill Conway, the inspired and inspiring Director of the Zoo, came up with the idea of "Wild Asia."
This meant leaving those forty acres wild, and peopling
them with animals from Asia. The animals would be
separated from each other, but they would have the run of
a large piece of land where they could live their lives almost as though they were still in the wilds of their
homeland.

I brought this idea before the Trustees, who were most
responsive. So we said that we would give five million if
the city would give five million. Mayor Lindsay pledged
the five million, but as time went by and he left office
there seemed no hope of ever getting anything more. The
Foundation decided to go ahead anyway and added another one million six hundred thousand to finish the job.
A monorail was built which crosses the Bronx River twice
and moves slowly along thirty feet above where the animals
are. The first day it opened the five Asian elephants, each
holding the tail of the one in front, dashed into their large
pond and, once there, joyously sprinkled water over their
heads with their trunks. It is a wonderful exhibit and is
extremely popular, as is the World of Darkness. When
Howard Phipps gave a dinner on the opening day of Wild
Asia, he said, "Brooke has done for the Bronx River what
Cleopatra did for the Nile." Mother would have indeed
repeated her famous quotation, "Brooke, you are getting
beyond yourself."

We gave two chairs, a million dollars each, to
Rockefeller University. One of the Astor professors is
Gerald Edelman, who was a Nobel Prize winner for his
work in Immunology. We have also made other gifts to
the University for the upkeep of the laboratories.

To the Pierpont Morgan Library we made a gift to a much needed building fund as they had outgrown their student facilities and needed room for stacks and study carrels. We have given over two million dollars to Channel 13, the New York City Public Broadcasting Station, for their facilities.

We have also given to the Museum of Natural History, to the Museum of the City of New York, and to New York University for a chair in science; to Columbia University for a floor of the Babies Hospital, a large gift in 1960 to the New York Hospital and last year a million-dollar chair for research at Memorial Hospital. We also gave a million dollars to the Episcopal Church last year. And this year a million dollars to the New York Hospital Cornell Medical School.

There is another feature of New York in which we at the Foundation are all most interested and that is the preservation of what is left of "old New York." Therefore we have supported South Street Seaport, helping them to reconstruct some of the old houses and also the old South Street piers. Against the chrome and glass of the giant skyscrapers, it is heartwarming to see the tall masts of the clipper ships that used to sail from these docks one hundred years ago. It was our hope that about five blocks that lead to the piers would be closed off to vehicular traffic and that the few early nineteenth-century houses that are left could be turned into profitable little shops with flats above them. This hope has been realized as the Rouse Co., which did such a successful job on Quincy Market and Faneuil Hall in Boston, has finally decided to put $60 million into the area, which includes building a large pier with good-quality boutiques of all types. Already, including the Rouse $60 million, $210 million has been raised with the assistance of state and federal funds. Again a pilot project of ours has been capped with success. We also gave a quarter of a million dollars to help to save the block around

Fraunces Tavern and have given to the magnificent Customs House in hopes that a good use can be found for it. All of these buildings are in the lower part of Manhattan, and when they are finished they could make quite an impact on the area, as Quincy Market and Faneuil Hall have done on Boston.

Lower Manhattan played a large part in my life during the Bicentennial and on July 4th, 1976, I had a particular triumph. The Vincent Astor Foundation, being so interested in South Street Seaport, was naturally interested in the tall ships that were to sail into New York Harbor on July 4th from many nations. The Foundation made a donation toward that day and so did I personally.

Three of us had been invited to come down and spend the day at the Seamen's Church Institute (to which the Foundation has given a one-million-dollar matching fund). We had tickets for lunch there, two nice rooms to rest in if we got tired and tickets to let us up on the roof to view the ships entering the harbor from below the Statue of Liberty and also to view the fireworks. Because of traffic we had to be down at the Battery by 9 A.M.—which we were. Six million people were expected to crowd into that one square mile and remain there for the twelve hours of festivities. There was a Guard of Honor of naval vessels all the way up the Hudson to the George Washington Bridge. The President was to be on the carrier *Forrestal*, and was to review all the ships from there. From the roof of the Seamen's Church Institute, we saw the first of the tall sails, a U. S. Coast Guard training ship, appearing behind the curve of Staten Island around 11 A.M. The tide was running out, and there was very little wind, so they came slowly—the *Amerigo Vespucci*, the Italian training ship with her cadets in white standing at attention all along the yardarm and up the mast to the crow's nest; the *Kruzenshtern*, the Russian entry and almost a sister ship of the *Peking*, which South Street Seaport owns, was the

largest and most impressive. In all there were 225 ships
representing thirty nations and when they had all disappeared up the Hudson, we walked through the crowded
streets. I have never seen such a friendly and good-natured
crowd: no one shoving or pushing, no irate parent slap-
ping a child, no drunks; in fact a police sergeant I spoke to
told me that from 6 A.M. to 6:30 P.M. there had only been
one arrest. There was singing and dancing, and ethnic food
booths and jugglers and just general happiness and good
nature. We had been asked to be back at the Seamen's
Church Institute at seven, and so we returned to be told
that we were expected at the bandstand at Battery Park.
We had a police escort, as the crowd was so great. Our escort estimated there to be about 100,000 but with the
help of our escort, and the good nature of the people, we
soon found ourselves in front of the bandstand, where the
Goldman band was playing. I was taken into a little room
where Mayor Beame and Brendan Gill were waiting for
me and was told that I was to receive an award. It was the
first I had heard of it; and I was quite overcome. Mayor
Beame and Brendan Gill walked me out and up onto the
platform. The band gave a flourish, and Mayor Beame,
looking very natty in white trousers and a blue blazer,
stepped forward and made a little speech which started
out about this being a great day for New Yorkers and then
suddenly turned into a speech about me. Brendan had had
a medal struck by the Municipal Arts Society proclaiming
in bronze my achievements. (There is nothing like a
friend to build up one's ego.) The Mayor presented it to
me, saying that I had done more for New York City than
any other one person. As I accepted the award Brendan
suggested they give a cheer for "Brooke"; and I looked
down upon 100,000 people all shouting, "Brooke." There
was nothing I could say. New York seemed like a glorious
overgrown village to me at that moment and I was really
overcome with pride in the good nature and humor of the

crowd. All I could stammer out was that the Astor Foundation believed in New York and would never leave it. A pretty dull response, but I was lucky not to have burst into tears.

Another incident that I enjoyed particularly during that week was when I stood on the South Street Seaport dock as the head of the Swedish Navy arrived in his admiral's barge rowed by twelve young sailors. The admiral stepped smartly ashore as the young sailors raised their oars in salute. The bands played the Swedish and American anthems. The Swedish admiral had come to return the ship's bell of the *Wavertree* as a cultural gift to the United States. Two sailors carried the bell on a bar between them and the admiral presented it to an American admiral.

It seems that the *Wavertree* had fallen on evil days and had been dismantled. A Swedish petty officer had bought her bell at an antique shop in South America. He had eventually presented it to the Maritime Museum in Stockholm, where it had been for thirty-seven years.

We celebrated the return of the bell by a luncheon at the Seaport Museum and after many "skoals" I remember saying that from now on the *Wavertree* bell would speak in two tongues—Swedish and English. There were more toasts all around after that!

During that week I was privileged to be one of thirty-two guests invited to dine with Her Majesty the Queen of England on board the royal yacht *Britannia*. The *Britannia* was anchored at the end of the Cunard dock in a full moon with some of the tall ships still anchored in the Hudson nearby her. Two hundred people came to a reception after dinner while a band played on the end of the pier close to the stern and the full moon shone upon us. It was a perfect ending to the week. The Queen herself had been down at the Treasury Building on Broad and Wall streets that morning and had then walked through the crowds up to Trinity Church. I was terrified by the crowds around her, but she was serene, smiling and totally unafraid. Never has New York been in such a good and festive mood. I think New York is very much like the child in the old nursery rhyme: "When she's good she is very very good, and when she's bad, she's horrid."

When I inherited the Foundation I immediately became a plum to be plucked. I was old enough in the ways of the world to know that it was not for my wit or my charm that I was so much in demand. I had scanned too many charity lists in my day, planning how much I could get for "The Benefit" of whatever it was from Mrs. Whosis or the Blank Foundation. I therefore knew how tempting a new name in the field of giving can be. So I felt that I could not simply be president of the Astor Foundation. I had to do other things. I wanted to broaden my knowledge of the city. I wanted to know as much as I could. When I was first married to Vincent I had been asked to join the Board of the Metropolitan Museum of Art, but Vincent was against it. Minnie was on it and he thought that the media might make something of "the two Mrs. Astors" (even though Minnie was Mrs. Fosburgh). That seemed to me rather farfetched, but in any case when Vincent was alive, I would never have had time to take an active part and would therefore have been a poor Trustee.

But when I was asked again after Vincent's death, I was very pleased to join the Board and have stayed on it ever since. I also went on the boards of the New York Zoological Society, the New York Public Library, the Pierpont Morgan Library and the Rockefeller University. I am on the Acquisitions Committee and Executive Committee of the Metropolitan Museum of Art and on the executive committees of all the others too. I am also a Trustee and on the Executive Committee of Channel 13, the public television station of New York, and the Foundation has helped them to buy their headquarters.

As an active trustee on the boards of these institutions,

all of which benefit the public, I have learned more about
the city, its funding and its needs, than I could have in any
other way. It has brought me into contact with a gamut of
activity, from high art to labor unions. I have known the
city under four different mayors and many commissioners
of Parks and Culture. But above all, in being a Trustee, I
have come into contact with, and benefited by the wisdom
of, my fellow Trustees—men like Douglas Dillon, Chairman of the Board of the Metropolitan Museum of Art;
Howard Phipps, President of the Zoological Society (and
vitally interested in housing); Laurance Rockefeller, not
only interested in the Zoo, but a leading conservationist
and dedicated Chairman of the Board of Memorial Hospital; Bill Conway, the imaginative and constructive Director of the Zoo; Richard Salomon, Chairman of the Board
of the New York Public Library; David Rockefeller,
Chairman of the Executive Committee of the Board of
Rockefeller University; Patrick Haggerty, Chairman of
the Board of Rockefeller University (Texas Instruments);
Bill Baker of the Bell Laboratories and of course, the ex-
presidents of Rockefeller University, Fred Seitz and the
present president, Joshua Lederberg. I find the Board meetings of Rockefeller University totally absorbing. Most of
the talk is way over my head. I know very little of DNA
and cloning and enzymes and antibodies; but when I hear
Gerry Edelman and Lewis Thomas and other scientists
talking, I feel overcome with wonder at what man is
capable of thinking and doing. I am a bit like one of the
old-fashioned coach dogs that ran under the fire trucks. I
am excited by the fire burning in the minds of these men
even if I can only bark incoherently.

At the Metropolitan, the association with Thomas
Hoving, Philippe de Montebello and their colleagues has
been another continuing form of education. The Acquisitions Committee in particular is better than any history of

art class. The curators present the object to be purchased, describe its history and provenance, and show photographs of other objects of the same type and period that are either in other museums or in a great private collection.

At the Pierpont Morgan Library again we are shown the most rare manuscripts, both plain and illuminated, from the beginning of the civilized world and gleaned from many countries; also superb drawings, and of course the magnificent objects and paintings accumulated by J. P. Morgan himself. Mr. Henry Morgan, the senior member of the family today, is very involved in this great gift that his father left to the public and Charles Ryskamp, the Director, is continually mounting magnificent loan exhibitions and filling the auditorium in the evenings with concerts and lectures by men and women of high reputation.

Channel 13 with Ethan Allen Hitchcock as Chairman of the Board and Jay Iselin as Director is an education of quite another kind. What does the public want to see? How shall we best serve them? How can we stay within our comparatively small budget and still produce quality? It means constantly going to corporations and foundations and having drives for membership. It is extremely gratifying that the response has been so rewarding. Every time the money comes in, we can afford to break out in a new field. Even our own Foundation has funded two pilot programs on modern art written by John Russell and narrated by his wife, Rosamund Bernier. I asked the Foundation to do it. "Wouldn't it be nice," I said, "to see 'Funded by the Vincent Astor Foundation' instead of Exxon or Mobil Oil or Ford Foundation?" They were all delighted and we can hardly wait to see them on Channel 13.

I have tried to keep out of politics because I feel, as the president of a foundation, I should not be political. However, on an entirely personal basis, giving only from my own income and of my own time, I did work for Nelson

Rockefeller in 1968. John Hay Whitney and I were co-chairmen of Nelson's national campaign fund. We raised one million five, which was quite a lot in '68 dollars. I was at the headquarters writing and telephoning from morning to night and also took trips around the country.

I always felt that Nelson could have been President (in spite of the old guard Republicans) if he had not withdrawn twice during the campaign. It was a sad night for all of us workers when, down in Miami, Nixon had the required number of votes even before getting to the count of New York State.

Nelson was an extraordinary man—a real Pied Piper: when one was with him, his enthusiasm and vitality created an aura of excitement that was contagious. When I walked through the rooms of the Americana Hotel in Miami with David Rockefeller that fateful night after Nelson had lost, the people who had worked so hard and long were crying. Politics is the toughest game of all—and to be on a losing team is a terrible disappointment.

Another friend of mine who might have been President was Adlai Stevenson. We often sailed together in the Caribbean, and he visited me in the summer in Maine. He was an intellectual, a scholar and especially, a student of history who consequently took a broad and objective view of world affairs. He was also, unfortunately, a person who was tormented by indecision, which was his Achilles heel. I went to a dinner party at Adlai's apartment at the Waldorf when he was our Ambassador to the United Nations. It was for the Shah of Iran and his new bride, the Empress Farah Dibba. Adlai had about sixty people at small tables of ten and he sat with the Shah on his right and the beautiful, bejewelled young Empress on his left. I was seated next to the Shah, and we started off talking merrily about a mutual friend, an Englishman who had lived in Iran. Then the conversation lagged and I searched in my mind for a new subject. The Shah had just come from Washington, so I asked him if he had enjoyed his visit there, and I was ashamed of myself for asking anything so dull. But his reaction was instant. His eyes flashed. "It was the same old thing," he said bitterly. "I went begging for money in order to carry out the reforms that are so needed in my poor country. We need modern hospitals, doctors, scientists, schools, sanitation, buildings. We need to modernize; and, every time I ask for a loan to accomplish these much needed projects, I am turned down by your government. I remain in the role of a beggar." That was in the early sixties. Looking back now, it seems ironic that when the golden oil was found and the Shah was able to fulfill his dream, he laid the foundation for losing his Empire.

In 1968 when Nelson was still Governor of New York, Martin Luther King, Jr. was assassinated. I read about it in the papers, but never thought I would be a part of this tragic event until Happy Rockefeller called me up late one night. She told me that she and Nelson were flying down to Atlanta the next morning in order to attend the King funeral. The plane was to be crowded with civic leaders whom Nelson, ever generous, had invited to be his guests for the trip; but Happy, in her modesty, thought that there would be no place reserved for her in the church, and she asked me to come so that I could sit with her in the car outside until the service was over. Of course I said yes, and so the next morning at 5:30 A.M. they picked me up and we drove out to La Guardia. The plane was crowded with such dignitaries as John Lindsay, Bishop Donegan, Harry van Ardsdale and Roy Jenkins, at that time the Chancellor of the Exchequer of the United Kingdom. When we arrived at the Ebenezer Baptist Church, Happy and I were not seated with the official group, but we had excellent seats near the front of the church. It was a very moving service, particularly since a recording of

Martin Luther King, Jr. was played—his voice ringing out loud and clear through the entire church—and must have had a very special meaning for his wife and children and his parents who were sitting in the front pew in dignified and silent grief.

After the service, we started on our funeral march through the streets of Atlanta to Morehouse College, three-and-a-half miles away. We passed the state house with its flag at half mast, then moved out slowly into the suburbs. There were thousands of us, and we sang as we marched, sometimes holding hands. I walked just behind Nelson and Happy with Roy Jenkins and young Laurance Rockefeller. It was a slow march, and as it was high noon on a spring day, it grew boiling hot. I had put on a wool dress and jacket at 5 A.M. because it had been cool in New York; but as hot as I was, my sense of participating in an historic event kept me from dwelling on this slight discomfort. The scene was almost biblical, particularly as we got to the district of small semidetached and detached houses— all neatly kept with small lawns in front. It was an all-black district and the elders had put out long tables on the lawns or sidewalks, carefully draped with long white cloths and covered with glasses and pitchers of cool water prepared for the thirsty walkers. As we passed and sang, these people joined in our singing and came out to us bearing their welcome water glasses.

Eventually, we arrived at the Campus of Morehouse College, which was already jam-packed. Happy, Nelson, and Roy Jenkins were escorted up to the steps of the college while I remained in the crowd below. The college glee club resplendent in scarlet blazers, sang spirituals and there were many tributes and prayers. But so many people began to faint because of the heat and the crowd that the service ended sooner than intended, called off by the president of Morehouse. So we drifted away quietly still feeling the impact of this spiritual experience.

During the time when Nelson was completely out of politics, between his defeat as a candidate and his being named Vice-President, he gathered a group together and formed six panels, calling them "Critical Choices." It was intended to look at life in our country today and come up with ideas, and possibly with solutions. Men like Daniel Boorstin, Librarian of Congress, were on it as well as Edward Teller and Walt Rostow and his wife, Lady Bird Johnson and Irving Kristol, Laurance Rockefeller, Bess Myerson, Nancy Hanks, and others. I was on the "Quality of Life" panel and our Foundation made a gift especially for its work; but alas, when Nelson became Vice-President, the life went out of the group although fourteen volumes of essays and papers have been published.

Speaking of publishing, I have myself published two books. *Patchwork Childhood* is all about me from zero to sixteen. As I kept a diary from the age of seven, I had my material at hand. As a lonely only child, I became a modern on-the-spot reporter. If I do say so, it is quite an amusing and touching book and I am not ashamed of it. The other book, *The Bluebird Is at Home*, is a fable founded on my early married life. It is not nearly as good, although in the London *Times* I was described as a "modern Jane Austen"—no wonder I love England!

In the midst of all this one of my great delights is my son Tony—three times an ambassador—Malagasy Republic, Trinidad and Kenya. Kenya was his last post, and he left just before President Kenyatta died.

As you see, I have turned myself into a sort of Public Monument—a monument in the name of Vincent Astor. That's what I wanted to do, while at the same time continuing my education and "stretching my mind," as Mother said. I don't mind being a monument, even though it sounds very stuffy. I have seen too much and done too much not to be very contented with my lot. "Don't die guessing," cautioned Mother, and I hearkened to her words. I am not guessing. I have led a full life. Now at my age I want to enhance the life of others by good humor and understanding. I want people to know that I really care for them.

I am no longer a private person and available at all times for a friendly gossip or a long lunch, but that is a price I have had to pay. At my age now, although my spirit is willing, I must give up something. I can never give up the Foundation work or the attendant duties that make me useful there, nor can I give up my weekends alone, walking with my dogs in my woods, listening to the first signs of spring, the peepers in the swamp announcing the season with their chorus; the strange cries of the pheasants, the territorial songs of the birds, and seeing the first crocuses on the hillside, the willows turning pale green—spring—then winter with the most glorious sunsets of the year, flinging red scarves from behind the hills of New Jersey to me across the river—my two favorite times of the year. In winter when the first star starts to twinkle, I go inside and light the fire. I read, I watch the news, and eventually I daydream. If someone were to ask me what I dream, I could not tell them, for it is a sort of happy doze. I get strength from it, and I feel in a strange way relieved just from letting myself be *nothing*.

Nature has a very special effect on me. Once when I was walking by myself in the Maine woods, I was so overcome with the beauty—the ancient gray rocks, the wonderful scent of the pine trees, the sparkling sea at my feet—that I stood still and began to recite the Lord's Prayer. When I came to the words "Deliver us from evil" it struck me like a bolt of lightning that instead of meaning "Deliver us from evil" the words really meant "Deliver me from doing evil." If someone hurts me, *they* are being evil. If I hurt someone, *I* am the carrier of evil. Since then I have always said the Lord's Prayer with that meaning in mind: "May I never do evil to anyone." I hope that I never have.

> My heart leaps up when I behold
>   A rainbow in the sky:
> So was it when my life began;
> So is it now I am a man;
> So be it when I shall grow old,
>   Or let me die!
>   —Wordsworth

POSTSCRIPT

At the Metropolitan Museum of Art, it is customary for the Chairman of the Board to appoint a Trustee-Visitor to each department of the Museum, the duties of the Trustee-Visitor being to become acquainted with the needs of the department and to be the spokesman for the curators of the department at the Board meetings. I was appointed Trustee-Visitor to the Far East Department in 1970. At that time I was told by Douglas Dillon and by the curators that they felt that in spite of the variety and strength of the collections, the department had been neglected and needed a spokesman.

I found the role difficult at first, which I knew it would be, as the trend in recent years had been more toward the European and Middle East acquisitions. However, there were some very dedicated collectors, and Friends of the Far East Department who rallied round, and when Professor Wen Fong of Princeton became Special Consultant for the Far East Department in 1971, he changed the whole atmosphere. New Friends of the Far East were found and meetings became more lively as we drew on outside talent. The Packard Collection of Japanese Art, consisting of 410 objects, was one of the first big acquisitions which was bought with the hope that there would be student exchanges between the two nations. A new Japanese gallery is now being built with the help of the Friends of the Far East Department and in May 1979 the Japanese Premier Ohira presented a check for a million dollars from the Japanese Government to Douglas Dillon at a small ceremony at the Metropolitan Museum.

The Vincent Astor Foundation had bought several years before some beautiful early Ming furniture—enough to furnish an elegant scholar's room. As things progressed and my interest increased, I thought to myself, "Why wait? Why not do something now?" I thought back to my childhood, to those four wonderfully happy years in Peking and in the Temple in the Western Hills. I remembered the Great Wall that encircled Peking, and watching the birds flying home to the Forbidden City "to get in before gate closes," as my diminutive Amah said. Next to remembering the Wall, I remembered vividly the courtyards of China—courtyards in the temples with their ancient trees and mysterious Buddhas in the darkened pavilions. I remembered too the quiet and peace of the city courtyards where, behind thick walls, Chinese families led a contemplative life, away from the noise and excitement of the city.

Would there be use for such an oasis in the museum? Would people like to sit and rest their eyes and spirit? Could such a place be re-created? I remembered the subdued grayness of those courtyards—the walls, the tiles, the pavement all embellished by the lacquered columns of the rooms that surrounded the courtyard and the pots of flowers which were changed with the seasons. I spoke to Wen about it, who was most enthusiastic, and who is that rare combination of scholar and "doer." We started planning and searching and miraculously space was found. Directly over one of the Egyptian galleries there was a large open space with a skylight. It was just what we wanted and the Museum administration let us have it. We started by putting down a very strong and substantial floor of steel (very expensive too) and from then on, Wen was calling every day with new ideas. We had sketches and plans and maquettes from all over, but Wen kept saying, "it must be Chinese. It must be real." I heartily agreed, as I wanted something permanent, not a stage set.

Fortunately for us, another miracle took place. The policies of the People's Republic of China had changed substantially and when told by Wen about our project, they were most enthusiastic. Letters went back and forth, and Wen shuttled up and down to Washington to the Chinese Liaison. The whole climate of Sino-American relations had become different, and in the winter of 1978–79 a delegation of construction and cultural men came from China to New York to see our "site." I gave a large lunch for the Chinese delegation and for the "Friends," and the Chinese toasted us, for our joint venture. They were going to build the prototype of our courtyard as a museum in a public garden in Soochow. It would be a copy of a still-existing early Ming garden (in Soochow) and some twenty-five workmen and five supervisors and a cook would come to New York when that was finished for eighty days, and working six days a week, would complete the courtyard for us. In addition they were going to open up an imperial kiln which has been closed for one hundred years in order to make the roof tiles. Also, only a very special and rare wood, "nan," would be used for the columns outside the Ming room, for the Ming room itself and for the garden pavilion. Over and above that they were going to produce "pedigreed rocks"—rocks over a thousand years old, sculptured by rushing water, being turned every twenty-five years or so to create the form. A magic wand had been waved, and all wheels started working. Wen went to China twice and returned with glowing progress reports. Finally, I was told that the Soochow work would be completed in May 1979. "Old Lady," they wrote, "come to Soochow where you will be revered as you are in New York." How could I resist—to be revered in two hemispheres is irresistible! I shed all my aches and pains as a snake sheds its skin and so set forth, supported by a gallant entourage: Dr. Edgar Riley and his wife, Daphne—my executive secretary and dear friend—and a young French lady, Mlle. Tissot. Wen and his wife, Connie, met us in China, which was marvelous as we had built-in interpreters. Wen with his knowledge and enthusiasm was exhilarating and taught me how to behave vis-à-vis Chinese customs. I took it all very easily, particularly as upon arriving in Peking, we were met at the bottom of the gangway of the plane by a large black limousine—"the red flag car"—with brown tulle curtains, two smaller gray cars and a van for luggage. There were two young lady interpreters and several officials. I got into the limousine with an interpreter, and off we went bowling along the tree-lined avenue to Peking. I was traveling like an old mandarin lady, and I felt like one. I felt Chinese, at home, and perfectly relaxed. It was a new sensation to have after traveling so many miles, but I never lost that feeling during my entire visit. I went to many ceremonial dinners and gave one for forty myself. I jumped up and answered toasts and felt absolutely bubbling over with good will, as, apparently, did my hosts.

I was told that I could go anywhere in China, and see anything I wanted. I kept my visit entirely on the cultural side—the Palace Museum, the Summer Palace, the Great Wall, the temples in the hills, our own courtyard in Soochow, where I found that all the things that had been promised were, in fact, a fait accompli. The beautiful gray tiles from the newly reactivated imperial kiln were on the roofs, the "nan" wood columns were in place and so were the magnificent pedigreed rocks. I was given a reception there, and the next day, I met with the workmen who are coming to New York. It seemed like a dream when I thought back to that lunch in New York just a few months before. Another thrill was the five-and-a-half-hour trip down the Li River on a barge, winding between the huge limestone conelike mountains with a hermit's hut or a pagoda nestled in a break in the mountain's steep side. These mountains go straight up from the river's edge, looking like a ring of misshapen dwarfs engaged in a ritual dance. There is range behind range, and the peaks are wreathed in clouds. Occasionally there is a rice paddy, or one sees an old man sitting contentedly on the back of a water buffalo. These mountains are the inspiration for so many Chinese paintings; and it was like moving through a dream to see that they really exist. It is all as it was a thousand years ago. Time did not seem to exist.

A similar experience of the feeling of timelessness was in the warehouse of the Palace Museum, where Wen took us to show us what he hopes to bring to the Metropolitan. It is the Bronze Age—210 B.C.—and I touched a life-sized statue of a young man of the period with a face so alive and full of character that I could recognize him if I saw him in a crowd. He was standing at attention, a young man in the cavalry holding the chain reins of his Mongolian horse's bridle. The horse was small and sturdy and beautifully saddled. There was also a tiger made of bronze with solid gold stripes—a tiger so lithe and sinuous, carrying a lamb in his mouth, his tail curved with the triumph of his kill. He, too, looked alive; but so elegant and sophisticated in his sculpture that I felt that man must have been very very civilized in the Bronze Age. There was nothing "primitive" about the objects in that warehouse.

Standing there before them, I again felt that time did not exist. Their curators were as enthralled as I was and I was left with the thought that during Chinese history, wars and political upheavals may not have left the deep impact we think, perhaps no more than a breeze blowing over a deep lake.

On my last morning in Peking, I went back to the house that we had lived in. As I peered through the gates, I could hear again in the distance of my memory the bugles sounding Colors in the morning as the Marines raised the American flag over the gates. I looked up—not at Mother's room, but at the room where a little girl called Brooke stood up in her bed when she heard those bugles; and in her long white nightgown was rigid at attention, her hand raised in a salute until the bugles died away and the flag was up. It seemed inevitable that I would return to China to rediscover not only the mystery and the beauty of the land, but also to rediscover myself. I found that I was still the child of John and Mabel. I am still their Brooke, and nothing will ever change that.